D1338161

The Everyman Wodehouse

P. G. WODEHOUSE

Performing Flea
A Self-Portrait in Letters

With an Introduction and Additional Notes
by W. Townend

EVERYMAN

Published by Everyman's Library
Northburgh House
10 Northburgh Street
London EC1V 0AT

First published by Herbert Jenkins Ltd, London, 1953
Published by Everyman's Library, 2014

Typography by Peter B. Willberg

ISBN 978-1-84159-191-9

A CIP catalogue record for this book is available from the British Library

Distributed by Random House (UK) Ltd.,
20 Vauxhall Bridge Road, London SW1V 2SA

Typeset by AccComputing, Wincanton, Somerset
Printed and bound in Germany
by GGP Media GmbH, Pössneck

Performing Flea

CONTENTS

Iт was only a few months ago – though I had been receiving them for more than thirty years – that the thought occurred to me that an amusing and instructive book could be made of these letters of P. G. Wodehouse, eliminating the purely private passages which would be unintelligible to anyone but myself.

Amusing? ... Well, they amused me. And instructive? Yes, I think so. It seems to me that they are full of sound advice on the art and craft of writing fiction, and to the aspiring author, who has to learn by the arduous and heart-breaking process of trial and error, advice from a writer of worldwide fame is more precious than rubies – or should be.

In my impecunious youth in San Francisco, an equally impe-cunious friend from Omaha, Nebraska, with whom I had toiled for a pittance on a ranch in Mendocino County, near Russian River, walked with me one day on Market Street – the world's finest thoroughfare – and revealed a scheme whereby we could both make what Plum's Ukridge would have called 'a vast fortune'.

He suggested that we should combine what small amount of cash we had and insert advertisements in the San Francisco newspapers, stating that we were prepared to criticize and revise short stories and novels at a fee of so much per thousand words, and for a further fee would advise the writers of these how best to earn a living from authorship. He said, with some accuracy, that most people in San Francisco either had written or were planning to write, so why should we not make a bit by instructing them how to do it?

I was horrified and firmly refused, much to his regret, but without impairing our friendship. I said I knew nothing about writing fiction. He said he knew rather less than I did, but seemed puzzled that I should think that that mattered. Was I, he asked, going to throw away a chance of picking up some easy money?

I was.

Now Plum, I think, would have been qualified even then to take on such a project. Almost from the very beginning he knew his job. As Peter Quennell wrote of him a year or two ago: 'Though not one non-literary reader in a thousand will lift his eyes from the page to consider Wodehouse as an artist, a fellow hack cannot fail to admire the extraordinary skill with which, judged by professional literary standards, he goes about his business. Every sentence has a job to do and – in spite of the air of lunatic irresponsibility which hangs around a Wodehouse novel – does it neatly and efficiently. Bertie Wooster may live in a perpetual haze, but P. G. Wodehouse knows at any moment of the story exactly what he is aiming for.' In these letters – the earlier ones, at any rate – he certainly gave me some excellent tips on how to write, from which I hope I have profited.

It is nearly fifteen years since I last met Plum, but I have a feeling that I know him even better now than when we saw each other every week or month or so; for even when he lived in Le Touquet in France my wife and I were living in Dover and he would call in and see us each time he crossed the English Channel on his many visits to London. I think that the

explanation for this is that with the passage of time his letters
have grown in depth and understanding, and one can read in
what he has written – written with no thought that they would
ever be seen by other eyes than mine – an awareness of what
life has come to mean, of man's responsibilities and duties in a
world beset by fear, of the narrowness of mind that leads to war
and the pettiness many men and more women show in their
contacts with other people, and of a tendency to see both sides
of a problem at issue.

I may be wrong, but this is my reading of much that Plum
has written. I am, however, right in saying that no one I have
ever met has in his disposition so great a zeal for friendship and
is so faithful to his ideals.

Plum and I were at school together at Dulwich College, a
school situated in delightful surroundings of field and wood-
land where one can imagine oneself – or could at the turn of
the century – in the heart of the country. We were in the same
house, slept in the same small dormitory, and shared the
same small study, but outside the house our paths divided.
Plum was in the Classical Sixth and a School Prefect, he played
for the school two years at cricket, but although tried for the
football fifteen occasionally in 1897 and 1898 did not get his
honour cap till the 1899 season, by which time I had left.

He was, in fact, someone of importance in the life of Dulwich, and was already at the age of seventeen an author, having
among other things written a series of plays after the pattern
of the Greek tragedies, outrageously funny, dealing with boys
and masters. I would give a good deal to have those plays in my
possession now.

Unlike Plum I was of no importance in the school: I had

been kept by my father at a private school far too long: my education was unbalanced and knowing a fair amount of Latin, but little Greek, a fair amount of French but no German, I was forced to specialize in mathematics which, fortunately for me, meant that I passed many hours each week by myself in the master's private library, surrounded by books, and with no supervision save my own conscience which was elastic.

I was at Dulwich for four terms only, but save for my four years on the Pacific Coast and my Army Service from 1915 to 1919, no period of my life has made so great an impression on me. I look back on those few short months as among the happiest I have ever known and I owe this happiness to Plum Wodehouse with whom I spent evening after evening, when we should have been preparing the next day's work, in reading and in conversation. One result of this early association with Plum is my vast knowledge of the novelists of the late Victorian era, and my discovery of Rudyard Kipling's short stories and the works of Gilbert and Sullivan.

Plum was the third son of the late Henry Wodehouse, C.M.G., of the Hong Kong Civil Service, who when he heard that Plum wished to be an author said that he had no objection but stipulated that he should first of all become a clerk in the Hong Kong and Shanghai Bank and write in his spare time. And so, most reluctantly, Plum entered the London office of the Hong Kong and Shanghai Bank where he remained until one happy day he realized that his income from writing stories and newspaper articles was greater than his salary and resigned to become a whole-time writer.

This was in 1902 and very soon after he had left the Bank he obtained employment on the *Globe*, the oldest London evening newspaper, thanks to W. Beach Thomas, who had at one time been his form master at Dulwich and now edited the *By the Way* column, the forerunner of all such columns. In due course when Beach Thomas, now Sir William, left the *Globe*, Plum succeeded him.

Should there be anyone in the year 1951 ignorant of but interested in the life of a great English public school in the last years of Queen Victoria's reign I suggest that a perusal of Plum's school stories would be advantageous. Wrykyn, the school about which he wrote, is Dulwich, a Dulwich not situated in a London suburb but in the country. But whereas the boys of Wrykyn are practically all boarders Dulwich, like Bedford and St Paul's, though with four large boarding-houses, now increased to five, is in the main a day school; nevertheless elderly men who were at Dulwich between the years 1895 and 1901 will recognize and appreciate Plum's masterly delineation of the life we lived so long ago. *The Gold Bat*, *The White Feather*, *The Head of Kay's* and *Mike* are still, I believe, popular with the present generation of schoolboys and the copies of these books in the Dulwich College Library became so torn and tattered as to be almost unreadable.

Had I, in the course of years, earned even a pittance as a black-and-white artist – which was what I tried to be on leaving Dulwich – the letters that form this book would never have been written, but Chance – I can think of no better term, rejecting Incompetence as too humiliating, however true – turned me to the writing of fiction as a means of livelihood.

In the year 1906 I was living in one room in Arundel Street, a cul-de-sac off Coventry Street, where Lyons' Corner House now stands, my expenses being paid by Plum, a *quid pro quo*, as it were, for a service I had quite unwittingly done him. I had one day, when in a talkative mood, a normal condition, I fear, insisted on telling him the story of an eccentric acquaintance who had helped another man, equally eccentric, so I gathered, to manage a chicken farm in Devonshire. Neither my friend nor the man who was his partner had known the first thing about the raising and feeding of chickens and they might with no more chance of success have embarked on the rearing of seagulls. Every mistake that could be made by a chicken farmer was made by these two and in the end creditors, like vultures about a carcass, arrived in force and the partnership was dissolved in scenes of incredible tumult.

Plum was so amused by this story that he asked if he could use it in a book. He wrote the book, *Love Among the Chickens*, and it was a success, and on my share of the proceeds I came to live in Arundell Street.

Toward the end of that wonderful summer of 1906, discouraged by my failure as an artist, I felt that I needed a new source of material for my pictures, though actually what I needed was talent. Someone suggested that I should go for a voyage in a tramp steamer. Plum said that if I really wanted to go – 'and rather you than me' – he would pay my expenses.

I went for my voyage, to Sulina in Roumania, and returned after three months with a broken nose and no hat, with no pictures, but with note-books filled with stories I had heard on board my tramp, scraps of fo'c'sle and engine-room gossip, local colour, details of every-day routine, anecdotes and so on, which I had jotted down more or less idly with no thought in my mind that in years to come they might be of use to me.

Later when I had finally decided that I should never earn a

living as an artist, I unearthed these note-books, read through them, much as I have read through Plum Wodehouse's letters, and set to work to write a sea story, *The Tramp*, the first of the thirty-nine books which I have had published in the last thirty years.

W. TOWNEND.

It is usually difficult to decide at what point to begin a book, fiction or otherwise, but the problem here is settled by the fact that the letters I received from Plum between 1899 and 1920 have, with very few exceptions, been either lost or destroyed.

From 1922 the letters follow at frequent intervals. If at times there are gaps in the sequence, this was because Plum and I lived near enough to each other to make letter-writing unnecessary.

I begin with one written twelve months after I was demobilized from the Army. Plum, who had gone to New York in 1909, was rejected for military service because of bad eyesight and had remained in America during the war, earning a precarious living as a free-lance writer.

* * *

Feb. 28th, 1920.　　　　　　　*Great Neck, Long Island, N.Y.*

Dear Bill:

Your letter arrived this morning, and it's great to know that you are in the pink as it leaves me at present. I have seen a lot of your stuff in *Adventure*, and I wrote to you care of them, but I suppose it never reached you. Letters are always going wrong these days.

Gosh, what a time since we corresponded! When you last

heard from me, I was living in Bellport, wasn't I? Or was it Central Park West? Anyway, I know that wherever I was I was having the dickens of a job, keeping the wolf the right side of the door. Nobody would buy my short stories. I couldn't sell a damn one anywhere. If it hadn't been for Frank Crowninshield, the editor of *Vanity Fair*, liking my stuff and taking all I could do, I should have been very much against it.

Vanity Fair is a swanky magazine 'devoted to Society and the Arts', and I used to write about half of it each month under a number of names – P. G. Wodehouse, Pelham Grenville, J. Plum, C. P. West, P. Brooke-Haven and so on. (Comic articles, not short stories. They don't use fiction.) The payment wasn't high, but high enough to keep me going. I also became the *V.F.* dramatic critic.

I was plugging along like this, when suddenly everything changed and the millennium set in. The *Saturday Evening Post* took my serial *Something Fresh*, an amazing bit of luck which stunned me, as it had never really occurred to me as possible that a long story by an unknown writer would have a chance there. Since then I have had three more in the *S.E.P.* – *Uneasy Money*, *Piccadilly Jim* and *A Damsel in Distress*. (I deduce that you saw one of them, as your letter was forwarded from the *Post*.) They gave me a raise with each one – $3,500, $5,000, $7,500, and for the *Damsel* $10,000 – so now I can afford an occasional meat meal, not only for self but for wife and resident kitten and bulldog – all of whom can do with a cut off the joint.

But my big source of income these last years has been from the theatre. Do you remember a song of mine called 'Mr Chamberlain' that Seymour Hicks sang in *The Beauty of Bath* in 1906? The music was by Jerome Kern, and I happened to run into Jerry over here – it was at the Princess Theatre the first night of a very successful small musical comedy which he had written with Guy Bolton – and he introduced me to Guy, who suggested that we three should team up, Guy doing the book and me the lyrics. I was delighted, of course, because I love writing lyrics. We wrote a fairly successful show called *Have a Heart* and then had a terrific smash with a thing called *Oh, Boy!* after which all the managers were after us with commissions. One season Guy and I actually had five shows running simultaneously on Broadway, and about a dozen companies out on the road.

Guy and I clicked from the start like Damon and Pythias. We love working together. Never a harsh word or a dirty look. He is one of the nicest chaps I ever met and the supreme worker of all time. I help him as much as I can with the 'book' end of the things, but he really does the whole job and I just do the lyrics, which are easy when one has Jerry to work with.

In spite of all this theatre work, I have managed to write a number of short stories for the *S.E.P.* – about a bloke called Bertie Wooster and his valet, and I am now doing a serial for *Collier's* and another for – if you'll believe it – the *Woman's Home Companion*. Heaven knows what a women's magazine wants with my sort of stuff, but they are giving me fifteen thousand of the best for it.

* * *

The short stories to which Plum refers were those later published by Herbert Jenkins under the title *The Inimitable Jeeves*. The *Collier's* serial was *Jill the Reckless*, the *Woman's Home Companion's*, *The Girl on the Boat*.

* * *

Here are the answers to your questions:

(1) I now write stories at terrific speed. I've started a habit of rushing them through and then working over them very carefully, instead of trying to get the first draft exactly right, and have just finished the rough draft of an eight thousand word story in two days. It nearly slew me. As a rule, I find a week long enough for a short story, if I have the plot well thought out.

(2) On a novel I generally do eight pages a day, i.e. about 2,500 words.

(3) Recently I have had a great time with my work. We have been snowed up here after a record blizzard, and nobody has been able to get at me for ages. As a rule I like to start work in the mornings, knock off for a breather, and then do a bit more before dinner. I never work after dinner. Yet in the old days that was my best time. Odd.

(4) Plots. They've been coming along fine of late.

(5) I think a good agent the best investment in the world. The point is that an agent can fight for your stuff as you can't possibly fight yourself. I would never have the nerve to refuse a fairly good offer in the hope of getting more elsewhere, but an agent will.

Funny you should have had that trouble about a story getting longer and longer in spite of yourself. I'm suffering that way now. This new novel of mine is already 15,000 words longer than anything I have done, and the worst is yet to come.

I must get hold of Alec Waugh's book *The Loom of Youth*, that you speak so highly of. I've heard a lot about it. He must be pretty good to be able to do anything big at seventeen. I was practically an imbecile at that age.

We sail on the *Adriatic* on April 24, as follows: Ethel, carrying the black kitten, followed by myself with parrot in cage and

Loretta, our maid, with any other animals we may acquire in the meantime. We shall have to leave Sammy, the bulldog, behind, worse luck, owing to the quarantine laws. It's a nuisance and we shall miss him sorely, but fortunately it won't break his heart being parted from us, as he is the most amiable soul in the world and can be happy with anyone. This is the dog I was given by one of the girls in the revue Guy and I wrote for the Century Theatre (Gosh, what a flop that one was!), and he cost us a fortune when we first had him, because he was always liking the looks of passers-by outside our garden gate and trotting out and following them. The first time he disappeared, we gave the man who brought him back ten dollars, and this got round among the local children, and stirred up their business instincts. They would come to our gate and call 'Sammy, Sammy, Sammy', and out old Sam would waddle, and then they would bring him back with a cheery 'We found your dog wandering around down the road, mister,' and cash in. I may add that the bottom has dropped out of the market and today any child who collects twenty-five cents thinks he has done well.

* * *

That I then received no letter of any importance from Plum until June, 1922, is explained by the fact that we were living within easy reach of each other in London and so met frequently.

* * *

June 27th, 1922.   *4 Onslow Square, S.W.7.*

I've just wired to you to say that I think the story is great. The only criticism I would make is that, as a reader, I wished that

Overeck (what ghastly names you give these poor blighters! – when you read your stamp story you will be pained to see that I have changed your characters to Smith, Evans, Jones and so on) had got it in the neck a bit more directly. Still, it's all right as it stands.

Listen, Bill, any funny plots you can send me will be heartily welcomed. I've got to start another series in the *Strand*, February number, and haven't any ideas except that I think I'll write some stories with Ukridge as the chief character. At the date of the series he is still unmarried and I can make him always in love with some girl or other, like Bingo Little, if necessary. The keynote is that he and his pals are all very hard-up, and a plot which has as a punch Ukridge just missing touching someone for two bob would be quite in order.

I am afraid your eyes won't be gladdened yet awhile by the sight of *Leave it to Psmith*. I have suddenly decided to introduce another character, and this has created the most extraordinary confusion in the earlier chapters, so that my MS. is all anyhow.

I have now contracted to finish a novel, six short stories and a musical show with Guy Bolton, by the end of October. I have no ideas and don't expect to get any. By the way, am off to Dinard on July 15th. Probably only for a fortnight, or three weeks, as rehearsals of *The Cabaret Girl*, the thing I've written with George Grossmith, for the Winter Garden – music by Jerry Kern – begin in August.

The puppy was run over by a motor bike the other day and emerged perfectly unhurt but a bit emotional. We had to chase him half across London before he simmered down. He just started running and kept on running till he felt better.

17 North Drive, Great Neck,
December 16th, 1922.   *Long Island, N.Y.*

Life has been one damned bit of work after another ever since I landed here. First, Guy Bolton and I settled down and wrote a musical comedy – tentatively called *Pat*, a rotten title – in two weeks for Flo Ziegfeld. It has been lying in a drawer ever since, Ziegfeld having been busy over another play, and doesn't look like getting put on this year. This, I should mention, is the play Ziegfeld was cabling about with such boyish excitement – the one I came over to do. You never heard anything like the fuss he made when I announced I couldn't make the Wednesday boat but would sail on the Saturday. He gave me to understand that my loitering would ruin everything.

I then sat down to finish *Leave it to Psmith*, for the *Saturday Evening Post*. I wrote 40,000 words in three weeks.

Since then I have been working with Guy on a musical comedy, *Sitting Pretty*, for the Duncan Sisters, music by Irving Berlin. This is complicated by the fact that Guy's new comedy has just started rehearsals, and he is up to his neck in it. So the work is proceeding by jerks.

The *Saturday Evening Post* has done me proud. Although they never commission anything, they liked the first 60,000 words of *Leave it to Psmith* so much that they announced it in the papers before I sent in the remainder. I mailed them the last part on a Wednesday and got a cheque for $20,000 on the following Tuesday.

The story will start late in January, I think. Do you get the *Post* now? If not, let me know, and I'll have it sent to you. I want you to cast a fatherly eye over the first two instalments in particular. There is a tremendous amount of plot to be got across in these and I want you to see if I could improve the construction. There is no possible way of avoiding telling part of the story twice over, which is a nuisance, but I think it's pretty good though I'm doubtful about the final chapter.

December 22nd, 1922.   *Great Neck, Long Island.*

More or less down with lumbago. It started by my putting my hip out while playing golf and this set up an irritation. I went to an osteopath yesterday who practically tore me limb from limb. I must say I feel better after the treatment, though not at all sure that all of me is still there. I wonder what an osteopath does if a patient suddenly comes apart in his hands. ('Quick, Watson, the seccotine!')

We are having the devil of a time over this Duncan Sisters show. All attempts to get hold of Irving Berlin about the music have failed. We went into New York last Monday to keep an appointment with him and found that he had had to rush off to the dentist. He then made a date with me over the phone to lunch with him on Thursday and work all the afternoon. I went in and called at his flat and he was out and had left no message. Heaven knows when the thing will ever be finished!

December 29th, 1922.   *Great Neck.*

Well, well, well. So everything's all right. Yesterday morning when I got down to breakfast, there was a letter from Hoffman, saying that he was buying your novel, *The Tramp*, for *Adventure*. I cabled you yesterday (cursing you violently for having such a long address). What I said was... 'Tramp Sold', but

I expect the cable people will think that that didn't make sense and will edit it. You probably got it as 'Trump Solid' or 'Stamp Gold', but anyhow, I hope you read the hidden meaning.

You don't know how bucked I am over this. I have been worrying myself like the dickens about this yarn. I felt that if they turned it down after you had sweated eleven weeks over it, you might turn your face to the wall and give up. But I think this proves that you are O.K.

I don't want to come the heavy expert, but I'll tell you what has been wrong with some of your stuff in the past – you have been too easily satisfied with the *bones* of a story. Every time you have had a good story to tell, you have done a corker. If you look back, you'll see that the only ones of yours which have failed are those which have had a weak plot.

Another thing. Your stuff is really too good for the ordinary magazine, so that when you don't have a plot which is all right for the flatheads anyway, editors are apt to turn you down.

All this sounds rather incoherent – but, well, look here: your story, *The Horse Thief*, was sure-fire for any magazine because the actual plot was so exactly right for any type of reader that it didn't matter that it was well written instead of cheaply. But *The Price of the Picture* was no good for popular magazines unless thoroughly cheapened.

And now I know what I am driving at is: When you get a plot, examine it carefully and say to yourself: 'Is this a popular magazine plot?' If it isn't, simply don't attempt to make it a popular magazine story. Just put all you know into it and write it the very best you can and confine its field to the really decent magazines like *Blackwood's*, the *Cornhill*, etc.

I think that now you have had such an instant response from the *Cornhill* you should follow up that line as hard as you can.

It may not be so immediately profitable as the more popular magazines, but you make up for that in reputation.

I have got to start the *Cosmopolitan* series at once, and the editor likes the character of Ukridge, so if you have any more plots, ship them over.

May 28th, 1923.   *Southampton, Long Island.*

I have at last got the *Strand* with *A Couple of Down-and-Outs* in it. I think the illustrations are good and the story reads fine. It has given me an illuminating idea about your work – to wit, that you make all your characters so real that you can't afford a grey ending. You simply must make a point of having them all right in the end, or the reader feels miserable. And you have got to make the happy ending definite, too, as in this story.

Another thing is: what you want to put your stuff over is ACTION. In *A Couple of Down-and-Outs* the story jumps from one vivid scene to another. The more I write, the more I am convinced that the only way to write a popular story is to split it up into scenes, and have as little stuff between the scenes as possible. See what I mean? Well, look here. I wrote a story the other day – *The Return of Battling Billson* – and the only thing that was arrived at in the first 1,500 words was that I met Battling Billson down in the East End and gave him Ukridge's address, which he had lost. But by having me go into a pub and get a drink and have lost my money and be chucked out by the barman and picked up by Billson, who happened to be passing, and then having Billson go in and clean up the pub and man-handle the barman I got some darned good stuff which, I think, absolutely concealed the fact that nothing had really happened except my giving him the address.

Do you see what I mean? I think that for a magazine story you *must* start off with a good scene. Of course, you probably know this already, but here it is again with my blessing.

I'm going up to New York tomorrow for a few days, as George Grossmith is arriving to work on the next Winter Garden show with me.

I was awfully glad to get your letter containing the welcome statement that you thought on reading it again that *Ukridge's Dog College* was all right. I had to rush that story in the most horrible way. I think I told you that the *Cosmopolitan* wanted it for the April number, and I had about five days to deliver it and got it all wrong, and had to write about 20,000 words before I got it set. And then, when I reached Palm Beach, I found that the artist had illustrated a scene which was not in the final version, and I had to add a new one by telephone!

I have done two more stories in the last three weeks, and am now well ahead again, having completed eight. I'm so glad you like the series. Now that I've got well into it, I think it better than any of the others. It was difficult at first having the 'I' chap a straight character instead of a sort of Bertie Wooster, but now I find it rather a relief, as it seems to make the thing more real.

I have had a stream of letters cursing the end of *Leave it to Psmith*, and I shall have to rewrite it. But what a sweat it is altering a story that has gone cold!

July 23rd, 1923.   *Easthampton, Long Island.*

Have you ever been knocked over by a car? If not, don't. There's no percentage in it. I was strolling along yesterday evening to meet Ethel who had gone down to the station in our Buick, and half-way to the village she sighted me and pulled in to the sidewalk. The roads here are cement, with a sort of No-Man's Land of dirt between sidewalk and road. I had just got on to this when I saw a Ford coming down behind our car. Naturally, I thought it would pull up when it realized that Ethel had stopped, but it must have been going too fast, for I suddenly observed with interest that it wasn't stopping but was swinging in straight for me on the wrong side of the road. I gave one gazelle-like spring sideways and the damned thing's right front wheel caught my left leg squarely and I thought the world had ended. I took the most awful toss and came down on the side of my face and skinned my nose, my left leg and my right arm. This morning all sorts of unsuspected muscles and bones are aching, and I can hardly move my right arm. But, my gosh! doesn't it just show that we are here today and gone tomorrow! If I had been a trifle less fit and active, I should have got the entire car in the wishbone. Oh, well, it's all in a lifetime!

Last night I went to bed early and read your story, *Peter the Greek*. For the first half I thought it was the best thing you had ever done, full of action and suspense. But, honestly, as you seem to think yourself from your letter, it does drop a bit after that. Mogger (my Heaven! what names you give your characters!) whom you have established as a sinister menace, is weakened by that scene where Teame hits him. It is an error, I think, ever to have your villain manhandled by a minor character. Just imagine Moriarty socked by Doctor Watson. A villain ought to be a sort of scarcely human invulnerable figure. The reader ought to be in a constant state of panic, saying to himself: 'How the devil *is* this superman to be foiled?' The only person capable of hurting him should be the hero.

Bill, I've spoken of this before and I want to emphasize it again – you *must not* take any risk of humanizing your villains in a story of action. And by humanizing I mean treating them subjectively instead of objectively.

Taking Moriarty as the pattern villain, don't you see how much stronger he is by being an inscrutable figure and how much he would have been weakened if Conan Doyle had switched off to a chapter showing his thoughts? A villain ought to be a sort of malevolent force, not an intelligible person at all.

I wish the deuce we could meet and talk these things over. It is so hard to discuss a story by correspondence. The time to wrangle over the construction of a story is when it is being shaped, not after it has set.

I wish, too, that you were in London and not Switzerland. I am sailing next Saturday for the rehearsals of *The Beauty Prize* at the Winter Garden, and I shall be in London for three weeks or so. I suppose your wanderings can't possibly take you home for August?

Herbert Jenkins' death was a great shock to me. I was awfully fond of him, but I always had an idea that he could not last very long. He simply worked himself to death. He was very fragile with a terrific driving mind and no physique at all, one of those fellows who look transparent and are always tired. One used to wonder how long he could possibly carry on. He shirked his meals and exercise and concentrated entirely on work. You can't do it.

August 24th, 1923.   *11 King Street, St James's, London.*

I am at the above address and should like to see a specimen of your typing, with all the latest gossip from Switzerland, but mark you, laddie, I sail for New York on September 5th, so make it snappy!

I have the honour to report that the old bean is in a state of absolute stagnation. I wrote the best golf-story I have ever done on board the boat coming over – *The Coming of Gowf* – but since I landed I have not had the ghost of an idea for a plot of any kind – so much so – or so little so – that I shall be obliged to drop the Ukridge Series – at any rate for the moment – at the end of the ninth story. I wanted the last two stories to be about how he got married, and it looked as if it would be pretty easy, but I'm darned if I can think of anything for him to do. It may come later. I've done a lot of work this last year – twelve short stories and half a novel, besides my share of *The Beauty Prize*, including all the lyrics – and it may simply be that I need a rest.

The kitten has had a fit, but is all right again now. I allude to the animal at the Wodehouse home at Easthampton, whom you have never met. A cheery soul, with a fascinating habit of amusing the master at breakfast by chasing a ball of paper all over the room, and then suddenly dashing up the curtain from floor to ceiling at one bound. Sammy, the bulldog, has had an attack of eczema, but is doing well. No other news from home.

c/o Guaranty Trust Company,
November 4th, 1923.   *44th St & 5th Avenue, New York City.*

I have been meaning to write to you for some time about *The Talking Doll*. It gripped me all through but if you are going to start anything in a story like the idea of the doll and Chutton, it is brutal to the reader to explain it away in the end. It is like the ghost turning out to be smugglers.

Just one more thing. I think you have made a mistake in starting interesting stuff and then dropping it. The principle

I always go on in writing a long story is to think of the characters in terms of actors in a play. I say to myself, when I invent a good character for an early scene: 'If this were a musical comedy we should have to get somebody like Leslie Henson to play this part, and if he found that all he had was a short scene in act one, he would walk out. How, therefore, can I twist the story so as to give him more to do and keep him alive till the fall of the curtain?'

This generally works well and improves the story. A good instance of this was Baxter in *Leave it to Psmith*. It became plain to me as I constructed the story that Baxter was such an important character that he simply had to have a good scene somewhere in what would correspond to the latter part of act two, so I bunged in that flower-pot sequence.

I wish we could discuss these stories, as we used to, before you finish them. It is so much easier to see where a scenario goes off the rails. Why don't you send me your next scenario for me to make suggestions? I always get my own scenarios passed by two or three people before I start writing. If one has finished a long story, one goes cold on it and alterations are a torture. I had this experience with *Leave it to Psmith*. You and a number of other people told me the end was wrong, as I had already suspected myself, but I couldn't muster up energy and ideas enough to alter it. I finally did it, and it has held up the publication of the book and caused much agony of spirit at the Herbert Jenkins office. Still, it is all right now, I think.

I am half-way through mapping out a new novel, which looks like being a pippin. I am going on a new system this time, making the scenario very full, putting in atmosphere and dialogue etc., so that when I come actually to write it the work will be easy. So far I have scenarioed it out to about the 40,000 word mark; and it has taken me 13,000 words to do it! I have now reached a point where deep thought is required. I am not sure I haven't got too much plot, and may have to jettison the best idea in the story. I suppose the secret of writing is to go through your stuff till you come on something you think is particularly good, and then cut it out.

* * *

The new novel Plum speaks about here was published under the title of *Bill the Conqueror*.

* * *

c/o Guy Bolton,
January 26th, 1924.   *17 Beverly Road, Great Neck, L.I.N.Y.*

Listen, Bill. Is this a crazy idea? I suddenly thought the other day, there are always rats on board ship, so why shouldn't one rat, starting by being a bit bigger than the others, gradually grow and grow, feeding on his little playmates, till he became the size of an Airedale terrier? Then there begin to be mysterious happenings on board the ship. Men are found dead with their faces chewed off, etc. And so on.

Is this any good to you? It certainly isn't to me. I give it you with my blessing.

* * *

An interesting letter – to me, at any rate. Plum's suggested giant rat story unexpectedly came to fruition ten years later when I wrote a story on the same theme, though dealing with an island in the South Pacific and not with a ship. This story was published in *Harper's Magazine* – and was, I suppose, one of the few good short stories I ever wrote, but the extraordinary part about the whole affair is that I had no idea Plum had given me the plot until, reading over his letter of January 26th, 1924, I suddenly realized that the theme of the story had come from him, and was not my own invention. I have a good enough memory, but this was one of the things I had forgotten in twenty-seven years!

* * *

May 8th, 1924.   *Hôtel Campbell, Avenue Friedmann, Paris.*

Our plans for the summer are still very undecided, but it looks as if we we were going to take a house in London in the autumn.

Are you working well these days? I haven't had an idea for a story for three months or more. I finished *The Adventures of Sally* at the beginning of April and since then my mind has been a blank. I had to write it under difficulties, as I was working with Guy and Jerry Kern on a musical comedy, the first we three have done together since the Princess Theatre days. It's called *Sitting Pretty*, and was doing all right when I left New York, but I have my doubts about it.

It's a good instance of the sort of trouble you run into when working in the theatre. Do you remember me telling you that Guy and I were doing a show for the Duncan Sisters with Irving Berlin? This is it. What happened was that we didn't plan to produce till October or later and the Duncans asked Sam Harris, our manager, if they could fill in during the summer with a little thing called *Topsy and Eva* – a sort of comic *Uncle Tom's Cabin* which they had written themselves.

They just wanted to do it out on the coast, they said. Sam said that would be all right, so they went ahead, expecting to play a couple of months or so, and darned if *Topsy and Eva* didn't turn out one of those colossal hits which run for ever. It's now in about its fiftieth week in Chicago with New York still to come, so we lost the Duncans and owing to losing them lost Irving Berlin, who liked *Sitting Pretty* but thought it wouldn't go without them. So we got hold of Jerry and carried on with him. He has done a fine score, but it still remains to be seen whether or not the show – written as a vehicle for a sister act – will succeed with its present cast. We have Gertrude Bryan and Queenie Smith for the two Duncan parts, and they are both very good, but in my opinion they aren't a team and this may dish us. A pity if it happens, as it's really a good show.

* * *

Sitting Pretty came off after a short run, the only one of the six Bolton-Wodehouse-Kern musical comedies that did not play a whole season in New York. Irving Berlin had been right.

* * *

September 23rd, 1924.   *Grand Hotel, Harrogate, Yorks.*

Awfully sorry I haven't written for so long. I've been very busy. I've done a couple of short stories since I got here and also practically completed the scenario of new novel.

Ethel left yesterday to see about getting our new house ready. We have taken 23, Gilbert Street, Grosvenor Square, from October 1st. Isn't there any chance of your being in town at any rate through November? I have a feeling that Dulwich are going to have a good team this year.

Harrogate is a terrific place for work. I wrote an elaborate scenario of the first third of my novel yesterday. I've got a new system now, as it worked so well with *Bill the Conqueror*: that is to write a 30,000 word scenario before starting the novel. (Perhaps I've told you already.) By this means you avoid those ghastly moments when you suddenly come on a hole in the plot and are tied up for three days while you invent a situation. I found that the knowledge that I had a clear path ahead of me helped my grip on the thing. Also, writing a scenario of this length gives you ideas for dialogue scenes and you can jam them down in skeleton and there they are, ready for use later.

Do you like the title: *Sam the Sudden*?

You remember how we condemned Harry Leon Wilson's *Oh, Doctor!* on the strength of the first instalment in the *Post*? I have just been reading it in book form, and it's excellent. I think a story has to be pretty good to stand up against publication in the *Post*, with that small print and those solid pages. But I must say I'm not keen on his new one. Are you reading it? How that man does work that Addison Simms joke to death!

*   *   *

I think it must have been within the next twelve months that the *Saturday Evening Post* discarded the small type, that was so hard on their writers and adopted larger print altogether, which was a great improvement in every way.

*   *   *

October 1st, 1924.   *Harrogate.*

The short story I've just finished, entitled *Honeysuckle Cottage*, is the funniest idea I've ever had. A young writer of thrillers gets left five thousand quid and a house by his aunt, who was Leila May Pinkney, the famous writer of sentimental stories. He finds that her vibrations have set up a sort of miasma of sentimentalism in the place, so that all who come within its radius get soppy and maudlin. He then finds to his horror that he is – but it will be simpler to send you the story, so I am doing so. I polished it up a good bit in typing it out.

Key to the Addison Simms mystery. I don't know if it is still going, but there used to be an advertisement of a memory training course in all the American magazines. It showed the man who had not taken the course embarrassed and floundering when he met the old acquaintance whose name he had forgotten. Whereas the man who had taken the course just stretched out his hand with a beaming smile and said: 'Why, certainly, I remember you, Mr Addison Simms. We met at the Rotary Club dinner at Seattle on October the Third, 1910. How are you, how are your wife and your three children? And how did you come out on that granary deal?'

*   *   *

In his letter of October 2nd, 1924, written once more from Harrogate, Plum discusses at great length the reasons why, in his opinion, my long story, *His Father's Son*, had been rejected when other of my stories which I considered not so good had been accepted and published. Plum wrote:

*   *   *

It seems to me that if you are to go on writing for popular magazines you will deliberately have to make your stuff cheaper. At present you are working from character to plot, and what they want, I'm convinced, is the story that contains only obvious characters who exist simply for the sake of the plot. Take a story like that one I thought was your very best, *In the Stokehold*. It was all subtlety. What they would have liked would have been the same idea with all the motives obvious. You've been trying to write for magazines that aren't good enough, and you are consequently caught in two minds. You can't bring yourself to start with a cheap, tawdry plot, and yet you torture the story to suit an editor by excluding everything he objects to.

Here is an exact parallel. Remember *The Luck Stone*, which with your assistance I wrote for *Chums*? School story full of kidnappings, attempted murders, etc. They were delighted with it. Then I tried them with a real school story and they threw a fit. 'What, no blood?' they cried, and shot the thing back at me.

* * *

I was thrilled and amused when on re-reading Plum's letters, I discovered by chance among them a note I had had from him, dated May 6th, 1906.

* * *

Dear Bill:

Here's a go. I've been commissioned by *Chums* to do a 70,000 word serial by July. They want it not so public-schooly as my usual stuff and with rather a lurid plot. For Heaven's sake rally round and lend a hand. I've written off today earnestly recommending you for the illustrations on the strength of those you did for *The White Feather*.

In any case, give me an idea or two.

PS. Your reward will be my blessing and at least a fiver.

* * *

Though a fiver was a fiver in those days, Plum sent me ten pounds for the small amount of help I was able to give him. It should be of interest to any student of the books of P. G. Wodehouse to obtain the numbers of *Chums* for the latter part of 1906, if any still survive, and read *The Luck Stone*, by – if I remember rightly – 'Basil Windham'.

A letter Plum wrote on October 28th from 23 Gilbert Street, Mayfair, contains some valuable advice.

* * *

When you're doing a long story you have got to be most infernally careful of the values of your characters. I believe I told you once before that I classed all my characters as if they were living salaried actors, and I'm convinced that this is a rough but very good way of looking at them.

The one thing actors – important actors, I mean – won't stand is being brought on to play a scene which is of no value to them in order that they may feed some less important character, and I believe this isn't vanity but is based on an instinctive knowledge of stagecraft. They kick because they know the balance isn't right.

I wish we could meet. How is the cottage working out? One thing about living in the country is that, even if the windows leak, you can get some work done. I find it's the hardest job to get at the stuff here. We have damned dinners and lunches which just eat up the time. I find that having a lunch hanging over me kills my morning's work, and dinner isn't much better. I'm at the stage now, if I drop my characters, they go cold.

I enclose a sheet of questions, which you will save my life by answering. They come in Chapter Three of *Sam the Sudden*, the chapter I ought to be working on now.

Chapter Three starts as follows:

Sam Shotter stood outside the galley of the tramp steamer *Araminta* in pleasant conversation with Clarence – ('Soup') Todhunter, the vessel's popular and energetic cook.

Now then:

(A) How was Sam dressed? (All his luggage had come over on the *Mauretania* and he had sea-clothes on. This is very important, as in the next chapter it is essential that Sam shall look like a dead-beat and be taken for a burglar.)

(B) What did Sam see, hear and smell, as he stood outside the galley?

(C) Sam is the stepson of a millionaire and has a penchant for travelling on tramps. He must have had at least one voyage on the *Araminta* before, because it is essential that he knows the skipper well. Therefore, in what capacity did he sail? Would it be ship's etiquette for him to chum up with the skipper as well as the cook?

(D) On the voyage the only thing Sam has had to look at has been a photograph of a girl cut out of the *Tatler*. Could he have a cabin to himself? And do you call it a cabin or a state-room?

(E) The *Araminta* is sailing from America to England. How long would the voyage take? Also, where would she start from, and where dock? Could she dock at Port of London, and be going on to Cardiff?

(F) I particularly want Sam to be in London when Chapter Three starts, so that he has an easy trip to the West End, which is the setting of the next chapter. Please give me some atmosphere for Port of London, or wherever it is, i.e. something for Sam to see from the deck of the ship.

(G) Can you possibly write me a description of Soup Todhunter from your knowledge of ship's cooks? It is immaterial what he looks like, of course, but it will help.

(H) I am probably taking Sam to the skipper's cabin, so what is the skipper doing when the boat has just docked? I mean, probably the boat is discharging cargo or has been during the day. I want Sam to get off the ship in nice time to take the skipper up to the West End for a bit of dinner.

Well, that's all I can think of at the moment. I'm keeping a carbon copy of these questions, so you'll only need to jot down notes under each heading.

I do hope you're not busy on anything just now, as I don't want to interrupt you. Also bear in mind that I can carry on quite well for at least three weeks without the information. I have got the story so mapped out that I can skip the sea stuff and go on working on the shore scenes till you are ready.

* * *

I answered all these questions with great care, but, alas, as you will see if you turn to *Sam the Sudden*, Sam Shotter never did stand outside the galley of the tramp steamer *Araminta* in pleasant conversation with Clarence ('Soup') Todhunter. In the final version the meeting took place off stage and is merely referred to in the words 'He had dined well, having as his guest his old friend Hash Todhunter' – not 'Soup', an honourable name bestowed later on Mr Slattery, the burglar in *Hot Water*. All I actually accomplished was putting Plum right about Sam's costume and

Hash's looks. But that formidable list of questions shows
the thoroughness with which he approached a job of work.

* * *

January 11th, 1925.   *23 Gilbert Street, Grosvenor Square.*

I think that their criticism of this story means that your stuff
is too real.

You have your heroes struggling against Life and Fate, and
what they want are stories about men struggling with octopuses
and pirates. You make the reader uneasy. He doesn't enjoy himself. He feels, 'Well, maybe this poor devil will struggle through
all right, but what a wretched thought it is that the world is full
of poor devils on the brink of being chucked out of jobs and
put on the beach.' You make them think about life and popular
magazine readers don't want to.

Another thought is that your method involves the elimina-
tion of comedy. Your hero, being real, can't approach his
difficulties gaily and meet them in a dashing way. I do hope
this is clear. What I mean is this: A man trapped in a ruined
mill by pock-marked Mexicans and one-eyed Chinamen can
be lively and facetious. A man in the position of most of your
heroes can't be anything but dead serious. This tends to make
a story heavy; it lifts it, in fact, into a class of literature in which
your intended public simply doesn't belong.

April 28th, 1925.   *23 Gilbert Street, Grosvenor Square.*

What an age since I wrote to you last. I have been in a sort
of trance since I finished *Sam the Sudden.*

It was a frightful rush – so much so that I hadn't time to

have it typed but had to send my original script (the only one in existence) over to America from Monte Carlo, and was in a considerable twitter till I heard that it had arrived safely, I having no confidence whatever in the postal arrangements of foreign countries. I sold it to the *Post* for $25,000, and they will eventually send proofs over here, which the Newnes people are anxiously waiting for. At present the Newnes editor has the first 30,000 words and no more. I do hate having to rush a thing like this.

I am having my usual struggle to get new ideas. So far I have got out what may be the framework of a novel, but the incidents don't seem to come.

I'm having lunch with Conan Doyle today. He has written a spiritualistic novel which starts in the July *Strand*.

Conan Doyle, a few words on the subject of. Don't you find as you age in the wood, as we are both doing, that the tragedy of life is that your early heroes lose their glamour? As a lad in the twenties you worship old whoever-it-is, the successful author, and by the time you're forty you find yourself blushing hotly at the thought that you could ever have admired the bilge he writes.

Now, with Doyle I don't have this feeling. I still revere his work as much as ever. I used to think it swell, and I still think it swell. Do you remember when we used to stand outside the bookstall at Dulwich station on the first of the month, waiting for Stanhope to open it so that we could get the new *Strand* with the latest instalment of *Rodney Stone* ... and the agony of finding that something had happened to postpone the fight between Champion Harrison and Crab Wilson for another month? I would do it today if *Rodney Stone* was running now.

And apart from his work, I admire Doyle so much as a man.

I should call him definitely a great man, and I don't imagine I'm the only one who thinks so. I love that solid, precise way he has of talking, like Sherlock Holmes. He was telling me once that when he was in America, he saw an advertisement in a paper: 'Conan Doyle's School of Writing. Let the Conan Doyle School of Writing teach you how to sell' – or something to that effect. In other words, some blighter was using his name to swindle the public. Well, what most people in his place would have said would have been 'Hullo! This looks fishy'. The way he put it when telling me the story was: 'I said to myself, "Ha! There is villainy afoot".'

May 27th, 1925.

I'm very bucked about the *Post* giving you $600 for *Bolshevik*. I remember Lorimer telling me that he had paid two hundred dollars for a story by Bozeman Bulger (What's become of him, by the way? Do you remember, he used to write a lot for the *Post*) – and that very soon they would raise him to two hundred and fifty. He seemed to think that lavish. They only gave me $400 for my first story or two, so evidently they must have been hard hit by *Bolshevik*. I don't wonder. I always said it was a whale of a story.

November 2nd, 1925.   *Hotel Marguery, New York.*

What a time since I wrote to you last. I don't know why it is, but when I'm staying with people, I can never write letters. I didn't write one while I was on Jim Stillman's yacht. However, now we have settled temporarily in New York.

Listen, laddie. I am putting together a serial plot and my

only trouble is that, wishing to use that shanghaiing stuff about which I once consulted you, I find it necessary that my hero should know a lot of tramp skippers. Otherwise, the fact that he is shanghaied on the one boat of which he happens to know the skipper becomes too much of a coincidence.

Well, then. What I want him to be is the godson – original touch, this. You thought I was going to say nephew – of Jones Mickelbury (I bet you wish you'd thought of that name), the eminent shipowner. He starts in the firm, and his job involves going down to the docks at all sorts of unearthly morning hours to interview skippers of incoming boats belonging to the firm. NOW, IS THERE SUCH A JOB?

It must be something that would irk a lazy man, because the effect on him when he chucks it is to make him stay in bed all day, which annoys the heroine and leads to a good situation.

I've just got out a good Ukridge plot. U pawns his aunt's diamond brooch to buy a half-share in a dog that is to win the Waterloo Cup, and the dog dies. O.K.

Extract from an undated letter written from New York.

Hotel Marguery, 270 Park Avenue.

Did I tell you that a man came up to me the other day and said: 'Mr Wodehouse, I want to thank you for the happy hours you have given me with your book *Forty Years in China!*'

June 26th, 1926.   *Hunstanton Hall, Norfolk.*

The above address does not mean that I have bought a country estate. It is a joint belonging to a friend of mine, and I am putting in a week or two here. It's one of those enormous houses, about two-thirds of which are derelict. There is a whole wing which has not been lived in for half a century. You know the sort of thing – it's happening all over the country now – thousands of acres, park, gardens, moat, etc., and priceless heirlooms, but precious little ready money. The income from farms and so on just about balances expenses.

I spend most of my time on the moat, which is really a sizeable lake. I'm writing this in the punt with my typewriter on a bed-table wobbling on one of the seats. There is a duck close by which utters occasional quacks that sound like a man with an unpleasant voice saying nasty things in an undertone. Beside me is a brick wall with the date 1623 on it. The only catch is that the water is full of weeds, so I can't swim in it as I would like to.

I've just had a cable from Guy Bolton asking me to sail on July 8th and do a new show with him for Gertrude Lawrence. I am trying to put it off till the 24th. Ethel isn't keen on going to America just now, so I am torn between a dislike of leaving her and a desire not to let a good thing get by me. Because there's no question that it is a good thing. Gertie is terrifically popular over there and a show for her can't miss, especially as

George Gershwin is doing the music. George being the composer means that Ira Gershwin will write the lyrics, so that I shall simply help Guy with the book as much as I can.

* * *

The show to which Plum refers was called *Oh, Kay!*, and was produced in New York in November, 1926, and in London in September, 1927. It had 256 performances in New York and 214 in London.

* * *

April 1st, 1927.   *17 Norfolk Street, Park Lane.*

We have got a new Peke, Susan, three months old.

I was awfully glad to hear about your Gaumont deal. It ought to help the sale of the book a lot. I went round to the Jenkins headquarters the day I got back from Droitwich and had a long talk with Askew about your work, Grimsdick being away. He was very enthusiastic and said they thoroughly believed in you and thought your stuff fine, and intended to stick to it and build it up.

He realizes what I have always felt, that your sort of work has to be built up. Mine was just the same. I didn't sell over two thousand till I went to Jenkins with *Piccadilly Jim*. I don't think you can expect a big sale with an early book unless it happens to be one of those freak winners. The thing to do is to bung in book after book with one publisher. I'm sure that's the wheeze, as then each book helps the next.

Do stick to Jenkins. The more I see of them, the more I think they are the best publishers of the lot. Askew has been right through the bookselling business, starting as an apprentice and this gives him an enormous advantage. Sometimes when I see those column ads of other publishers in the Sunday papers, I get rather wistful, but I always come back to feeling that the Jenkins people do much more for you than any of them. I mean to say, while these other blokes are buying column ads, Askew is going round and taking some bookseller whom he used to play marbles with out for a drink and landing him with a hundred copies of your book.

May 5th, 1927.   *Impney Hotel, Droitwich.*

Isn't that writing blurbs stuff the devil! You ought to let me write yours and you write mine. I simply can't put down on paper the sort of thing they want. What they would like from you is something on the lines of 'When you meet Mr Townend, you are struck at once by a look in his eyes – it is the look of a man who has communed with his soul in the teeth of nor'-easters. One winter not many years ago, on a tramp steamer in the North Atlantic – etc.' It's hopeless trying to do that sort of thing yourself.

I am just finishing an adaptation (for America) of a serious play from the German. I was talking to Gilbert Miller, and Al Woods was there and I said to G. M.: 'I wish you'd give me Molnár's next play to adapt!' He said: 'You couldn't do it. It's not in your line. It's a serious play!' I said: 'Boy, I can write anything!' And Al Woods said: 'I have a serious German play,' and I said: 'Gimme!' purely with the intention of scoring off Gilbert by showing him how I could do the heavy dramatic stuff, too. So I hope I don't flop. I'll bet I do! Of course, I can't really write serious stuff, and why I ever let myself in for the damned thing, I can't imagine. I must have been cuckoo.

*   *   *

Later Plum adapted Molnár's *The Play's the Thing*, which was a great success in New York, not only when put on in 1928, but also when revived after the Second World War in 1948. It was, strangely enough, considering Plum's reputation in this country and his vast following, a failure in London.

*   *   *

July 27th, 1927.   *Hunstanton Hall.*

I've just read your story in the *Strand*. It's fine. I love Captain Crupper, and you have the most extraordinary knack of making your minor characters live.

Listen, laddie. Have you read a thing of mine called *Pig-Hoo-o-o-ey*? I have a sort of idea you once wrote a story constructed on those lines, i.e. some perfectly trivial thing which is important to a man and the story is apparently how he gets it. But in the process of getting it he gets entangled in somebody else's love story and all sorts of things happen but he pays no attention to them, being wholly concentrated on his small thing. If you never did a yarn on these lines, try one with Captain Crupper. It's a good formula.

Anyway, bung-oh! I'm sweating blood over *Money for Nothing*, and have just finished 53,000 words of it. Meanwhile, I have to anglicize *Oh, Kay!*, by August 9, attend rehearsals, adapt a French play, write a new musical comedy and do the rest of *Money for Nothing*, as far as I can see, by about September 1st. It'll all help to pass the time.

November 28th, 1927.   *14 East 60th Street, New York.*

I would have written before this, but ever since I landed I have been in a terrible rush. I came over here with George Grossmith, to do *The Three Musketeers* for Flo Ziegfeld, and we finished a rough version on the boat. But like all work that is done quickly, it needed a terrible lot of fixing, which was left to me, as George went home. I was working gaily on it when a fuse blew out in Ziegfeld's Marilyn Miller show – book by Guy Bolton and Bill McGuire – owing to the lyrist and composer turning up on the day of the start of rehearsals and announcing that they had finished one number, and hoped to have another done shortly, though they couldn't guarantee this. Ziegfeld fired them and called in two new composers, Sigmund Romberg and George Gershwin, and asked me to do the lyrics with Ira. I wrote nine in a week and ever since then have been sweating away at the rest. Meanwhile Gilbert Miller wanted a show in a hurry for Irene Bordoni, so I started on that, too – fixing the *Musketeers* with my left hand the while. By writing the entire second act in one day I have managed to deliver the Bordoni show on time, and I have now finished the lyrics of the Flo show and the revised version of the *Musketeers*, and all is well – or will be until Flo wants all the lyrics rewritten, as he is sure to do. We open the Bolton-McGuire-Ira Gershwin-Wodehouse-George Gershwin-Romberg show in Boston next week. It's called *Rosalie*, and I don't like it much, though it's bound to be a success with Marilyn and Jack Donahue in it.

Just at present I feel as if I would never get another idea for a story. I suppose I shall eventually, but this theatrical work certainly saps one's energies. As I write this, it is six o'clock, so the play I wrote for Ernest Truex, *Good Morning, Bill*, must just be finishing in London. I hope it has got over, as I know Gilbert Miller is waiting to see how it is received in London, before putting it on here.

New York is noisier than ever. I found my only way of getting any work done on the Flo lyrics, was to take a room at the Great Neck Golf Club and work there. So I am the only man on record who commutes the wrong way. I catch the twelve o'clock train from New York every day and return after dinner. Flo thinks I play golf all day out there and is rather plaintive about it, but I soothe him by producing a series of lyrics.

* * *

Good Morning, Bill was a success. It ran for 146 performances at the Duke of York's Theatre and was revived seven years later at Daly's with Peter Haddon as the hero.

Rosalie – the Bolton-McGuire-Ira Gershwin-Wodehouse-George Gershwin-Romberg piece – turned out a credit to its platoon of authors and composers, doing 335 performances in New York at the New Amsterdam Theatre. It was never produced in London. Plum was later to undergo some headaches out in Hollywood, trying to turn it into a motion picture for Marion Davies.

* * *

March 10th, 1928.　　　*17 Norfolk Street, Park Lane, London.*

Can you get anything to read these days? I was in the *Times* Library yesterday and came out empty-handed. There wasn't a thing I wanted. To fill in the time before Edgar Wallace writes another one, I am re-reading Dunsany. I never get tired of his stories. I can always let them cool off for a month or two and then come back to them. He is the only writer I know who opens up an entirely new world to me. What a mass of perfectly wonderful stuff he has done. (All this is probably wasted on you, as I don't suppose you have read him, unless you were attracted to his stories by the fact that they used to be illustrated by S. H. Sime. He has exactly the same eerie imagination as Sime. In fact, he told me once that quite a lot of his stuff was written from Sime's pictures. They would hand him a Sime drawing of a wintry scene with a sinister-looking bird flying over it and he would brood on it for a while and come up with *The Bird of the Difficult Eye*.)

His secret sorrow is that he wants to write plays and can't get them put on. I spent the afternoon with him once at his house down in Kent, and he read me three of his plays one after the other. All awfully good, but much too fantastic. One of them was about an unemployed ex-officer after the War who couldn't get a job, so he hired himself out as a watch-dog. He lived in a kennel, and the big scene was where he chased a cat up a tree and sat under it shouting abuse. I laughed heartily myself, but I could just picture the fishy, glazed eye of a manager listening to it.

Dunsany told me a story about the Troubles in Ireland, which amused me considerably. Lord Whoever-It-was had a big house near Cork somewhere, and one day a gang of Sinn Feiners rolled up and battered down the front door with axes. Inside they found a very English butler, a sort of Beach of Blandings Castle. He looked at them austerely and said coldly: 'His lordship is not at home.' They paid no attention to him and went in and wrecked the place from basement to attic, finally setting fire to it. On leaving, they found the butler still in the hall. Flames were darting all over the place and ceilings coming down with a bang, but Fotheringay – or whatever his name was – was quite unperturbed. 'Who shall I say called, sir?' he asked.

I've got Michael Arlen coming to dinner. Nice chap.

I had a profitable week-end at Droitwich, getting the missing links in *Summer Lightning*, which I had by me for eighteen months, and also a sort of lay-out for a novel, which, if I don't change the title, will be called *Big Money*. The short story jam also shows signs of breaking. The fact was I came back from America dead tired and then stayed in London for six weeks. What I needed was a few days among the trees. I feel fine now.

Edgar Wallace, I hear, now has a Rolls Royce and also a separate car for each of the five members of his family. Also a day butler and a night butler, so that there is never a time when you can go into his house and not find buttling going on. That's the way to live!

April 30th, 1928.   *17 Norfolk Street, Park Lane.*

So sorry not to have written before, but I have been much tied up with a very difficult story. *Company for Gertrude*, I'm calling it. I wish to goodness you were here to help me with it. It's one of those maddening yarns where you get the beginning and the end all right, and only want a bit in the middle. The idea is that Lord Emsworth has been landed with a niece at the castle, said niece having got engaged to a man her family disapproves of, a pal of Freddie Threepwood's. Freddie has seen a film where the same thing happened and the man, disguised with false whiskers, went and curried favour with the family, and then when they were all crazy about him, tore off the whiskers and asked for their blessing. So he sends the young man to stay at Blandings, telling Lord E. he is a friend of his named Popjoy. He tells the young man to strain every nerve to ingratiate himself with Lord E.

Now, you see what happens. The fellow spends his whole time hanging round Lord E., helping him up out of chairs, asking him questions about the gardens, etc. etc., and it simply maddens Lord E., who feels he has never loathed a young man more.

See the idea? Well, what is bothering me is the getting of the cumulative details which lead up to Lord E. loathing the young man. Can you think of any? What *would* a young man in that position do, thinking he was making a big hit with the old man when really he was driving him off his head? It all leads up to my big scene, where Lord E., having at last, as he thinks, eluded the young man, goes and bathes in the lake and is so delighted at having got away from him for a couple of minutes, that he starts to sing and kick his feet from sheer joy. Which causes the young man, who is lurking in the bushes, to think he is drowning and dive in and save him, starting, of course, by beating him over the head to keep him from struggling.

I've done the first 2,500 words, up to the moment of the young man's arrival at the castle, and I think it's good. I now have to think of some more details to fill in with before the rescue scene.

July 26th, 1928.   *Rogate Lodge, Sussex.*

We have been getting quite social lately. Guests in every nook and cranny. John Galsworthy came to lunch yesterday – he has a house near here – and we also had Leslie Howard, who is going to play opposite Tallulah Bankhead in that show

I adapted, *Her Cardboard Lover*. Did you know that Leslie was at Dulwich a year or two after our time? Leslie Howard is a stage name, so it's no good searching the school records. Probably Slacker knows all about him. He – L. H. – is an awfully nice fellow and a very good writer on the side. He wrote some excellent short things, very funny, which he showed me one day in New York, and I was able to get Frank Crowninshield, the editor of *Vanity Fair*, to use them.

Don't you think the tragedy of an author's life is the passion printers have for exclamation marks? They love to shove them in every second sentence. I've just been re-reading *Piccadilly Jim*, of which I did not correct the proofs, being in New York, and the book is bristling with them. Specimen sentence: 'But wait a minute! I don't get this!' It gives an impression of febrile excitement which spoils the whole run of the dialogue.

Ian Hay has been here, too, dramatizing *A Damsel in Distress*. Tom Miller and Basil Foster are putting it on. It opens in London on August 14th. We have formed a syndicate – the management, Ian and I each putting up five hundred quid. We needed another five hundred to make up the necessary two thousand, and A. A. Milne gallantly stepped forward and said he would like to come in. I don't think we shall lose our money, as Ian has done an awfully good job.

September 28th, 1928.   *Rogate Lodge.*

The two shows are doing marvellously. Both were well over the two thousand pounds last week. *Her Cardboard Lover* hasn't dropped below two thousand two hundred yet, but I have an uneasy feeling all the time that it is one of those plays that may go all to nothing at short notice, though Tallulah is terrific, as is Leslie Howard. *Damsel in Distress* looks solid and ought to run a year. It has gone up steadily every week.

I have spent the summer writing and rewriting the first thirty thousand words of *Summer Lightning*, and must have done – all told – about a hundred thousand words. It is one of those stories which one starts without getting the plot properly fixed and keeps going off the rails. I think all is well now, but I am shelving it to do some short stories.

How about C. E. Montague? Do you ever see his stuff? I've just found a good thing by him called *Judith*. Apart from that, I seem to have read nothing lately. Oh, yes, H. G. Wells' *Mr Blettsworthy*. Only fair, I thought.

(Nature note. A local cow starts mooing before dawn and goes steadily on and on. I now get, in consequence, about five hours sleep a night.)

Listen, Bill, something really must be done about Kip's *Mrs Bathurst*. I read it years ago and didn't understand a word of it. I thought to myself: 'Ah, youthful ignorance!' A week ago I re-read it. Result, precisely the same. What did the villain do to Mrs Bathurst? What did he tell the Captain in his cabin that made the Captain look very grave and send him up country where he was struck by lightning? Why was the other chap who was struck by lightning, too, introduced? And, above all, how was Kip allowed to get away with six solid pages of padding at the start of the story?

Have you any short story plots you want to dispose of? I need a Lord Emsworth plot and also a Ukridge. I am planning a vast campaign. I want to write six short stories simultaneously. I have three plots to begin with and I want three more. Don't you feel, when writing a story, that if only it were some other story you could write it on your head? I do. I'm sure it's the best way to have two or three going at the same time, so that when you get sick of the characters of one you can switch to another.

*   *   *

I laughed when I read Plum's 'I am planning a vast campaign', for in these words the creator of Ukridge is so clearly revealed. Again and again this is precisely what Ukridge planned to do, to be invariably in Plum's stories robbed of the fruits of his ingenuity.

The stories of Rudyard Kipling no longer seem to be popular and I wonder how many young men or women under thirty have read *Mrs Bathurst*, a great short story in spite of its leisurely start. But even now, fifty years after that story was written, I should dearly like to know the solution to the mystery.

Can anyone explain what happened between Vickery and Mrs Bathurst or why Vickery, having seen her walking toward the camera in a motion picture of the arrival of a train at an English railway station, shown at a circus in Durban – or was it Capetown? – should have expressed such consternation? It was true, I know, that he had thought of her as still living in New Zealand, but why, even supposing that they had had a love affair, should her arrival in England when he was in South Africa have so disturbed him? Why, too, should he have made that cryptic remark to Pyecroft that his lawful wife had died in childbirth? I often think I should like to insert a notice in *The Times* personal column asking if some clever person would clear up the mystery of *Mrs Bathurst* before it is too late.

*   *   *

October 18th, 1928.   *The Impney Hotel, Droitwich.*

I've just got a copy of *The Ship in the Swamp*. I think it's marvellous. My introduction is all wrong, of course, much too flippant. A book like that ought to have had something worthy of it. It's the best collection of short stories that has been published since *Where the Pavement Ends*. How infinitely better your stuff reads in book form than in magazine small print.

You've got to hand it to Grimsdick. This time he really has made a book. That jacket is terrific. And I feel now he was right in insisting on *The Ship in the Swamp* as the title. It's one of the few titles I've seen that grips the imagination. With that jacket, with the yellow flowers growing over the ship; you wonder what the deuce it is all about and you feel you must find out.

The only way to get a book public is to keep plugging away without any long intervals. They don't know you're writing till you've published about half a dozen. I produced five books which fell absolutely flat, and then got going with *Piccadilly Jim*. And when I say five I mean seven. I suppose if *Piccadilly Jim* had been published first it would have fallen as flat as the others, but all the time I must have been creating a public bit by bit and I feel it's going to be the same for you.

I enclose some letters in answer to some I wrote. Arnold Bennett's is a bit obscure. I also wrote to the *Daily Express*, etc. Are there any other reviewers you think would help? Why not send signed copies to all the editors who have used your stories – e.g. *Strand*, *Nash's*, *Storyteller*, etc.? You never know how much that sort of thing helps.

I'm going to write to Conan Doyle and Rudyard Kipling about it. After all, they can only snub me.

Dulwich have got a red-hot team this year. Nine old colours

from last year's side, which lost only to Bedford. Unfortunately, I hear Sherborne and Haileybury have got special teams, too. Still, I'm hoping we beat Bedford next Saturday. You must come up and see at least one game. Why not St Paul's at West Kensington on Saturday week?

*   *   *

Here is yet another instance of what trouble Plum went to in order to help a friend. His efforts regarding *The Ship in the Swamp* bore fruit as I had a succession of excellent notices for the book.

Owen Seaman wrote:

My dear Wodehouse:

> *The Ship in the Swamp* is being sent out to be reviewed by our maritime expert. I look forward to seeing you soon at the Beefsteak, especially as I want a personal talk with you.

Arnold Bennett wrote:

Dear Wodehouse:

> Thank you for your letter of the 12th, about Mr Townend. If I come across the book, and if I think it is better than yours, I will say so. But I very much doubt whether this will happen. As a contributor to the *Evening Standard*, I am the most callous fellow that God ever created.

which, though obscure, as Plum said, shows a sturdy and commendable independence, at least, and a belief that God created Arnold Bennett.

*   *   *

December 1st, 1928.   *17 Norfolk Street.*

I had a letter from New York on November 10th, saying that *Collier's* must have my serial by January 1st! Only 30,000 words written then and those all wrong. I have rewritten them and another 20,000, sweating like blazes! They now say that January 15th will be all right, so I think I'll deliver on time. But, my gosh, what a rush!

*   *   *

And now, omitting pages of advice and guidance on dead-and-gone stories, let us turn to a topic that has for more than a quarter of a century been dear to Plum Wodehouse's heart: Pekes.

There is a tendency for people, young people especially, to despise Pekes as pampered lapdogs, but though small in size no breed of dog is more courageous or attractive than the Pekinese. The Wodehouses' Peke, Susan, had lately had puppies and Ethel Wodehouse had asked my wife if she would like one. The answer was that she would, of course. In a long letter, dated December 15th, 1928, Plum wrote:

*   *   *

In *re* Bimmy. The great point is that a Peke needs a frightful lot of petting. Is Rene game to leave off doing whatever she is doing in order to pick Bimmy up and pet her?

*   *   *

Plum need have had no anxiety. Bimmy became the centre around which our household life revolved, as it were, and no more lovable or more sporting little dog ever breathed. She was quite without fear and used to paralyse us by dashing excitedly at the big farm bull when she met him being exercised on the road by the cowman. The bull, a normally sullen beast, was never hostile as he might have been toward a larger dog, merely a little confused and perplexed.

Bimmy, a miniature red brindle, was friendly toward all other animals, cows, horses, pigs – though pigs puzzled her – and cats. Only once did we see her angry and that was when an Alsatian who lived nearby rushed out of his garden gate as Bimmy went racing by and hustled her roughly. Bimmy, without checking her pace, turned, snarling, and snapped at him fiercely, resenting his interference, and the Alsatian halted and gazed after her in consternation, astounded that so small an animal should dare quarrel with him.

*   *   *

April 13th, 1929.

If you haven't been paid in advance for your stuff, you must be rolling now. I see nothing but your stories wherever I look.

Now about America. Harold Ober, Reynolds' partner, is in London now, and I should very much like you to meet him. Couldn't you come up one day next week and stay the night? I shall have a show on at the Golder's Green theatre (it comes to the *Globe* Monday week), and you and Rene could see that. We could give Ober a lunch and have a valuable talk about your work.

I was down at Southsea a week ago, opening this new show by Ian Hay and me, called *Baa, Baa, Black Sheep*, and I don't wonder you used to hate living there in the old days. What a particularly melancholy place it is with that beastly common between you and the sea. I like Portsmouth, but I can't stand Southsea. The show went marvellously there. Terrific enthusiasm, and we took £1,150 in the week, which, of course, is very good for a try-out. I only hope London will like it as well.

April 27th, 1929.   *Hunstanton Hall.*

I would have written before, but I have had a hell of a week. On Sunday I had to condense *Good Morning, Bill* into a sketch for Heather Thatcher. (She opens at the Coliseum on Whit Monday.) From Monday to Thursday night I was writing a Jeeves story in response to an urgent demand from America that I get it off by Saturday's boat, which meant mailing it from here not later than noon on Friday. (And why they wanted it so soon I can't think. It is for the October number of the *Cosmopolitan*.) On Friday and yesterday I was so exhausted I couldn't write. (Incidentally, you surely aren't aiming at writing a story a week? The strain would be too awful. Three a month is just possible, but even so, don't you think you would lose in merit what you gained in production? I find that if I work really quick on a story, I become incapable of judging it, and have to lay it aside for a week to let it get cool.)

It's wonderful being back at Hunstanton again, though things aren't so frightfully bright at the moment, as host has had a row with butler, who has given notice. The butler is a cheery soul who used to be the life and soul of the party, joining in the conversation at meals and laughing appreciatively if one made a joke, but now he hovers like a spectre, very strong and silent. I'm hoping peace will be declared soon.

I think I like Hunstanton as well in winter as in summer, though, of course, I don't get the moat in the winter months. I laid the scene of *Money for Nothing* at Hunstanton Hall.

What bloodstained books you seem to read! I haven't seen any of them. Down here I am limited to what there is in the house – principally Elizabethan dramatists – and what I can get from the twopence-a-go library in the town. How are you on the Elizabethan dramatists? My opinion, now that I have read them all, is that they are a shade better than Restoration dramatists, but as you rightly remark, that is not saying much.

These seaside libraries are a bit apt to have nothing later than *By Order of the Czar*, but the Hunstanton one is quite good. I have been able to get a number of tuppennyworths of E. V. Lucas and W. B. Maxwell, which I had read before, of course, but found I could read again. Do you know Lucas's novels – *London Lavender*, etc? He takes a character and sends him wandering around and meeting all sorts of odd people, or else he tells the thing in letters. I've read them all about a dozen times each, but I can always go back to them.

The first time I met Lucas was soon after I had begun writing 'By the Way' on the *Globe*. He had been doing a column a year or two before with C. L. Graves. The thing I can't understand about him is that in those days – 1903 or thereabouts – he was morbidly shy, so shy that it was really agony for him to meet people. He told me once that he would often bury his face in his hands just to avoid seeing his fellow men for a minute or so. Yet now he seems to be a regular mixer. Odd.

And talking of Maxwell. He came to dinner one night at

Norfolk Street when I wasn't there, and Ethel, greeting him in the library, told him that he was one of my favourite authors (which was quite true), and that I was never happier than when among his books, so to speak. And then to her horror she saw his eye swivelling round the shelves and realized that there wasn't a single Maxwell book there. The solution, of course, was that all his were in my study upstairs where I keep the books I like best. But I suppose for the rest of his life he will regard me as a fraud and a humbug. No means of letting him know the truth, of course.

I don't think any of those books you mention really amount to much. It seems to me that at least two-thirds of the stuff published nowadays is by one-book people. You know, *A Stirring Revelation of a Young Girl's Soul*, by Jane Emmeline Banks, who never writes another damn book in her life. The test is, can you write three?

August 17th, 1929.   *Hunstanton Hall.*

I did curse when I got your letter saying that Rene had been staying at her sister's for a week and that you had been all alone – just the very week I was up in London by myself. You could have come and stayed with me, and we could have sat up all night talking. All that week – which was given up per day to duty lunches and rehearsals – I used to get back to the house at 9.30 and sit reading till one a.m. It never occurred to me to try to get in touch with you, as I knew you were working, and my days were full up. Blast it! However—

The day before yesterday I was rung up and told that Flo Ziegfeld wanted to speak to me from New York. After a lot of waiting, I was told that the phone call had been cancelled.

He cabled instead. He wants me to go out immediately to help with a musical comedy. I had been wavering about going out for the production of *Candlelight* and this has decided me. His last cable said that he was arranging my passage through an agency who would communicate with me. It might mean next Wednesday, though I hope not. I don't expect to be over more than six weeks this time, and hope to return early in October.

Susan's devotion is beginning to affect my liver. I can't get a bit of exercise. She won't let me out of her sight, and she won't come for long walks. If I try to take her, she just sits down and looks pathetic. What she likes is to lie in the middle of the lawn and have me walk round and round her. She won't let me go on the moat, and if I bicycle to the town I have to take her along, tucked into my sweater. I hope she won't miss me too much when I leave. I don't think she will, as she will be with Ethel and will have Winks.

I lunched with Askew and Grimsdick the other day and they both almost wept at the idea of your not doing another long novel. Askew looks on you as the greatest sea story writer going and Grimsdick said he knew your stuff would sell, if you kept up the supply.

I'll try to see the *Saturday Evening Post* people when I'm in New York and ask them about your stuff. I might get a line on what they want. Broadly, of course, they like action as opposed to subtlety. The longer I write, the more I realize the necessity for telling a story as far as possible in scenes, especially at the start.

October 2nd, 1929.   *14 East 60th Street, New York.*

I am having the usual Ziegfeld experience. I have been here six weeks and nothing has happened yet. I don't expect to be back in England before Christmas.

The show I'm doing is a musical version of a – lousy in my opinion but very successful – play called *East is West*, done in 1918, all about a Chinese girl who goes around saying 'Me love Chlistian god velly much' and that sort of thing, and turns out in the end to be the daughter of an American missionary, kidnapped by Chinese in her infancy. I think it's frightful, but I suppose Flo is fascinated by the thought of how he will be able to spread himself over the costumes, and anyway I haven't anything to do with the writing of the book. Bill McGuire is doing that, at least he's supposed to be, but as far as I can make out he hasn't started yet. You would love Bill McGuire. He is exactly like Ukridge. Remind me to tell you when I get back, the story of him and the gangsters and the diamond ring. Much too long to relate here, but a laugh in every line.

The music is by Vincent Youmans, if he ever gets around to doing any, and I am collaborating on the lyrics with a very pleasant lad named Billy Rose, who broke into the Hall of Fame with a song entitled: 'Does the Chewing-Gum Lose its Flavour on the Bedpost Overnight?' As far as I can make out, Billy and I are the only members of the gang who are doing a stroke of work. I go around to his hotel every morning and we hammer out a lyric together and turn it in to Youmans, after which nothing more is heard of it.

So what with this and what with that it seemed to me a good idea to take a few days off and go to Hollywood. I wanted to see what the place was like before committing myself to it for an extended period. I was there three days, but having in an absent-minded moment forgotten to tell Flo and Gilbert Miller that this was only a flying visit, I created something of an upheaval in the bosoms of both. Flo wanted to have me around, as he expected Bill McGuire and Youmans to come out of their respective trances at any moment, and rehearsals of my adaptation of *Candlelight* for Gertie Lawrence were nearing their end and the out-of-town opening coming along, so Gilbert wanted me around, too. It was a nasty jar, therefore, when they were told that I had gone to Hollywood, presumably for good.

It hit Flo hardest, because he loves sending thousand-word telegrams telling people what he thinks of them, and he had no address where he could reach me. From what Billie Burke (Mrs Flo) told me later, I gather that he nearly had apoplexy. However, all was forgotten and forgiven when I returned on the ninth day. I went to Baltimore, where *Candlelight* was playing, and got a rather chilly reception from Gertie, but was eventually taken back into the fold.

Candlelight has since opened in New York and looks like a hit. We did $18,060 the first week. Gertie is wonderful, as always. This is the first time she has done a straight show without music, but she is just as good as she was in *Oh, Kay!* I don't believe there's anybody on the stage who can do comedy better.

I liked what little I saw of Hollywood and expect to return there in the summer. I have had three offers of a year's work, but I held out for only five months.

The only person I knew really well out there was Marion Davies, who was in the show *Oh, Boy!*, which Guy Bolton, Jerry Kern and I did for the Princess Theatre. She took me out to her house in Santa Monica and worked me into a big lunch at Metro-Goldwyn which they were giving for Winston Churchill. All very pleasant. Churchill made a speech at the lunch, and when he had finished Louis B. Mayer said: 'That was a very good speech. I think we would all like to hear it again,' and it was played back from an apparatus concealed in the flowers on the table. Churchill seemed rather taken aback.

I wanted to go to Chula Vista, but of course hadn't time. I must do it when I come here again.

I have reluctantly come to the conclusion that I must have one of those meaningless faces which make no impression whatever on the beholder. This was – I think – the seventh time I had been introduced to Churchill, and I could see that I came upon him as a complete surprise once more. Not a trace of that 'Why, of course I remember you, Mr Addison Simms of Seattle' stuff.

* * *

Chula Vista which Plum speaks of was in my day – 1910 to 1913 – a small ranch town south of San Diego some eight miles from the Mexican line. I lived there for some time and earned a precarious living at sundry jobs while writing stories in the evenings after the day's work was done. Chula Vista was a lovely little place, situated between the Pacific Ocean and the Coast Range of mountains in a setting of orange and lemon orchards, and palms and pepper and eucalyptus trees. Quite recently, Raymond Chandler in one of his letters told me that if I saw the place I would not like it, so greatly changed was it from the little town I had known.

The Billy Rose whom Plum mentions as his collaborator in the lyrics of the Chinese musical play shortly afterwards became a millionaire. During the great fair, he ran what was called the Acquacade, a swimming-and-diving-belle entertainment out near La Guardia airfield. His expenses per week were thirty thousand dollars, and he never failed to take in a hundred thousand, one bumper week topping two hundred and sixty thousand. This went on all through the summer, and it was at a time when the American income tax was a mere nineteen per cent.

* * *

November 11th, 1929.   *17 Norfolk Street.*

I'm longing to get down and see you all, but I'm in the middle of a story, which I must finish before I can make any move. I've gone and let myself in for one of those stories which lead up to a big comic scene and now I'm faced with writing the scene and it looks as if it was going to be difficult to make funny. It's a village Rugger match, where everybody tries to slay everybody else, described by Bertie Wooster who, of course, knows nothing about Rugger. It's damned hard to describe a game you know backward through the eyes of somebody who doesn't know it. However, I suppose it will come. These things always do. But it isn't easy.

I went down to Dulwich and saw the Mill Hill game. It was very one-sided and dull. We have a great side this year and I'm hoping we beat Haileybury on Saturday. It's rather funny how we regard the Bedford match. Nobody seems a bit pleased at having beaten them by twenty-five points. They take it for granted that Bedford must have a very bad team, and not that we have a good one. They appear to think there's something rather indecent about beating Bedford by twenty-five points.

Aren't Peke puppies the most fascinating things on earth? What are you going to do with them?

I want to talk to you about that story you sent me. It doesn't seem to be quite right, and I think I have spotted the flaw.

* * *

The remainder of the letter is taken up by another of Plum's masterly analyses of where a story had gone wrong and some suggestions as to how it could be improved.

* * *

December 9th, 1929.

What a sweat a novel is till you are sure of your characters. And what a vital thing it is to have plenty of things for a major character to *do*. That is the test. If they aren't in situations, characters can't be major characters, not even if you have the rest of the troupe talk their heads off about them.

I have just had a cable from Hollywood. They want me to do a picture for Evelyn Laye. This may mean a long trip out there pretty soon, but I don't expect to stay very long. I shall know more on December 21st when Sam Goldwyn arrives in England.

January 8th, 1930.   *17 Norfolk Street.*

My novel, *Big Money*, is coming out terrifically, and I am very nearly half-way through. The aunt has been eliminated altogether, and so has the hero's father – after four distinct and concrete versions were scrapped.

My main trouble is that my heroine refuses to come alive,

and what makes it worse is that the second girl is a pippin. I'm afraid the reader will skip all the stuff dealing with the hero and heroine and concentrate on the scenes between the second man and the second girl.

It looks as if Hollywood was off. I had some sessions with Goldwyn, but he wouldn't meet my price. The poor chump seemed to think he was doing me a favour offering about half what I get for a serial for doing a job which would be the most ghastly sweat. He said, when he sailed today, that he would think things over and let me know, but I'm hoping I have made the price too stiff for him. I don't want to go to Hollywood just now a bit. Later on, in the Spring, I should like it. But I feel now I want to be left alone with my novel.

I'm glad Christmas is over. I came in for the New Year festivities at Hunstanton, and had to wear a white waistcoat every night.

* * *

Four months later Plum set out for Hollywood. Ethel Wodehouse, who had gone to New York at the end of 1929, arranged a contract for him with Metro-Goldwyn-Mayer – six months at $2,500 a week with an option for another six months.

* * *

Metro–Goldwyn–Mayer Studios,
June 26th, 1930.   *Culver City, California.*

I have been meaning to write to you for ages, but I have been in a tremendous whirl of work ever since I arrived in Hollywood. For some obscure reason, after being absolutely dead for months, my brain suddenly started going like a dynamo. I got a new plot for a short story every day for a week. Then I started writing, and in well under a month have done three short stories, an act of a play, and all the dialogue for a picture.

There is something about this place that breeds work. We have a delightful house – Norma Shearer's – with a small but lovely garden and a big swimming-pool, the whole enclosed in patio form. The three wings of the house occupy three sides, a high wall, looking on to a deserted road, the other. So that one feels quite isolated. I have arranged with the studio to work at home, so often I spend three or four days on end without going out of the garden: I get up, swim, breakfast, work till two, swim again, have a lunch-tea, work till seven, swim for the third time, then dinner and the day is over. It is wonderful. I have never had such a frenzy of composition.

One of the stories I have written is your cat plot. The story of Webster, do you remember – the artist and the dignified cat? I have added a lot to the plot. It now ends differently. Hero has a row with his girl, flies to whiskey bottle, sees cat staring gravely and rebukingly at him, drops bottle, cat laps up whiskey, gets tight, springs through window and cleans up an alley cat which has been saying rude things to him for weeks. Hero realizes cat is one of the boys after all, and all is well. It has worked out as one of the best things I have ever done.

How is everything your end? I hope you have been selling stuff lately. Write and tell me all about everything.

I haven't made my pilgrimage to Chula Vista yet. Nor has Ethel arrived. I shall wait till she comes.

California is all right. It's a wonderful relief not having to worry about the weather. Incidentally, it is only in the past few days that it has been really hot and sunny. We had three weeks of dull English weather. Still, it never rained.

I don't see much of the movie world. My studio is five miles from where I live, and I only go there occasionally. If I ever dine out or go to parties, it is with other exiles – New York writers, etc. Most of my New York theatre friends are here.

Odd place this. Miles and miles of one-story bungalows, mostly Spanish, each with a little lawn in front and a pocket-handkerchief garden at the back, all jammed together in rows. Beverly Hills, where I am, is the rather aristocratic sector. Very pretty. Our house has a garden the size of the garden of any small house at Dulwich, and we pay two hundred quid a month for it.

August 18th, 1930.　　　　　*Metro-Goldwyn Studio, Culver City.*

Awfully glad to hear from you. That's fine about the story the *Saturday Evening Post* bought.

There is a writer here called John Farrow. Have you ever heard of him? He was saying something to someone the other day about how much he liked your work, especially *Tiger Bay.* He is a man who served before the mast. I met him not long ago and he said how well you know the sea and wanted to know if you had ever been a sailor.

Ethel arrived a month ago, with Winks under her arm. Winks has settled down finely and seems to be very happy. We are devoted to her, and she seems to have taken on a lot of Susan's characteristics. She barks furiously at our Japanese gardener.

I expect to be out here till next Spring. I might dash back to England for a week or two before that, but I am not counting on it, as I expect they will want me to stick on without going away.

As regards ideas I have had another barren spell. Isn't it the devil, how you get these brilliant periods when nothing seems easier than to plot out stories, and then comes the blank? Oddly enough, Hollywood hasn't inspired me in the least. I feel as if everything that could be written about it has already been done.

As a matter of fact, I don't think there is much to be written about this place. What it was like in the early days, I don't know, but nowadays the studio life is all perfectly normal, not a bit crazy. I haven't seen any swooning directors or temperamental stars. They seem just to do their job, and to be quite ordinary people, especially the directors, who are quiet, unemotional men who just work and don't throw any fits. Same with the stars. I don't believe I shall get a single story out of my stay here.

* * *

This letter was written about ten months before Plum was to shake the film industry to its foundations and, quite unintentionally, bring about what amounted to a major revolution. His forebodings about not getting a single story out of his stay in Hollywood were quite unjustified. Before he left for home he wrote the funniest skits on film stars and the making of films ever written. The yes-men of his stories became portents of the financial storm that was to break with such devastating fury. They can be found among the stories in the book entitled *Blandings Castle*.

* * *

October 28th, 1930.   *Metro–Goldwyn Studios.*

I was delighted to get your long letter. What a shame you had to alter the title of the new book. I agree I can't see why, in these days when there are so many books coming out, it matters if two titles clash. I see a man has just published a book called *Seventeen*. Well, you'd have thought Booth Tarkington had established the sole right to that title, but I'll bet nobody notices anything funny.

Well, laddie, it begins to look as if it would be some time before I return to England. The Metro people have taken up my option, and I am with them for another six months and Ethel has just taken a new house for a year. Which means that I shall probably stay that long.

If you came over here and settled down, I think I would spend at least six months in every year here. I like the place. I think Californian scenery is the most loathsome on earth – a cross between Coney Island and the Riviera – but by sticking in one's garden all the time and shutting one's eyes when one goes out, it is possible to get by.

As life goes on, though, don't you find that all you need is a wife, a few real friends, a regular supply of books, and a Peke? (Make that two Pekes and add a swimming-pool.)

M-G-M bought that musical comedy *Rosalie* – the thing Guy Bolton, Bill McGuire, George Gershwin, Sigmund Romberg, Ira Gershwin, and I did for Ziegfeld for Marilyn Miller – for Marion Davies. Everyone in the studio had a go at it, and then they told me to try. After I had messed about with it with no success, Irving Thalberg, the big boss (and a most charming fellow incidentally, about the nicest chap I've run into out here – he is Norma Shearer's husband) worked out a story on his own and summoned me to Santa Barbara, where he was spending a few days, to hear it. I drove down there with a stenographer from the studio, and he dictated a complete scenario. When he had finished, he leaned back and mopped his brow, and asked me if I wanted to have it read over to me. I was about to say Yes (just to make the party go), when I suddenly caught the stenographer's eye and was startled to see a look of agonized entreaty in it. I couldn't imagine what was wrong, but I gathered that for some reason she wanted me to say No, so I said No. When we were driving home, she told me that she had had a latish night the night before and had fallen asleep at the outset of the proceedings and slept peacefully throughout, not having heard or taken down a word.

Fortunately, I could remember the high spots of the thing, well enough to start working on it. Unfortunately, for some inscrutable reason Thalberg wants me to write it not in picture form but as a novelette, after which I suppose it will be turned into a picture. The prospect of this appals me, and I am hoping that the whole thing will eventually blow over, as things do out here.

What did Sheila Kaye-Smith object to in *Angel Pavement*? I thought it a splendid book. Curious method of writing Priestley has, though. Have you noticed it? A lot of characters with practically no connection with each other are attended to in turn, e.g. Smeeth and Dersingham. You get fifty pages of Smeeth at home, then fifty pages of Dersingham at home. Then a chunk of some other character. I always feel that I have got to link up, and that I couldn't show Dersingham at home without bringing Smeeth on, too, to play a scene with him.

I am still bathing vigorously three times a day, though in the early morning the water is pretty chilly. They tell me that with care you can bathe all through the winter.

Winks is barking like blazes in the garden. I think it must be the Japanese gardener, whom she hasn't accepted even after seeing him every day for six months.

Last night Maureen O'Sullivan brought her new Peke round here, and Winks was very austere. Do you remember the day you and Rene and Bimmy arrived in Norfolk Street? I had been looking forward sentimentally to the reunion of the two sisters and as I came downstairs I heard the most frightful snarling and yapping, and there was Winks trying to eat Bimmy. Odd, too, how the row stopped directly we took them out on to the steps. Apparently a Peke only resents Peke visitors in the actual house.

Leave it to Psmith seems to have got over all right in London. Thanks for the notices. Of course no one else ever thought of sending me any. (Aren't people funny about that? They write and tell you there was something awfully nice about you in the *Phoenix (Arizona) Intelligencer*, and take it for granted that you must have seen it yourself.)

Psmith did twenty-four hundred pounds at Golder's Green and two thousand and seventeen the first week at the Shaftesbury, during which week, of course, a lot of free seats had to be given away. *Damsel in Distress* only did sixteen hundred its first week in London.

I am at last reading *The Good Companions*. I love it. That's the sort of book I would like to write.

February 25th, 1931.

Only time for a scribble. The studio has just given me a job which will take up all my time for weeks, though I'll bet when I've finished it, it will be pigeon-holed and never heard of again.

I'm afraid just now is a bad time for stories unless commissioned. All the Mags, except the *S.E.P.*, are living on their accumulated stuff. This can't last much longer, and business conditions seem to be improving already.

I have been away for a week at Hearst's ranch. He owns 440,000 acres, more than the whole of Long Island! We took Winks, who was a great hit.

The ranch is about half-way between Hollywood and San Francisco. It is on the top of a high hill, and just inside the entrance gates is a great pile of stones, which, if you ever put them together, would form an old abbey which Hearst bought in France and shipped over and didn't know what to do with so left lying by the wayside. The next thing you see, having driven past this, is a yak or a buffalo or something in the middle of the road. Hearst collects animals and has a zoo on the premises, and the ones considered reasonably harmless are allowed to roam at large. You're apt to meet a bear or two before you get to the house.

The house is enormous, and there are always at least fifty guests staying there. All the furniture is period, and you probably sleep on a bed originally occupied by Napoleon or somebody. Ethel and I shared the Venetian suite with Sidney Blackmer, who had blown in from one of the studios.

The train that takes guests away leaves after midnight, and the one that brings new guests arrives early in the morning, so you have dinner with one lot of people and come down to breakfast next morning and find an entirely fresh crowd.

Meals are in an enormous room, and are served at a long table, with Hearst sitting in the middle on one side and Marion Davies in the middle on the other. The longer you are there, the further you get from the middle. I sat on Marion's right the first night, then found myself being edged further and further away till I got to the extreme end, when I thought it time to leave. Another day, and I should have been feeding on the floor.

March 14th, 1931.   *M-G-M Studio.*

I wish you were here for this weather. It is as warm as summer, and I am bathing regularly. The pool is a nice 62 degrees.

I am doing a picture version of *By Candlelight* now for John Gilbert. This looks as if it really might come to something. Everything else I have done so far has been scrapped. But I doubt if they intend to give me another contract. The enclosed paragraph from *Variety* can only refer to me, and it looks darned sinister. My only hope is that I have made myself so pleasant to all the studio heads that by now I may count as a cousin by marriage or something.

I must stop now, as we have to go out to dinner. Corinne Griffith.

Winks is in great form, and has got quite reconciled to having Johnnie, Maureen O'Sullivan's Peke, as a guest. We are putting Johnnie up while Maureen is in Ireland. Sex female in spite of the name, and age about a year. Very rowdy towards Winks, who disapproves rather. Johnnie is the only ugly Peke I have ever seen. She was run over by a car some months ago and has lost an eye. She looks like one of your tougher sailors.

*　　*　　*

This was the paragraph from *Variety* to which Plum refers:

Following *Variety*'s report of the ludicrous writer talent situation, eastern executives interrogated the studios as to instances such as concerned one English playwright and author who has been collecting $2,500 a week at one of the major studios for eleven months, without contributing anything really worth while to the screen.

I personally, having seen many bad Hollywood films and very few good ones, am convinced that Plum's non-success was due to the fact that the people responsible for making films were unable to recognize a good idea when it was given them. Unless a story conformed to their low standards, it was no use to them.

* * *

May 19th, 1931.   *Metro-Goldwyn Studio.*

Everything is very wobbly and depressed over here these days. We seem to be getting a sort of second instalment of the 1929 crash. The movies are in a bad state, and M-G-M showed no desire to engage me again when my contract lapsed last week. Meanwhile I am plugging along with *Hot Water* and have done 60,000 words, but it looks like being one of those long ones and I doubt if I shall finish it before mid-August.

Two Hollywood stories, one previous to that interview of mine, the other more recent. The first is supposed to illustrate the Hollywood idea of poverty. A supervisor was giving a writer instructions about the picture he wanted him to work on. He said the outline was that a father has a ne'er-do-well son and gets fed up with his escapades and thinks the only thing to make a man of the young fellow is to force him to battle with the world for himself. So he cuts him off with $500 a week. The other story is quite a recent one, and has to do with the current depression. A man standing in the crowd outside a movie theatre here after a big opening hears the carriage starter calling for 'Mr Warner's automobile', 'Mr Lasky's automobile',

'Mr Louis B. Mayer's automobile', and so on, and he shakes his head. 'At an opening a year from now,' he says, 'there won't be any of this stuff about automobiles. You'll hear them call for Mr Warner's bicycle, Mr Lasky's kiddie car and Mr Louis B. Mayer's roller-skates.'

I'm afraid that interview of mine has had a lot to do with the depression in the picture world. Yet I was only saying what everybody has been saying for years. Apparently what caused the explosion was my giving figures and mentioning a definite studio in print. But, damn it all, it never ought to have been in print. It was just a casual remark I happened to drop off the record (though, like an ass, I didn't say that it was off the record). It just shows that with these American reporters you must weigh every word before you speak.

Another story, not a Hollywood one. Wilton Lackaye, the actor, was playing in San Francisco and invited the editor of one of the San Francisco papers to dinner one night. The editor said he was sorry but he couldn't come, because he had a conference. 'A conference?' said Lackaye. 'What's that for?' The editor explained. 'We get together every day for an hour or so and decide what is to be in the next day's paper – matters of policy, emphasis on news and all that sort of thing.' 'Good heavens!' said Lackaye, amazed. 'Do you mean to tell me that you get out that paper *deliberately*?'

We have been having a heat wave for the last week. I never noticed the heat last year, but this has been terrific. At that, though, it isn't as bad as it was sometimes in the East. I remember when Guy Bolton and I were at Great Neck writing *Oh, Kay!*, for Gertie Lawrence in the summer of 1926, I used to have to change my shirt three times in a morning.

Heather Thatcher has turned up to spend a couple of

months with us. We gave a big party for her yesterday, which I found rather loathsome, as it seemed to pollute our nice garden. There was a mob milling round in it from four in the afternoon till eleven at night. About twenty people in the pool at one time. The only beauty of having a party in your own home is that you can sneak away. I went upstairs to my room at five and only appeared for dinner, returning to my room at eight sharp. (The perfect host.) I re-read *Cakes and Ale*. What a masterly book it is. Have you read it? Incidentally, if they were going to pick on anyone for being irreverent towards the old Victorian master, why not Hugh Walpole for his *Hans Frost*? Did you read that one?

I can't remember if you said you liked or disliked Dorothy Parker's *Lament for the Living*. I have just got it out of the library, and it's good.

We are toying with a scheme for going round the world in December on the *Empress of Britain*. Sometimes we feel we should like it, and then we ask ourselves if we really want to see the ruddy world. I'm darned if I know. I have never seen any spectacular spot yet that didn't disappoint me. Notably, the Grand Canyon, and also Niagara Falls.

Personally, I've always liked wandering around in the background. I mean, I get much more kick out of a place like Droitwich, which has no real merits, than out of something like the Taj Mahal.

Maureen O'Sullivan's Peke is still with us. She – the Peke, not Maureen – snores like twenty dogs and sleeps under my bed. I'm getting used to it. She is the ugliest and greediest hound I ever met, but full of charm.

*   *   *

The first intimation we had at home that anything had gone wrong was reading in *The Times* a brief report of the interview that was to rock Hollywood.

Although his contract had lapsed the Metro-Goldwyn-Mayer people rang Plum up one day to ask if he would give an interview to a woman reporter for the *Los Angeles Times*. Plum said he would be delighted.

The woman reporter duly arrived and was received by Plum politely and cheerfully. She asked Plum how he liked Hollywood. Plum said amiably that he liked Hollywood and its inhabitants immensely; he said how much he had enjoyed his stay and added, to fill in time and make conversation before the interview proper began, that his one regret was he had been paid such an enormous sum of money without having done anything to earn it.

And that was that.

The interview then got under way and was conducted by both parties on normal question and answer lines. The woman reporter withdrew, having got her scoop.

Early the next morning before Plum was out of bed the telephone rang. Someone wanted to speak to Mr P. G. Wodehouse. Plum answered: rather sleepily, I take it. A voice at the other end of the line said it was Reuter's Los Angeles correspondent speaking, and would Mr Wodehouse kindly say if the interview with him in that day's *Los Angeles Times* was authentic. Plum, rather startled at having been aroused at that hour to be asked so trite a question, said that it was. Reuter's correspondent then asked if he might have Mr Wodehouse's permission to cable it across to London and Plum, even more startled, said that he might!

A brief interval elapsed and then the telephone bell rang again. This time an agitated voice demanded if Mr Wodehouse had seen the interview in the *Los Angeles Times*, because if he had—

Plum dashed downstairs and grabbed the *Times* and almost the first thing he saw under scare headlines was the interview that was destined to revolutionize the motion picture industry and put it on a sound basis and cut out the dead wood, the woman reporter having printed every word he had said about his regret at having been paid such an enormous sum of money without having done a thing to earn it!

Before nightfall Plum was the most talked of man in the United States of America and the bankers went into action.

Some years later I read what the well-known American writer, Rupert Hughes, had to say about this strange episode in the *Saturday Evening Post*.

Many authors have been badly treated in Hollywood, but Hollywood has paid high for this idiocy. One of the gentlest and one of the most valuable for Hollywood – P. G. Wodehouse – quietly regretted that he had been paid a hundred thousand dollars for doing next to nothing. This remark was taken up, and it stirred the bankers deeply, as it should have done. But Mr Wodehouse has written no ferocious assaults on those who slighted him.

* * *

September 14th, 1931. *Beverly Hills.*

This business of writing to you has taken on a graver aspect, the postal authorities here having raised the ante to five cents per letter. I can bear it bravely as far as you are concerned, but I do grudge having to spend five cents on a letter to some female in East Grinstead who wants to know if I pronounce my name Wood-house or Wodehouse.

My art is not going too well at the moment. I have six more stories to do for the *American Magazine*, and ye Ed has put me right out of my stride by asking me to make them about American characters in an American setting, little knowing that if I try to do American stuff, the result is awful. Apparently he doesn't care for Mulliner stories, though I'll swear things like *Fate* and *The Fiery Wooing of Mordred* aren't bad, always provided you like my sort of stuff. What puzzles me about it all is that when he commissioned the series he must have known the sort of thing I wrote. It can't have come on him as a stunning shock to find that I was laying my scene in England. What did he expect from me? Thoughtful studies of life in the Arkansas foothills?

I suppose I ought to have taken a strong line and refused haughtily to change my act, but I'm all for strewing a little happiness as I go by, so I told him I would have a pop at some Hollywood stories.

Talking of taking a strong line, a negro out west somewhere had been cheated at a street-fair gambling concern and was pretty sore about it. He said to the man running the thing, 'I shall get even with you.' 'How?' said the gambler. 'You are coming here next year?' asked the negro. The gambler said he was. 'Well,' said the negro, 'when I see a white man coming up to gamble with you, I shall stand nearby and say "Oo! Oo!" '

We dined last night with Douglas Fairbanks and Mary Pickford. She is a most intelligent woman, quite unlike the usual movie star. I talked to her all the evening. (Probably bored her stiff.)

Have you read A. A. Milne's serial, *Two People* in the *Daily Mail*? It's colossal. The sort of book I shall buy and re-read every six months or so. What a genius he is at drawing character. Did you ever see his *The Dover Road*? My favourite play.

Hollywood story. Couple of boxers at the American Legion stadium put on a very mild show, and a spectator, meeting one of them after the fight, reproached him for giving such an inadequate exhibition. The boxer admitted that he had not mixed it up very vigorously, but had a satisfactory explanation. 'Couldn't take no chances of getting mussed up,' he said, 'not with a part in Mae West's new picture coming along.'

A New York actress has just got back to Broadway after a year in Hollywood. She says that she has been so long among the false fronts and papier-mâché mansions on the set that nowadays she finds herself sneaking a look at her husband to see if he goes all the way round or is just a profile.

Non-Hollywood story. Inez Haynes Irwin, wife of Will Irwin, applied for a passport the other day and, assisted by Will Irwin and Wallace Irwin, started to fill up the 'description' form. One of the questions was 'Mouth?' Well, that was all right. She wrote 'Brilliant crimson Cupid's bow with delicious shadowy corners', but the next question 'Face?' puzzled her. 'What do I say to that?' she asked. 'Write "Yes",' said Wallace Irwin.

Domaine de la Fréyère,
March 6th, 1932.   *Auribeau, Alpes Maritimes.*

The above is now our address. We move in on Thursday. We have taken it for a year. It is a sort of Provençal country-house, with a hundred acres of hillside and large grounds and a huge swimming-pool. It ought to be lovely in summer. Just at the moment it is a bit bleak.

I have written one goodish story since I got here, and two others which aren't right. I think I can fix them, but a comic story which goes off the rails is worse than any other kind. One gets the feeling that one's stuff isn't funny, which is deadly.

Do you ever read Claude Houghton? Writes darned well.

I bought Aldous Huxley's *Brave World* thing, but simply can't read it. What a bore these stories of the future are. The whole point of Huxley is that he can write better about modern life than anybody else, so of course he goes and writes about the future, blast him. Michael Arlen is down here, writing a novel the scene of which is laid in the future. It's a ruddy epidemic.

I have had rotten luck with books lately. All my favourite authors have let me down, and I've had to fall back on the French. I've read everything by Colette I could get hold of, including her autobiography, *Mes Apprentissages*. In *re* Colette a thing I've never been able to understand is how her husband,

Willy, got away with it. Did you ever hear of Willy? He must have been quite a chap. He was a hack journalist of sorts, and shortly after they were married he spotted Colette could write, so he locked her in a room, and made her turn out the four *Claudine* books, which he published under his own name – 'par Willy' – and made a fortune out of. He would give her an occasional bit of the proceeds and expect her to be grateful for it, and he used to tell interviewers that his wife had been of considerable assistance to him in these works of his, helping him quite a bit.

Right. One can faintly understand that aspect of his literary production, because she was very young and scared stiff of him, so I suppose she didn't dare to object. But why did all the other fellows whose work he published as his own put up with it?

What he used to do was get a central idea for a novel, and write a page or two, then he would send it to a friend with a letter saying that he had got as far as this but what was needed now was the friend's magic touch. Would he, the friend, mind dashing off a few thousand words in his own inimitable style, just to get the thing going?

When the script came back with the added stuff, he had it typed and sent it to another friend. 'To the rescue, old man! You will see that enclosed is beginning to shape, but it needs you to add the touches. Could you take the time to etc.' The script – plus the added stuff – would then go to a third friend, then a fourth and possibly a fifth, until eventually it was finished and another novel 'par Willy' was in the bookshops.

How did he *do* it? It must have been hypnotism or something.

We have settled down here very comfortably. Weather bad

so far, but they say from now on we get six months of unbroken sunshine. It's a good place for work. I have written sixty-four pages of *Thank You, Jeeves*, in seventeen days, and would have done more but I went off the rails and had to rewrite three times. That is the curse of my type of story. Unless I get the construction absolutely smooth, it bores the reader. In this story, for instance, I had Bertie meet the heroine in London, scene, then again in the country, another scene. I found I had to boil all this down to one meeting, as it was talky. By the way, it's not all jam writing a story in the first person. The reader can know nothing except what Bertie tells him, and Bertie can know only a limited amount himself.

I have just got Denis Mackail's *David's Day*. Very good. You ought to read it.

Grimsdick wants me to do a preface for the Bindle Omnibus book. Damned difficult. Easy enough if I could do a kidding preface like I did for *The Ship in the Swamp* – I could describe a Jenkins day, with H. J. doing everybody's work including the office boy's. But, dash it, the man killed himself by overwork, so bim goes that.

* * *

If there is any reader who does not yet know how a writer's mind works and would like to know, let him ponder on how in the course of writing this letter Plum's Bertie Wooster story developed. To me the most interesting and remarkable feature of Plum's methods of writing a story is that, however many false starts he may have made and however difficult it may have been for him to find the right way of presenting his theme, the finished result always reads as though the story had simply poured out without check.

* * *

April 23rd, 1932.   *Domaine de la Fréyère.*

The stuff you sent me about the house with monkeys and mice in it is just what I needed for *Thank You, Jeeves*. It fits in perfectly. (This sounds like Willy, doesn't it?) Bertie's pal Chuffy lives at Chuffnell Hall, Chuffy's aunt and her small son at the Dower House in the park. The son breeds white mice. They smell, and the aunt thinks it's drains, so they shift to the Hall and only a caretaker is in the Dower House. So when Bertie breaks in to get a night's lodging, with his face covered with black boot polish ... Golly, what rot it sounds when one writes it down! Come, come, Wodehouse, is this the best you can do in the way of carrying on the great tradition of English Literature? Still, I'll bet the plot of *Hamlet* seemed just as lousy when Shakespeare was trying to tell it to Ben Jonson in the Mermaid Tavern. ('Well, Ben, see what I mean, the central character is this guy, see, who's in love with this girl, see, but her old man doesn't think he's on the level, see, so he tells her—wait a minute, I better start at the beginning. Well, so this guy's in college, see, and he's come home because his mother's gone and married his uncle, see, and he sees a ghost, see. So this ghost turns out to be the guy's father. ...')

I haven't read *Magnolia Street*, so I don't know how good it is, but as a rule I think most novels would be better, if shorter.

I think we shall open Norfolk Street in March next, when we get it back.

August 13th, 1932.   *Domaine de la Fréyère.*

How's everything going with you? I liked your 'Before and After' story in *Collier's*.

Would this idea be any good to you? Downtrodden young peer, much snootered by aunts, etc., has become engaged to two girls at once, and feels that the only way out is to vanish. He runs away to sea and has adventures. It might work out into something.

I am hoping that this rise in the American stock market means the beginning of better times out there. There is no doubt that the magazines in New York are having a bad time. Fancy the *Saturday Evening Post* people having to pass their dividend! Two years ago they were paying eight dollars a share. I sold *Thank You, Jeeves* to the *Cosmopolitan* for $50,000 – my record – and they are paying me so much a month and not the whole amount down in a lump. I've never heard of that happening before. Hearst can't be as hard up as all that.

August 24th, 1932.   *Domaine de la Fréyère.*

Odd your not getting *Louder and Funnier*. I sent it off quite a month ago. This confirms my view that only about one letter in five sent out from this bally place ever arrives anywhere, and parcels simply haven't a hope. The postman probably drops anything at all heavy down a ravine. And I don't blame him. The poor devil has to walk miles up and down hill in the blazing sun. I'll write to the Fabers to send you a copy. The best thing about *Louder and Funnier* is the jacket by Rex Whistler.

H. G. Wells lives not far from here, and I have been seeing him occasionally. He lunched here yesterday. I knew him slightly in London, at the time when he had some complicated row on with a man who had worked for him on his *Outline of History*. He asked a bunch of authors to dinner to hear his side of the thing. Why he included me, I don't know. Arnold Bennett was there and we walked home together. He was pleasant but patronizing.

I like Wells. An odd bird, though. The first time I met him, we had barely finished the initial pip-pippings when he said, apropos of nothing, 'My Father was a professional cricketer'. If there's a good answer to that, you tell me. I thought of saying, 'Mine had a white moustache', but finally settled for 'Oh, ah', and we went on to speak of other things.

Don't you find that the chief difficulty in writing novels is getting the love interest set? Boy meets girl. Right. But what happens then? I'm gradually assembling a plot where a rising young artist is sent for to Blandings to paint a portrait. He says to himself 'Ah, some prominent Duchess, no doubt', and of course it turns out that Lord Emsworth wants a portrait of his pig, to celebrate her winning the silver medal at the Shropshire Agricultural Show in the Fat Pigs class. Artist, deeply offended, speaks disparagingly of pigs and Lord E. kicks him out. On his way out, he – the artist – sees a wonderful girl, falls in love at first sight and realizes that he has now made it impossible for himself ever to enter the Blandings premises again. So he is obliged to hang round the place, seeking furtive meetings.

Now then. Who is the girl? Why is she at Blandings? I can't get on till I find out what her position is.

Which reminds me of a story I read somewhere – by S. J. Perelman? I can't remember – about a movie magnate who had a wonderful idea for a picture, and he sends to New York for an author, telling him, when he arrives, that every writer on the payroll has been stumped for three months by one detail in the story. Get that one small detail, and the thing will be set.

'We fade in on a street in London,' he says, 'and there's a guy in rags dragging himself along through the fog, a Lon Chaney type guy. He's all twisted and crippled up. He comes to a colossal house in Berkeley Square and lets himself in with a latchkey, and he's in a gorgeous hall full of Chinese rugs and Ming vases, and the minute he's inside he straightens up, takes off his harness and unties his leg, and by golly, he's as normal as you and me, not a cripple at all. Then we truck with him through a door, and he's like in a hospital corridor, and he pulls on rubber gloves and an operating gown and he goes into a room where there's ten, fifteen beautiful dames chained to the wall with practically nothing on. We follow him to a bench that's full of test tubes and scientific stuff, and he grabs a hypodermic needle and he goes around laughing like a hyena and jabbing it into these beautiful dames. And that's where you got to figure out this one thing: *What kind of a business is this guy in?*'

December 1st, 1932.   *Dorchester Hotel, London.*

When I see you I want to talk over an idea for a secret collaboration on a series of sensational stories. I think it would be fun having a shot at these. I don't suppose we shall be able to do anything till I settle in London again, but it now looks as if we should open Norfolk Street in March or earlier.

I never in my life experienced such suspense as during that second half of the Sherborne match, culminating in Billy Griffith scoring that superb try. Isn't it strange that one can still be absorbed by Dulwich footer? I never saw such splendid defensive work as we put up. It was easily the best school match I have seen.

Don't you find, as you get on in life, that the actual things you really want cost about two hundred a year? I have examined my soul, and I find that my needs are a library subscription and tobacco money, plus an extra bit for holidays.

When I see you, I want to take away a pile of your stories. I feel there must be so many of them that just need a bit of fixing. We might use some of them for the collaboration. Shall we revive Basil Windham?

January 4th, 1933.   *Domaine de la Fréyère.*

I hope to have my novel finished before I return to England. If I put off my return till March, that is to say. At present, we plan to come back at end of January and open Norfolk Street.

I shall be glad to be settled in England again. This country is fine, but we are too far from everything. And if one lives in Cannes, there is the constant temptation of the Casino. London is the best spot, all round.

How have you been doing? Any luck? I'm afraid it is still a bad time for the magazines.

Second Test Match. How about it? What a bunch of rabbits! Isn't it odd how cricketers during the county season seem such marvels yet no good in Australia.

Have you ever read Warwick Deeping? I hadn't till the other day when Ethel took *New Wine and Old* out of the library. He is good. His stuff reminds me a little of yours.

The catch about that sort of stuff, of course, is that it is quiet and does not make a punching appeal, so that it is necessary to build book on book and get a public gradually.

I have had a devil of a time with my new one. It is a sequel to *Summer Lightning*, to be called *Heavy Weather*, and the first chapters were terribly hard to write, because I had to be careful not to assume that people had read *S. L.* and at the same time not put in yards of explanation which would have bored those who had. In order to get one hundred pages of O.K. stuff, I must have written nearly a hundred thousand words.

This place is congested with Ethel's adopted cats, all having kittens.

February 9th, 1933.   *Domaine de la Fréyère, Auribeau, A.M.*

Sorry I haven't answered yours of January 23rd before. I have been sweating at *Heavy Weather*, and must be getting a bit stale, as I simply hadn't any energy left to write a line after the day's work. It's a curious thing about this novel, and probably means that it's going to be good, but I must have written at least 200,000 words so far. For a long time I couldn't get the thing straight. I kept getting dissatisfied with the first 30,000 words and starting again. Today I reached page 254 and have a very detailed scenario of the rest, and all up to page 254 now looks all right. It really reads as if I had written it straight off without a pause.

My plans are a little uncertain. I am waiting to hear from Ethel, who left on Sunday to open Norfolk Street, leaving me with Winky! I think the idea is that she is going to find out about quarantine and then write me. I expect a letter tomorrow.

If she says come along, I shall start at once. I am thoroughly sick of this place. These last four days have been rather trying. I am alone in the house with the caretaker and his wife, who cooks for me. I take my meals on trays.

94

I could go and stay at a hotel in Cannes, of course, but Winky would be such a burden at a hotel. My God, she's bad enough here! She won't let me out of her sight. I feel rotten if I don't get an exercise walk in the afternoon, but every time I try to start on one Winky sits on the terrace and just looks at me. You can hear her saying, 'Going to leave me, eh? Well, of all the dirty tricks!' So I say, 'Well, come along, too.' And she says: 'What, sweat down that mountain and have to sweat up again? Not for me.' So it ends in my strolling about the garden.

November 5th, 1933.   *17 Norfolk Street.*

Thanks for card about telephone number. This will ease the situation a lot. I shall now be able to let you know of my visits on the day instead of having to give notice a week ahead.

Since returning from Hunstanton, I have been having rather a lull. I sold *Right Ho, Jeeves* to the *Saturday Evening Post*, and they are starting it on December 2nd, which will be a nasty knock for the *Cosmopolitan* who, after postponing publication for two years, God knows why, are starting *Thank You, Jeeves* on December 10th. I got the same price as for *Heavy Weather* – $40,000.

March 10th, 1934.   *The Dorchester, Park Lane.*

I've just had the foulest week of my career.

Which reminds me of the story of the engine-driver. This engine-driver overslept himself one morning, had to shave in a hurry, cut himself, went down to breakfast, found the coffee was cold and the toast burned, raced off to his train, tripped over a loose stone and barked his shin, and, finally, got aboard and started off. The train had just rounded a corner when he suddenly saw another train on the same line coming at him at fifty miles an hour. He heaved a weary sigh. 'Do *you* have days,' he said to the stoker, 'when *everything* seems to go wrong?'

But about this week. It included two visits to the dentist, a cold in the head, the opening of Crockford's Club (one of those ghastly functions where you're invited for ten o'clock and don't have any dinner because you think supper will be served the moment you arrive and then don't get any supper), an American interviewer who caught me just as the cold was at its worst, and a snack luncheon to celebrate the publication of a young author's new book. And, finally, the shifting of our fifteen trunks, twenty suitcases and two Pekes from Seamore Court here.

I must say that luncheon was the limit. It seemed to take one into a new and dreadful world. Can you imagine giving a lunch to celebrate the publication of a book? With other authors, mostly fairies, twittering all over the place, screaming 'Oh Lionel!' and photographs of you holding the book, etc. Gosh! Dumas was the boy. When he had finished a novel he kept on sitting and started another. No snack luncheons for him.

Thrilling about your voyage. Can't we manage to combine our trips? My idea is to go to Cannes again, but I am game to do anything. Why wouldn't a week or two at Marseilles do you just as well as the trip to Port Said? You ought to see the South of France, it would be very valuable to your work, and you have the gift of being able to collect material on a very short stay.

The Riviera isn't much good to me, but I should have thought you could have got a lot out of it. You have Marseilles, which is right up your street, and all the tough quarters of

Nice, etc. Anyway, if we could arrange to meet at Marseilles and then think what to do next, it would be fine.

June 11th, 1934.   *Hôtel Prince de Galles, Paris.*

I've been meaning to write for ages, but I've been tied up with *The Luck of the Bodkins*. I find that the longer I go on writing, the harder it becomes to get a story right without going over and over it. I have just reached page 180 and I suppose I must have done quite 400 pages! Still, it is in good shape now.

Paris is fine. I don't go out much, as I am working all the time. I have been here for exactly five weeks, except for one day at Le Touquet. I may be going to Le Touquet again for a few days soon, to talk with Guy Bolton about our play for Vinton Freedley *Anything Goes*. But this address will always find me.

I had an offer from Paramount the other day to go to Hollywood, and had to refuse. But rather gratifying after the way Hollywood took a solemn vow three years ago never to mention my name again. Quite the olive branch!

Do you know, Bill, what was one of the most interesting periods in history? The year 1822 in France, when the ex-officers of the Old Guard were plotting to bring Napoleon's son to the throne. I am reading a book called *Les Demi-Soldes* (The Half-pay Officers) by Desparbes (which sounds like the sort of name you give the characters in your stories). It's thrilling.

August 2nd, 1934.   *Royal Picardy, Le Touquet-Paris-Plage.*

Thanks for yours. I'm glad the novel is coming out well. What a sweat all that sea stuff must be.

The big item of news is that we have bought a house here. Isn't it odd? The only reason I came to Le Touquet was because I was writing this musical comedy with Guy Bolton, and he doesn't like Paris, so I said, all right, we'll meet half-way, I'll come to Le Touquet.

At first I didn't like the place, and then suddenly it began to get me, and it struck both Ethel and me that as regards situation, it was the one ideal spot in the world. I can get over to England by boat in a few hours and by plane in one hour. It is only two and a half hours from Paris and within motoring distance of Cherbourg.

We shan't be moving in, I suppose, till next Spring, as the house wants fixing up.

I'm having a devil of a time with *Anything Goes*. I can't get hold of Guy or the composer, Cole Porter. What has become of Cole, Heaven knows. Last heard of at Heidelberg.

September 13th, 1934.   *Golf Hotel, Le Touquet.*

The Ship in the Fanlight arrived this morning. I am looking forward to reading it tonight in bed. Don't you think they have given you a good jacket this time? It really seems as if they have turned over a new leaf in that respect.

Idea for a story for you: Mate of ship murders Captain to get his job, sets fire to ship to destroy all traces, becomes hero and lives happily ever afterwards – except for the moment when the Captain's ghost comes and breathes down the back of his neck, just as he is addressing his old school on *How to Succeed*.

I have been musing over what you say at the end of your letter about the passage of Time. I feel just the same. My particular trouble is that what I feel I should really like is to vegetate in one place all my life, and I spend my whole time whizzing about.

Of course, the trouble is that one is never quite happy unless one is working – and by working I don't so much mean the actual writing as the feeling that one could write if one wanted to. It is the in-between times that kill one.

I am now faced with a difficult job – a 16,000 word story for the *New York Herald Tribune*, to run in four parts. But I can't seem to get the right idea. A short story of 7,000 words is simple, and a novelette of 30,000, too, but this in-between length is trying. I haven't room to build up an elaborate plot, and yet the story must not be thin and must have at least a passable curtain for each instalment. Oh, well, I suppose it will come.

Hutchinsons have just sent me the *Century of Humour*. Have they sent you a copy? Your *Interlude in a Quiet Life* looks very good.

October 5th, 1934.   *Low Wood, Le Touquet.*

I have been meaning to write to you for weeks, but I have been working on the 16,000 word story for the *New York Tribune Magazine*.

I finished it this morning, after much sweat.

Thanks for the ideas for stories. That one about sitting down on the chair that wasn't there is fine, but, laddie, did you ever read a *Saturday Evening Post* story by Nunnally Johnson called *There Ought To Be A Law*? It was about a wife who would keep moving the furniture, and the big scene was very similar. There the husband chucks himself into bed in the dark, to find the bed is over in another corner of the room.

I'm much bitten with the idea of writing some stories under

another name. I've been brooding on one you sent me, *The Old House*. I believe that if one got a slightly different angle on it, it would go? Do you remember the story? Young American wife shown over English country house by shabby old man, who turns out to be the owner. Arthur Morrison once did a very good one where a caller was shown over house by bloke who had just murdered the owner, whose body was lying in next room. Couldn't we do something on those lines?

I am very fit. The air here is wonderful, and I have to go and fetch our papers every day from Paris Plage. That means a four-mile walk, so what with taking the dogs for runs and generally messing about, I suppose I do a steady fifty miles a week. I notice the difference in my condition very much. In London, my four-mile walk used to leave me not exactly tired but feeling I had had all I wanted, but here I hardly feel it.

December 4th, 1934.   *Low Wood, Le Touquet.*

Lady Dudley (Gertie Millar) lives a few doors off us and when she went to England asked me to exercise her spotted carriage dog occasionally. Well, of course, after I had taken it with me for two days on my walk to get the papers, it proceeded to regard this walk as a fixed ceremony. The day I had to go to Lille, I hear it refused all food and would not be comforted.

I finished *The Luck of the Bodkins* on November 20th, and ever since have been in a sort of coma. Do you get like that after a big bout of work?

As a matter of fact, my present collapse is the result of a strain that has gone on now for almost six months. While in the middle of *The Luck of the Bodkins*, and just beginning to see my way through it, I had to break off and start plotting out that musical comedy, *Anything Goes*, for New York with Howard Lindsay, the director. We toiled all through that blazing weather in Paris, and then we came down here and started all over again with Guy Bolton. In the end we got out a plot, and I wrote a rough version, and sent it off to Guy to rewrite.

Well, I eventually started on *The Luck of the Bodkins* again. Then I got the commission for the novelette for the *New York Herald Tribune*, to be done in a hurry. So I started sweating at that and, just as I was in the middle of it, a cable came from America from Vinton Freedley, the manager, saying that the stuff which Guy and I had sent over wouldn't do, and that he was calling in two other people to rewrite it. So there I was, presumably out of that.

I got the novelette finished and sent it over, but was naturally in a panic about it after the débâcle of the musical comedy which, incidentally, had been preceded by the complete failure of the Bolton-Wodehouse comedy in London, because, though it was a commission, I wouldn't have felt able to stand on my rights and demand the money unless the stuff was acceptable. And for weeks I heard nothing.

Meanwhile, *The Luck of the Bodkins* was coming out with great difficulty. Have you had the experience of getting out what looks like a perfect scenario and then finding that it won't write and has to be completely changed?

And then suddenly – or, rather, not suddenly, but in a sort of series of bits of good news – everything came right. My arrangement about *Anything Goes* was that I was to get 2% of the gross, if I was able to go to New York and attend rehearsals, but if I couldn't I was to give up half of the 1% to Howard Lindsay. So I was looking on it all the time as $1\frac{1}{2}$% job ($1\frac{1}{2}$% being the ordinary musical comedy royalty).

You can imagine my relief when I found that the rewriting was not going to affect my royalty very much. Russel Crouse, the rewriter, had consented to do the work for half of 1%, so I am only down a quarter of 1% on the normal royalty. Then we heard that the show was a huge success in Boston, and now it has been produced in New York and is the biggest hit for years and years and Cochran has bought it for London.

Meanwhile, I had had a cable from the *New York Herald Tribune*, which said 'Happy about Lord Havershot' (that was the name of the hero of the novelette), from which I inferred that it was all right – though don't you hate these ambiguous cables? I mean, the editor might quite easily really have written 'Not happy' and the French postal officials cut out the word 'Not' as not seeming to them important.

Finally, however, a letter arrived with the cheque, just about the time I heard the news of the success of the show.

By that time, I was struggling with the last chapters of *The Luck of the Bodkins*. Usually when I get to the last fifty pages of a story, it begins to write itself. But this time everything went wrong and I had to grope my way through it all at the rate of two pages a day. I began to get superstitious about it and felt that if I could ever get it finished my luck would be in. On November 29th I was within four pages of the end and suddenly all the lights in the house went out and stayed out!

Still, I finished it next day, and it is pretty good, I think. Frightfully long – 362 pages of typescript – it must be over the 100,000 words.

All this, added to the fact that Ethel has gone to London, and it has been raining from the moment she left, has left me pretty limp. I suppose I shall be all right in a day or so.

One of your old letters mentioned that you had been reading

J. D. Beresford and that you admired his work a lot. I think he's darned good, too. Did you read a weird little story of his in the *Daily Express* about a dog?

Have you been following public school footer form this year? I have never known it so in and out.

> Bedford 30, Dulwich nil
> Dulwich nil, Haileybury 3
> Haileybury 9, Bedford 5
> Tonbridge 3, Haileybury 5
> Dulwich 11, Tonbridge nil.

Dulwich beat Mill Hill, Mill Hill beat Brighton, Brighton beat Dulwich.

* * *

The *Herald Tribune* novelette Plum subsequently expanded into a full-length novel, *Laughing Gas*.

No letter ever illustrated more completely the trials and torments of even an eminent writer than this. Plum was, at the time his letter was written – December, 1934 – pre-eminent in his profession, yet even he, as his letter showed, had his rebuffs, his moments of doubt and his difficulties. It must have been a consolation to him to read soon after this Hilaire Belloc's introduction to the book, *Week-End Wodehouse*. Mr Belloc wrote:

> Some two or three years ago I was asked in the United States to broadcast a few words on my own trade of writing – what I thought of it and why I disliked it.

I understand that this broadcast was heard by a very large number – some millions, it seems. Now in the course of this broadcast I gave as the best writer of English now alive, Mr P. G. Wodehouse.

It was not only a very sincere, but a reasonable and well-thought-out pronouncement. Yet I got a vast number of communications asking me what I exactly meant. Not that those who had heard me doubted Mr Wodehouse's genius. They had given proof of their perception of that genius by according him the very wide circulation which he enjoys on that side of the Atlantic, as I am glad to say he does elsewhere. No; their puzzlement was why I should call the author who was supreme in that particular line of country the 'best' writer of our time: the best living writer of *English*: why I should have called him, as I did call him, 'the head of my profession'.

I shall quote no more of this profoundly erudite essay on Plum Wodehouse's art, so often decried by those without real understanding as being merely 'verbal' wit, but suggest the book in which Mr Belloc's essay appears should at once be either bought or borrowed from the nearest library because in *Week-End Wodehouse* there will be found what a critic in the *Observer* described as 'A ravishing anthology from Mr Wodehouse's novels, some of his lighter papers, and choice morsels of comment and description.'

*　　*　　*

January 23rd, 1935.   *Low Wood.*

When I got to page 100 of *Voyage Without End*, I rushed to my typewriter and wrote a letter to Arthur Waugh, the head of Chapman & Hall, raving about the book. As I don't know him, this will probably cause him to reject the thing immediately. Still, I meant well.

Bill, it's an absolute masterpiece. It's the only book I've read for years that did really take me out of myself into another atmosphere, so that I got the sense of coming back to another world when I finished reading. I just live with those people. What Ivor Nicholson's reader can be suffering from, I don't know, because it defeats me how anyone can say those characters aren't real. There isn't one of them that you can't visualize with perfect clearness as you read.

One of the best tips for writing a play is 'Never let them sit down' – i.e. keep the characters buzzing about without a pause, and that's just what you have done here. There isn't a moment till you come to the end of Part One where you can stop reading. You always feel there is something round the corner.

Let's see what Chapman & Hall do. If they fail, I will write to Sir Tresham Lever, who is Thornton Butterworth, or E. V. Lucas.

I am contemplating writing to Ivor Nicholson, cursing his reader – who, I imagine, is a novelist of sorts. By the way, how does a publisher ever accept a novel on a reader's report? If you told the story of any book in the form of a reader's report, it would sound awful.

Reader's report of Henry Fourth, Part One, by W. Shakespeare: 'This is a story of life in London. The plot is improbable and does not carry conviction, as it deals with a Prince of Wales who apparently visits public houses. There is a fat man named Falstaff.'

I'll tell you one thing. From now on, in your novels, let yourself go, regardless of what the reader is going to think. For magazines one more or less has to study the public, but not for the novel public. I believe there are two ways of writing novels. One is mine, making the thing a sort of musical comedy without music, and ignoring real life altogether; the other is going right deep down into life and not caring a damn. The ones that fail are the ones where the writer loses his nerve and says: 'My God! I can't write this, I must tone it down.'

If you will let me have a copy of *Greenside Island*, I'll send it to young Lorimer on the *Saturday Evening Post*, telling him that it was submitted before, but that you have rewritten it. I gather that he has taken Costain's place, and Costain was the man who read it before. Costain is now Eastern editor of Fox Films – a good job, I suppose, so long as you stay in it, but I wouldn't trust myself to a movie company. You dine with the President on Monday, and he slaps you on the back and tells you you are the salt of the earth, and on Tuesday morning you get a letter from him saying you are fired. Still, I suppose Costain has a long contract.

Here's an idea you might be able to use: I see a man at Ascot with a rich-looking but unpleasant wife. I pity him, and you, who know him, tell me he is one of the happiest men you know. You tell me his story.

The point of this is that he is in love with a *house*. He is of hardish-up family, went to school in some awful suburb where he lived – not Dulwich, as Dulwich is too pleasant. He had some distant cousins who owned a lovely country house, a place like Hunstanton Hall. Out of pity they used to have him to stay for two weeks every summer, and those two weeks were his real life. He worshipped the house. I mean, really worshipped. It was the core of his whole inner life.

Then there came the war. The distant cousins lost all their sons, and in addition became broke. (Note: He stopped going to stay at the house when he was seventeen, when he went into an office, so it has remained a remote Paradise all this time.)

Some profiteers bought the house, and a chain of circumstances – she might be in the profiteer's office – brought him into contact with profiteer's daughter, a spoiled, awful girl.

You will have to give hero some quality of attraction. He might be very handsome. Because the daughter wants him and insists on having him. And he marries her, though thoroughly disliking her, because it will mean that he will get back to the house.

So there he is when I meet him. He is snubbed by the parents, and the girl nags him, because her brief infatuation is over and she realizes that she is landed with a nobody as a husband. He has a rotten time as far as his outward life goes, but he is perfectly happy. He has the house and can potter about and dream.

I think you could make something of that. It has something of the quality of your *The Rose House*.

* * *

I wrote Plum's story about the man in love with a house and it failed badly, which in a way did not surprise me as I felt when I had finished it that it was a thoroughly poor effort. But I know now what was wrong with it; it was not a short story plot at all, but the theme for a novel.

* * *

February 4th, 1935. *Low Wood.*

Hell's foundations quivering briskly just now. The *Saturday Evening Post* have rejected *The Luck of the Bodkins* – my first rejection in America in twenty-one years. I have re-read the book as critically as if it were someone else's – all right someone's else, if you prefer it – and see now what's wrong. Gosh, isn't it awful the mistakes one can make and not see till too late? It's 25,000 words too long.

Do you know, I believe over-longness is the worst fault in writing. I had such a good farcical plot in this one that I got all hopped up and felt that it wasn't possible to give 'em too much of this superb stuff, so every scene I wrote was elaborated till it lost its grip. To give you some idea, I now reach on Page 45 a situation which in the original I got to on page 100! That's 15,000 words out for a start. I expect to cut 30,000.

Just got the *Anything Goes* script from America. There are two lines of mine left in it, and so far I am receiving £50 a week apiece for them. That's about £3 10s. a word, which is pretty good payment, though less, of course, than my stuff is worth.

Letter from Arthur Waugh. *11 Henrietta Street,*
Chapman & Hall, Ltd. *Covent Garden, W.C.2.*

Dear Mr Wodehouse:

I was delighted to get your kind letter about Mr Townend's MS., and, as it happened, it could not have arrived at a more opportune moment. For only a couple of hours before it came, I had started on the MS. and was struck at once by the conviction that these deck-hands, seagoing men, and their womenkind were the real thing, drawn from life – not the stock figures from the novelist's cardboard tray. I must admit that I thought their world a bit sordid to please the general public; but when they get to sea the atmosphere may change. I was much helped by your letter, and encouraged at the start of my task of reading the MS. – no very light one, for it looks like 130,000 words at least. Thank you very much for writing to me about it.

Yes; it is true that we have never met in the body, but in the spirit we have travelled a good many miles together. There was a time, in Alec's schooldays, when we used to read your books together with enormous enjoyment; and, though we are never long enough together nowadays – to read more than a telegram – we have still preserved a sort of freemason's code of Psmithisms, which continually crops up in our letters. Indeed, I can truly say, in emulation of Wolfe, that I would far rather have created Psmith than have stormed Quebec.

Again thanking you for your very pleasant letter and hoping that I may like *Voyage Without End* as much as you do.

Sincerely yours,
Arthur Waugh.

March 6th, 1935.   *Hôtel Lincoln, Rue Bayard, Paris.*

I have been at above address since February 24th. I return to Low Wood on Saturday.

Your letter, forwarded on from Le Touquet, reached me last night. I am frightfully bucked that Chapman & Hall have taken *Voyage Without End.*

I must say I feel a bit uneasy about that huge cut they want to make, and particularly at your saying that they had cut 30,000 words already themselves. I think you should be in sole control of any cutting that has to be done.

Can you hang on for a few days, till I can get back to Le Touquet and read the story again? The only living soul at Low Wood at present is a Jugo-Slavian butler, and any attempt to get him to mail you the script would result in your receiving either (a) the MS. of *The Luck of the Bodkins* or (b) a handsomely bound copy of the *Encyclopædia Britannica*.

This cutting business is frightfully tricky, as I know from my own experience. I got 25,000 words out of *The Luck of the Bodkins* without any trouble at all, but not by paring down scenes. I reconstructed the first half of the story entirely, taking advantage of a really sound criticism from Reeves Shaw to eliminate one situation entirely. Isn't it odd how one can spoil a story by being too leisurely in telling it?

I thought your briar pipe thing in the *Strand* the best short story you had written for ages. Surely in Captain Shuffley you have got the character you were looking for, who would run through a series! He seems to me as good as Bob Pretty. I see him as a chap who might have adventure after adventure, doing the most chivalrous things but always making a bit out of them. You know what I mean – saves girl from low-down *café* in Buenos Aires and you find at end that his main motive in starting the big rescue scene was that he hadn't any money to pay his bill, and wanted a way of creating a diversion.

Have you ever noticed how if you are expecting an important telegram some absolutely unimportant one arrives? I remember in 1922 when *The Beauty Prize* was produced at the Winter Garden, I sailed the day it opened, expecting a wireless about how it had gone. On the first day out along came a wireless and I tore it open and it was from Leslie Henson, wishing me Bon Voyage.

The same thing has happened now. I am on tenterhooks about the fate of some stuff I sent over to New York. I got a letter from my agent saying that the editor of the *Red Book* liked the stories, but that a snag had arisen in the shape of the president of the company, which also owns *McCall's*, because in 1922 I contracted to do six short stories for *McCall's* and never delivered them! The president has been brooding on it ever since, and agent says it rather looks as if he may have to shade our price a bit as compensation.

Well, as anything I get out of America nowadays with this income-tax dispute going on is like a bone sneaked from a dog, I cabled 'Close deal at any price you can get and cable at once'. Sure enough, a telegram arrived that night. It was from Gertie Millar at Le Touquet, thanking me for having exercised her Dalmatian dog in her absence.

* * *

March 10th, 1935.   *Low Wood.*

What asses Pekes are! We took Winky to Paris, leaving Boo behind. Ten days later I bring her back. But was there a joyful reunion? No, sir. Each poor fish had completely forgotten the other, and each, seeing a stranger in her home, prepared to fight to the death. They had six fights in the first ten minutes and one the next morning, but have now settled down.

One of the fights was the funniest thing you ever saw. I had put my typewriter case down in a corner and Winky was behind it. Boo came up in front and they both reared up on their hind legs and stood with their noses touching, snarling and growling, but unable to get at each other. This went on for about five minutes.

March 28th, 1935.   *Low Wood.*

Thank God, the sun has broken through the clouds and the United States Marines have arrived just as the savages were storming the stockade. A cable from my New York agent came, saying that he had sold *The Luck of the Bodkins* and three short stories to the *Red Book*. $25,000 for Bodkins as against the $40,000 *The Post* would have paid, but what of it?' Oo-la-la!' as we say over here.

That hound Boo as near as a toucher got killed last night. We were walking on left side of road. Two girls on bikes came along on right side. Boo dashed across and gave chase, spilling one girl. I stopped to pick her up, and Boo legged it after the other one, spilling her also. I was twenty yards behind when I saw a car coming and at that moment Boo swerved to the left. I gave a yell and the car stopped with the wheel right over her. Another revolution would have killed her. She then trotted to Ethel and lay on her back, which is her idea of passing off a delicate situation.

No date.   *Low Wood.*

I have just had a review of *Blandings Castle* in some provincial paper, criticizing in an adverse spirit a scene which is not in the book at all, but in Eric Linklater's *Ripeness Is All*.

Just had a testing job – reading the page proofs of the *Mulliner Omnibus* book. 864 pages! It humbled me a good deal, as the stuff didn't seem good. Still, I suppose nothing would, if you read 864 pages of it straight off.

I can't get an idea for a novel. Maddening, as except for that I am fixed so solidly for the coming year – for there will be four companies of *Anything Goes* playing, not counting the London one, and I have an original play for Ralph Lynn – *The Inside Stand* – and an adaptation coming on in London, and I am well ahead with short stories. But all is useless unless I can get started on a novel.

Oh, this will interest you. Askew was saying why doesn't Townend stick to sea stories, and said that one single bookseller in Glasgow sold a thousand copies of the half-crown edition of *The Tramp*. Of course, this is a hell of a time to tell you this, when you are in the middle of a non-sea novel, but as a guide for the future apparently what they want from you is the sea stuff.

P.S. – I thought your old address was pretty bad, but the new one beats it. I look on it as a good morning's work addressing an envelope to you now.

September 12th, 1935.   *Low Wood.*

In *re* short story series. My own experience is that you can't – unless you are extraordinarily inventive – write a series bang off. I started writing in 1902, and every day I said to myself: 'I must get a character for a series.' In 1916 I wrote the first *Jeeves* story. About a year later I wrote another. But it wasn't till I had done about six at long intervals that I realized I had got a series-character.

You remember that story you gave me, about the woman telling lies about the girl's relations, so that she could marry the humble suitor? It comes out in the Christmas *Strand*, called

Uncle Fred Flits By. Now, in Uncle Fred I'm sure I have got a character, but at the moment I simply can't think of another plot for him. I'm just waiting and hoping one will come.

It's different if you have got a man with a definite job – Sherlock Holmes or Raffles. Then you can think of things for him to do. But I wouldn't sit down and do a series of *Adventures of Psmith,* because there is no definite line that he would take.

I expect to be over again very soon. Jack Waller's new musical comedy opens tonight, and I suppose that almost immediately after that he will start rehearsals of my Ralph Lynn show. In which case I shall stay over till the opening.

November 15th, 1935. Telegram.

Motoring Portsmouth stopping tea Cooden hotel five. Plum.

* * *

I met Plum for tea. Rain was pouring down and a high wind was blowing. He had motored from Le Touquet to Boulogne, had crossed to Folkestone, where he had hired a car to take him all the way to Portsmouth to attend the first performance of his new play. How he endured so dreadful a journey in pitch-black darkness I cannot imagine. He told me when I said goodbye to him, that he proposed to use the time involved in thinking out a new story; which was a convincing proof of Plum's power of concentration.

* * *

December 2nd, 1935.   *Hilbre, Le Touquet.*

Isn't it perfectly rotten – my old typewriter on which I have been working since 1911, has gone phut. I had it patched up in Boulogne, but now the shift key won't work, so I have had to discard it. I am writing this on a machine which has been knocking around for a year or so, while Ethel buys me a new one in London. I think she is getting a Royal. I believe that's what you use, isn't it?

Do you know if there is any way of having my old machine entirely rebuilt? Expense no object. My trouble is that this is a Monarch, and there is no Monarch firm now. Perhaps if I buy a Royal, the Royal people would fix it up.

Don't you find that after you've used a typewriter for a long time, you can't get used to the touch of any other?

I have been alone here with the dogs for exactly two weeks tomorrow. It's extraordinary how well one gets along – once one has fallen into a routine. I find the great thing is having something good to read after dinner. The rest of the day takes care of itself.

Talking of reading and the publisher's reader who said your stuff was 'nasty', the other evening, routing among the shelves of this house we're living in till Low Wood is ready, I came upon Faulkner's *Sanctuary*. Have you ever read it? It's one of the few books that have really given me the horrors and made me feel sick as well. Those Southerners! What a set! – as Matthew Arnold would say.

I'm glad you liked 'Uncle Fred'. But unless you give me another story as good as that one, I can't think of anything for him to do. He is really a sort of elderly Psmith, and I can see in a vague way that he ought to go about helping people – and at the same time getting Pongo into trouble – but it's details that are so hard to think of. I wish I had a more inventive mind.

Here's a rummy thing, Bill. For six months I have been hammering away at a plot, trying to make it come out, with no success. Last night I suddenly said: 'Could this be a Ukridge story?' Ten minutes later I had the plot complete. It's the treatment that matters, isn't it?

The Ralph Lynn play, alas! is not doing any too well. Whether this is due to its being no good or whether it is simply the pre-Christmas slump, I don't know. One good thing is that we can keep running at a low figure. But I rather think it has missed fire.

I've been bitten to pieces by mosquitoes – of all things in December! They must have turned in for the winter in the rooms here and woken up to find a square meal in their midst.

January 20th, 1936.   *Low Wood.*

Just off to Carlton Hôtel, St Moritz, where I expect to stay for a few weeks. I don't know how I shall like it. I've always avoided Switzerland up to now.

Doesn't Kipling's death give you a sort of stunned feeling? He seems to leave such a gap. I didn't feel the same about Doyle or Bennett or Galsworthy. I suppose it is because he is so associated with one's boyhood. It has made me feel older all of a sudden.

I am writing this on my new Royal. I have got quite used to it now, but I still can't feel as easy as I did on the old Monarch – which, I hope, some expert will be able to repair. I don't like these metal things which stick up and hold the paper down, so that you can't get a clear view of what you're writing.

Winks and Boo do nothing nowadays but fight. I think it is because they are not getting enough exercise. Have you ever studied the psychology of the Dirty Look in Pekes? Winks and Boo will be sleeping quite happily in their baskets at different ends of the room, and then suddenly one of them will lift her head and stare. The other then stares. This goes on for about ten seconds, and then they rush at one another snarling, and start a terrific battle. My theory is that dogs say things which the human ear can't hear, and during this period they are exchanging inaudible cracks. By the way, we're taking both Pekes to St Moritz.

Do you ever read Claude Houghton's stuff? (C. H. Oldfield, Dulwich, circ. 1908). His last book *Christina* is good. He sends me his books as they come out, but we've never met.

Low Wood is in a hideous mess now, but will emerge as a very nice house when it is finished. I hate being in our present place, which is just a shack and as cold as ice.

* * *

What Plum had said in his letter about the death of Rudyard Kipling found an echo in my heart. Ever since our schooldays Kipling had stood for something stable and permanent in our lives.

Plum and he corresponded quite often, having met at the Beefsteak Club of which both were members. Plum told me once, more or less in jest, that if he were to predecease me he would leave me Kipling's letters but added that I should find that Kipling invariably spelt his name *Woodhouse*. This puzzled me until I reflected that he was remembering the name he had used in two of his stories, or in one story, at least.

*　　*　　*

April 2nd, 1936.　　　　　　　　　　　　　*Hilbre, Le Touquet.*

I'm sorry you are going through a mistrustful phase in your book, but I am pretty certain it is only because you have been working so hard at it. I have had just the same experience with the one I am doing now – *Laughing Gas* – a novel-length version of a short serial which came out in *Pearson's* last year – did you see it? – about the man whose soul goes into the body of the child film star. A few days ago it all seemed absolutely idiotic, but it looks quite all right again now.

Listen. Extract from a book by Arnold Bennett called *How to Become an Author.*

He should take care to produce books at regular short intervals. He may continue this process for years without any really striking result in fame or money, and he may pessimistically imagine that his prolonged labours are fruitless. And then newspapers will begin to refer to him as a known author, as an author the mention of whose name is sufficient to recall his productions, and he will discover that all the while the building of his reputation has been going on like a coral reef.

Even mediocre talent, when combined with fixity of purpose and regular industry, will, infallibly, result in a gratifying success.

But it must never be forgotten that while the reputation is being formed, the excellent and amiable public needs continuous diplomatic treatment. It must not be permitted to ignore his existence. At least once a year, and oftener if possible, a good solid well-made book should be flung into the libraries.

He also advises against frittering away energy on a lot of small things – e.g. short stories.

That seems to me to sum up your position, except that you certainly can't call yours a 'mediocre talent'. Really good stuff like yours is bound to succeed if you keep turning it out. I think this plan of yours of doing a lot of novels is the right one. What you've got to remember is that, in a sense, you really started with *Voyage Without End*, because the other books were buried.

Arnold Bennett's own case was just the same. His early books didn't sell. But gradually one began to see his name about.

May 13th, 1936.   *Hilbre, Le Touquet.*

I finished *Comox* last night, and I see exactly what you mean. It is a hybrid. It starts off as a leisurely, Arnold Bennett sort of novel and then turns into a story of action, and the effect of this is to make the last part seem all out of key. It seems to me that you will have to abandon the leisurely note and go for the action.

In writing a novel, I always imagine I am writing for a cast of actors. Some actors are natural minor actors and some are natural major ones. It is a matter of personality. Same in a book. Psmith, for instance, is a major character. If I am going to have Psmith in a story, he must be in the big situations.

Right ho, then. In this book, Sennen stands out as a major character. You have taken so much pains to make him live that you can't exclude him from the main thread of the story. What is the main thread of the story? Andrew's married life. Therefore, Sennen must affect that. But he doesn't. Comox does. And Comox is essentially a minor character. (And if you say he isn't, I come right hack at you – quick as a flash – by saying that in that case you can't drop him casually into the story on page 200. He must run right through.)

I believe the solution of this book is to give Comox's stuff to Sennen.

Is there any particular point in having the action in the nineties? I imagine that this is a leftover from your original idea of the story being a manuscript found in the cabin of a dead, elderly man, isn't it? As I read, I couldn't see any reason why it all shouldn't be happening in the present.

It's awfully hard to put all I want to in a letter.

The main thing is, PULL THE STORY TOGETHER. At present it lacks grip. The stuff is all there, but the construction is wrong.

The thing that made *Voyage Without End* so marvellous was the way it zipped along. You can get just the same effect into this one, and I really think you've got a stronger theme.

ONE BIG CHARACTER IS WORTH TWO SMALL ONES. Don't diffuse the interest. Generally, the trouble is that you can't switch Character B's stuff so that it fits Character A, but here Comox can blend into Sennen without a hitch.

The absolute cast-iron good rule, I'm sure, in writing a story, is to introduce *all* your characters as early as possible – especially if they are going to play important parts later.

It will probably be agony to rewrite this book, as you must be sick of it, but I know you have got something just as big as *Voyage Without End*, if you only sweat at it. If you send it out in its present form, it won't be a failure, but it won't be nearly so successful. Even if it means later publication, do have a go at it.

I think the success of every novel depends largely on one or two high spots. The thing to do is to say to yourself 'Which are my big scenes?' and then get every drop of juice out of them. You are a bit apt to give the same value to a minor scene as to a major. I believe that when one has really got a bit of action going, it can extend as long as you like.

July 23rd, 1936.   *Golf Hotel, Le Touquet.*

I've just returned from a hurried visit to England, but simply couldn't get a moment to get in touch with you. I had a phone call from Ethel saying that Guy Bolton had been rushed into hospital at Worthing with acute appendicitis and nearly died, and I had to spend my time travelling up and down. He seems to be all right now, thank goodness, but it was a near thing.

Listen. How far are you from Folkestone? Couldn't you catch the morning boat, lunch here and spend the afternoon, and go back on the evening boat – unless you could stop the night? It's nothing of a trip. You pop into a taxi at Boulogne and say Hôtel du Golf, Le Touquet, and you're here in forty minutes. You wouldn't have to leave till six, which would give us the whole afternoon.

Enclosed will give you a laugh. Me and Mussolini!

* * *

In due course, within the week, we went to Le Touquet for the day by way of Folkestone and Boulogne where we were met and put into a taxi. Plum was waiting for us at the Golf Hotel, and took us to Low Wood to meet the

Pekes, Winks, Bimmy's sister, and Boo, whom Rene had taken care of for some weeks at the end of 1931. There was, to be sure, a moment of apprehension when we entered Low Wood, which was in the hands of the builders and occupied only by Madge, the cook, and her husband, an Englishman, an ex-soldier of the 1914–18 War. Would the Pekes regard us as interlopers in their home; enemies to be driven off the premises, or would they show themselves friendly? Although neither dog could have remembered us, they accepted us at sight, which was a compliment, Boo, in particular, being apt to take an illogical dislike to strangers and bark furiously until soothed and assured that no actual harm could come to her or her home.

We had lunch with Plum at the Picardy, walked in the sun among sand dunes and pine trees, talked, saw what sights Le Touquet had to offer, had tea and then departed to catch the evening boat back to Folkestone and a train to Walmer.

Readers may regard all this talk of Pekes and public school football and cricket as being 'small beer'. This may be so, but a celebrity's life is not confined solely to the major achievements with which his name is associated, the books he has written, the pictures he has painted, the battles he has taken part in, the money he has made, the public offices he has held and the honours he has received; to gain a full understanding of the man and his calibre it is necessary to know something about his hobbies and tastes and interests. It is, I find, almost impossible to think of Plum without a Peke as a companion.

* * *

A letter from the president of the International Mark Twain Society gives the explanation of 'Me and Mussolini'.

* * *

June 26th, 1936.   *Webster Groves, Missouri.*

Dear Mr Wodehouse:

In recognition of your outstanding and lasting contribution to the happiness of the world, it gives us much pleasure to offer you the Mark Twain Medal. The list enclosed will show you to whom the Medal has been given in the past.

> With all good wishes,
> Yours sincerely,
> Cyril Clemens.

* * *

The list included Mussolini.

In October Plum went to Hollywood for the second time.

* * *

1315 Angelo Drive,
November 7th, 1936.   *Beverly Hills, California.*

I am sending this to Watt, because I am not sure if you are still at the flat.

Well, here we are, settled in a house miles away up at the top of a mountain, surrounded by canyons in which I am told rattlesnakes abound, and employing a protection agency to guard the place at nights! We looked at a lot of houses in the valley part of Beverly Hills, where we were before, but couldn't find one we liked, so took this, which is a lovely place with a nice pool, but, as I say, remote. Still, that's an advantage in a way, as we don't get everybody dropping in on us.

Did you ever hear anything from Doubleday? I wrote to him, urging him to publish your books in America, but have heard nothing, except that Watt told me D. had had a 'very nice' letter from me. What I wanted to know, of course, was if he was going to publish your books.

Winky has taken on a new lease of life through association with the puppy. (Did I tell you Ethel bought a female puppy just before we sailed?) She ignored her for six weeks, and then suddenly became devoted to her. She races about the garden, chased by the puppy.

The puppy is a comedian. In New York, we had put on Winky's lead and let it trail on the carpet, and we went out, but no Winky followed, though we called to her. When we went back, we found Winks trying hard to get out, but the puppy had seized the lead and was tugging at it.

Everything is very pleasant and placid here, and I am having a good time. But it doesn't seem as interesting as it was last time. I miss Thalberg very much, though I like Sam Katz, for whom I am working. I am collaborating on a musical picture with a man I last saw twenty years ago, when I was sympathizing with him for being chucked out of the cast of one of the Bolton-Wodehouse-Kern musical comedies. He is a wild Irishman named McGowan, who seems to be fighting the heads of the studio all the time. I get on very well with him myself.

Before starting for California, I went to Philadelphia to see Lorimer at the *Saturday Evening Post*. He was very friendly. Rather funny, when he bought *The Crime Wave At Blandings* after I had had nothing in the *S.E.P.* for a couple of years owing to my American income-tax trouble, he paid me $2,000 and wrote me a letter asking if that was all right. I wrote back: 'Dear Mr Lorimer. I am so intensely spiritual that money means nothing to me, but I must confess that that $2,000 was a bit of a sock on the jaw, as I had always thought that a short story was supposed to fetch a tenth of the price of a serial, so I had been looking forward to $4,000.' This apparently touched his heart, for the first thing he said to me when I came into his room was that he would give me $4,000.

He seemed a little taken aback when I walked in, as he had not seen me since the days when I had thick black hair on my now bald head. Did I ever tell you about that? He bought *Something Fresh* as a serial, and when I wrote *Uneasy Money*, he asked me to spend the week-end at his house, bringing the script with me. On the Sunday he curled up on a sofa and started to read the script, with me sitting there, pretending to be absorbed in a bound volume of the *Post* but really, of course, listening in anguish in the hope of hearing him laugh. Which presently he began to do, and after about half an hour he said: 'I like this one better than the other.' I never heard such beautiful words in my life. At the end of the first hour he said he would buy it and give me $5,000. For *Something Fresh* he had given me $3,500. He said he would have given me $5,000 for *Something Fresh*, but he had had a row with my agent and wanted to score off him. Tough luck on a writer to be caught in the middle of a feud like that, don't you think?

I've always thought that his buying *Something Fresh* showed what a wonderful editor he was. Here was a story by an absolutely unknown man, and a story, what is more, about life in England, a country he didn't like, but it amused him, so he decided without any hesitation that the public of the *Saturday*

Evening Post were jolly well going to be amused by it, too, and he didn't give a damn if they weren't.

I think the reason the English magazines die off like flies is that the editors are wondering timidly all the time what their readers are going to like, and won't take a chance on anything that isn't on exactly the same lines as everything else they have ever published. Lorimer has always had an unswerving faith in his own judgment. His attitude is 'I like this story, and to hell with what anyone else thinks'. That's how he has made the *Post* such a success.

He is retiring in January, to be succeeded by Wesley Stout.

I still swim every morning, but the water is beginning to get a bit chilly.

Haven't seen many celebrities yet. We don't see much of anybody except our beloved Maureen O'Sullivan and her husband, John Farrow. He is the man who likes your sea stories so much. I met Clark Gable the other day. Also Fred Astaire. I think Fred is going to do a picture of my *A Damsel in Distress*, with music by George Gershwin. I shall know more about this later.

* * *

The puppy Plum mentions in this letter, which was soon to be known as Wonder, became in due course the most travelled, the most celebrated and the longest-lived of all the Wodehouse Pekes, and the only one we never met.

* * *

December 28th, 1936.   *1315 Angelo Drive.*

Thanks for your long letters with all the news about the school footer. Isn't it extraordinary how we never seem to get the breaks against Haileybury? I remember one very wet day when we scored four tries and they also scored four and converted one from the touchline, a thing that wouldn't have happened again in a hundred times.

I call it a very good performance beating St Paul's. If they could take fifteen points off Bedford, they must be a good side.

(Incidentally, isn't it amazing that you and I, old buffers of 55, with Civilization shortly about to crash, can worry about school football? It is really almost the only thing I do worry about.)

By the way, a word about stories. Don't regard the rejected ones as hopeless. I wrote a Ukridge story last year which I tried to feel was all right, but inside me knew was not. It was sent to the *Red Book*, which chucked it. I have rewritten it, making it a Bingo Little story, and it is now fine. (I haven't actually sent it out yet, but I shall be amazed if the *Saturday Evening Post* don't take it.) See what I mean? The thing was wrong, because I told it in one way. Telling it in another made it all right.

I haven't finished my novel yet. I have had rather a big job to do at the studio, and this particular story – *Summer Moonshine* – is so tricky that I can't just dash off a chapter at odd times. In my spare time I have been rewriting a couple of short stories. The one I mentioned above is one of them, and the other I have sold to the *Post*.

I have a story coming out in *S.E.P.* week ending January 30th, which they think is the best I have ever done. It was sent to the *Red Book*, and they offered $2,000 for it, having given me $3,000 for my others, I refused this, and on landing in America rang up the editor and asked him to return my story – having called on Lorimer the previous day and, as I believe I told you, got him to agree that he would pay $4,000 for any stories of mine which he accepted. The editor of the *Red Book* raised the offer to $2,500; but I believed in the story so much that I turned it down, and am glad that I did, because the *Post* jumped at it. Title – *All's Well with Bingo.*

I heartily concur, as Watt would say, with your remarks about *Reggie and the Greasy Bird.* In that shape, rotten. It just shows how much depends on the telling of a story – which is what I mean about your rejected stuff. Half of it may be quite all right, except for one little thing that has put an editor off without his knowing why he was put off. That was what was wrong with the Ukridge story (see above). I had to have a scene where the hero gets in bad with the man who is about to give him a job, and I had a bad scene and, what was worse, a very long one. Even when I had changed it to a Bingo Little story, I could see it was not quite right, and finally I spotted that what was wrong was this one scene.

I had Ukridge meeting the man at Charing Cross station – while they are talking, along comes one of U.'s creditors and U. breaks off in the middle of a sentence and legs it with the creditor after him, thus making the prospective employer feel that he is a bit too eccentric to employ.

Why that wasn't right, I'm still darned if I know. It sounds a good enough scene, and I may quite possibly use it somewhere eventually. But it was all wrong for this story. I have now substituted a quite short and simple scene at the employer's club.

We have now reached the rainy season here. Funny how one never minds rain in England, but in California it seems to upset everything.

March 7th, 1937.   *1315 Angelo Drive.*

I meant to send you a lot of clippings about the frosts here, but forgot. Anyway, the gist is that we have had a foul winter and the valley below this house has been wrapped in a dense London fog for weeks, because of the smudge pots which they have been burning to try to save the lemon crops.

Did smudge pots enter into your lemon-life at all when you were out in California? Or was it always warm here then in winter? Lemons have been practically wiped out this year.

I am leading a very quiet life here. Unless I have to go and see my producer, I stay around the house all day except for an hour's walk, and we go up to our rooms at 8.30 and read and listen to the radio. I enjoy it, though I must say I would like to be nearer home. This place seems very far away sometimes.

Winks is very well. Also the puppy, who now has a new name – Wonder. My day starts when I hear the puppy bark in Ethel's room. I open the door, and the puppy comes leaping out. Winky then pokes her head out of my bed, in which she has been sleeping, and I take them downstairs and let them out. I bring them in when I come down to breakfast, and they then have to be let out again in order to bark at the gardener, whose arrival is always a terrific surprise and shock to them, though he has turned up at the same time every morning for four months.

Woman out here has just got a divorce. Stated that her husband had not worked for months and was a pretty low-down character altogether. 'He was always going to dances,' she said, 'and when he wanted to go to one the other night, he took the only pair of silk stockings I had and cut the tops off so that he could wear them as socks.'

March 24th, 1937.   *1315 Angelo Drive, Beverly Hills.*

I finished *Summer Moonshine* yesterday. Young Lorimer, of the *Saturday Evening Post*, called on me about two weeks ago and took away 80,000 words of it, leaving me about another 10,000 to do. I must say the *S.E.P.* are extraordinary. Lorimer left on a Friday, read the thing in the train, arrived Philadelphia Monday night, presumably went to the office Tuesday morning and gave the MS. to somebody else, who must have read it Tuesday and given it to Stout, the chief editor, on Wednesday morning and Stout must have read it on Wednesday night, because on Thursday morning I got a telegram saying it had been accepted.

I don't see how they manage to be so quick. They get 75,000 MSS. a year, all of which are read.

Price – $40,000.

Against this triumph I have to set the fact that Metro-Goldwyn-Mayer are not taking up my option, which expires in another two weeks. I have had another flop with them. I started gaily in working on a picture with Bill McGuire, and I gradually found myself being edged out. Eventually, they came out into the open and said they had wanted McGuire to write the thing by himself, all along. There seems to be a curse over M-G-M, so far as I am concerned.

Since then, I have had a number of offers from other studios for one picture apiece. It seems pretty certain that in about two weeks I shall be working on my *Damsel in Distress*, which R.K.O. bought for Fred Astaire. Selznick wants me to do a thing called *The Earl of Chicago* and Walter Wanger asked me to go round, as he had something right in my line. It turned out to be Clarence Budington Kelland's *Stand-In*. I turned it down. I got myself in bad enough last time by criticizing Hollywood, and I didn't want to do a picture which would have been an indictment of the studios.

Raining in buckets today, and snow on the foothills yesterday! The latest gag here is about the New York man who came to Southern California for the winter – and found it!

May 6th, 1937.   *1315 Angelo Drive.*

Listen. What has become of the old-fashioned California climate? We had a couple of warm days last week, and then went right back to winter weather again. Today is absolutely freezing. And it's been the same ever since I got here.

I wish we had taken this house for six months instead of a year. There seems to be a probability that I shall do a four weeks' job on the *Damsel in Distress*, but except for that nothing is stirring. I was told that I was going to do *The Earl of Chicago*, but I see that Ben Hecht is doing it. The fact is, I'm not worth the money my agent insists on asking for me. After all, my record here is eighteen months, with only small bits of pictures to show for it. I'm no good to these people. Lay off old Pop Wodehouse, is the advice I would give to any studio that wants to get on in the world. There is no surer road to success.

May 7th, 1937.

I have been seeing a lot of G. O. Allen, the England cricket captain, who came home from Australia via Hollywood. He told me the inside story of the bodyline crisis. He is a bit sick about the last English team, as everybody failed enthusiastically on every occasion, and the fast bowlers had to do all the work.

Our butler got home last night tight as a drum and is still sleeping it off. Over here, the help take every Thursday off, and he employed his holiday in getting thoroughly pickled.

I can't fathom the mentality of Pekes. Yesterday Roland Young came to tea and sat on the sofa with Winks snuggling up to him on one side and Wonder on the other. The moment he got up and started to leave, both Pekes sprang down and attacked his ankles with savage snarls. You would have thought they had never seen him before, and had spotted him breaking in through a window.

Interesting that about your visit to the specialist. It's nice to know that your heart is all right. Isn't it difficult to get accustomed to the idea that one is now at the age when most people settle down and don't do a thing? I am now exactly the age my father was when I left Dulwich, and I remember him as tottering to his armchair and settling in it for the day. That's one thing about being a writer – it does keep you young. Do you find you can't walk as far as you used to? I do out here, but I remember last year in Le Touquet I used to do my seven miles without feeling it. I think it's mainly the California climate.

Big strike now in the picture industry, which may close all the studios. That'll teach them not to take up my option.

June 24th, 1937.   *1315 Angelo Drive.*

Life here at present is a bit like being on your *Lancing Island*. We can't go on the mountains because of the rattlesnakes, the butler killed two Black Widow spiders in the garden (deadlier than snakes), and last night and this morning the following episodes occurred. We were taking the dogs for a stroll after dinner, and Wonder didn't follow. We went back and found her playing with a tarantula on the drive! And this morning, when I came out from my swim, I heard her gruffling at something on the steps of the pool, and there was another tarantula, bigger than the first one!

I am sweating away at a picture. The Fred Astaire one, *A Damsel in Distress*, with musical score by George Gershwin. When they bought it, they gave it to one of the R.K.O. writers to adapt, and he turned out a script all about crooks – no resemblance to the novel. Then it struck them that it might be a good thing to stick to the story, so they chucked away the other script and called me in. I think it is going to make a good picture. But what uncongenial work picture-writing is. Somebody's got to do it, I suppose, but this is the last time they'll get me.

June 25th, 1937.

Your letter of June 15th has just arrived.

We have got a big party on tomorrow night – seventy people coming – and there is no room for them all in the house, so we shall have to feed in the garden, and the fear that is haunting us is that it will be too cold. Up here in the mountains we get an odd sort of white mist which comes up from the sea. They don't get it in the valley. The days now are scorching, but it always cools off a lot at night. Still, last night was lovely.

I'm glad you liked the Peke story. I have a good one coming out next week. But I haven't had a short-story idea for ages. They don't seem to come nowadays.

I shall be glad to get away from California. It is too far away.

As far as I can make out, the American magazines are doing all right now, but prices have gone down a lot. The *Post* seems away ahead of the rest, and Lorimer's resignation doesn't seem to have hurt it at all.

September 4th, 1937.   *1315 Angelo Drive.*

I finished my work on *Damsel in Distress* three weeks ago, and with only one day's interval started on a picture with Eddie Goulding – Englishman whom I used to know in London before the war – now a director here. I am not finding it very pleasant, because he has his own ideas about the thing and rewrites all my stuff, thus inducing a what's-the-use feeling and making it hard not to shove down just anything. Also, I don't like the story.

The money is fine – $10,000 for six weeks and $2,000 a week after that – but this blasted Administration has just knocked the bottom out of everything by altering the tax laws, so that instead of paying a flat ten per cent as a non-resident alien I now have to pay ordinary citizen rates, which take away about a third of what one earns.

The taxes are fantastic here and very tough on Hollywood stars because they make so much over a short period and then go into the discard. Nelson Eddy, my neighbour, made $600,000 last year, and when all his taxes and expenses were paid found that he had $50,000 left. Well, not bad, even so, one might say. But then the point is that in 1939 his income may be about tuppence! Stars shoot up and die away here before you can breathe.

I'm not enjoying life much just now. I don't like doing pictures. *A Damsel in Distress* was fun, because I was working with the best director here – George Stevens – and on my own story, but as a rule pictures are a bore. And just now I'm pining to get at a new novel, which I have all mapped out. I sneak in a page or two every now and then, but I want to concentrate on it.

October 11th, 1937.   *1315 Angelo Drive.*

Just a line to say that we are not staying here for the Spring, after all, but are sailing on October 28th, and I shall be back at Le Touquet on November 4th.

November 9th, 1937.   *Low Wood, Le Touquet.*

Just had a misfortune with the old typewriter. Arrived here with a very faint ribbon and took out a spare, and found, after I had taken off the old ribbon that the new one was a Remington, and wouldn't fit. So I have been three days with the machine out of action.

I am coming over on Tuesday the sixteenth. I am not quite certain where I shall go.

Frightful lot to talk about. Remind me to tell you about my visit to the *Saturday Evening Post*. One of the editors is Erd Brandt, who used to be your agent. He spoke very highly of you, and said you were now living in Brazil. I said yes, you were, and were looked on locally as quite one of the nuts, so you can now start writing a lot of Brazil stories for them. They want to see your stuff. They all remembered it and liked it.

November 22nd, 1937.   *Low Wood.*

Two things combined to make me scratch my visit. I shrank from a journey probably in rotten weather, and secondly I got a letter from Reynolds, enclosing one from the *Saturday Evening Post* about my serial, which made it necessary for me to pitch in on the thing.

It looks as if *The Post* are taking it for granted that they are going to buy the story – I sent them the first 50,000 words – but they felt that the early part needed cutting. 'Too many stage waits' was what Brandt said. And when I looked at it, I saw they were right.

Here is the lay-out, as I had it.

1. Bertie goes to see his Aunt Dahlia.
2. She tells him to go and buy flowers for Aunt Agatha, who is ill.
3. Bertie goes back to his flat and she rings up and says she forgot to say that she has another job for him – which will necessitate a visit to an antique shop.
4. Bertie goes to flower shop and gets into trouble.
5. Bertie goes back to his flat and sobs on Jeeves's shoulder.
6. Bertie goes to antique shop and gets into more trouble.

Now, can you imagine that I had written that part quite a dozen times and only now spotted that it ought to go thus:

1. Bertie goes to Aunt Dahlia. She tells him to go to antique shop.
2. Bertie goes to antique shop, plays the scene which originally took place in flower shop, then plays the antique shop scene.

It cuts out fifteen pages without losing anything of value. And what I am driving at is that isn't it ghastly to think that after earning one's living as a writer for thirty-seven years one can make a blunder like that. Why on earth I kept taking Bertie back to the flat, where nothing whatever happened, I can't think.

This necessitated five days of intense work, and I now feel

that I might as well get on with the thing and postpone my visit to England till December 16th.

Did you ever read an old book called *Helen's Babies*, about a young bachelor getting saddled with some kids? *The Ladies' Home Journal* editor has got a fixation that a splendid modern version could be done, and he has offered me $45,000 if I will do it. And here's the tragedy. I can't think of a single idea towards it. When *Helen's Babies* was published, all you had to do was to get the central idea and then have a monotonous stream of incidents where the kids caused trouble. Nobody seemed to mind in those days that you were being repetitious. But surely that sort of thing wouldn't go now. In any case, I can't work it. I'll never do a story, however much I'm offered, unless I like it and feel I can make it good.

The *L.H.J.* editor is Bruce Gould, who used to write those wonderful stories in the *Post* about a literary agent. Do you remember them? They were superb.

*   *   *

Even now, whenever I read one of Plum's books, I find it difficult to realize that he ever had the slightest difficulty in the construction or writing. In a way it was a comfort to me to learn that even he had written a book that limped at the start, because I had always thought that, if there was one thing he excelled in more than another, it was in the way he began his stories. As a reader, I felt that my attention and interest were captured from the very first sentences. Consider, for instance, the beginning of *The Luck of the Bodkins*:

Into the face of the young man who sat on the terrace of the Hôtel Magnifique at Cannes there had crept a look of furtive shame, the shifty, hangdog look which announces that an Englishman is about to talk French. One of the things which Gertrude Butterick had impressed upon Monty Bodkin when he left for this holiday on the Riviera was that he must be sure to practise his French, and Gertrude's word was law. So now, though he knew that it was going to make his nose tickle, he said:

'Er, garçon.'

'M'sieur?'

'Er, garcon, esker-vous avez un spot de l'encre et une pièce de papier – note-papier, vous savez – et une enveloppe et une plume?'

'Bien, m'sieur.'

The strain was too great. Monty relapsed into his native tongue.

'I want to write a letter,' he said. And having, like all lovers, a tendency to share his romance with the world, he would probably have added 'to the sweetest girl on earth', had not the waiter already bounded off like a retriever, to return a few moments later with the fixings.

'V'là, sir! Zere you are, sir,' said the waiter. He was engaged to a girl in Paris who had told him that when on the Riviera he must be sure to practise his English. 'Eenk – pin – pipper – enveloppe – and a liddle bit of bloddin' pipper.'

This brings the reader to the end of Page One. He will now turn to Page Two and read on.

The book with which Plum was having such trouble was *The Code of the Woosters*, and it is in this book, in Chapter VIII, that you will find the funniest of the Jeeves and Bertie scenes where the girl, Stiffy, enters her bedroom to find them treed on the top of the chest of drawers and the cupboard because of the menace of her Aberdeen terrier, Bartholomew.

* * *

January 4th, 1938.   *Low Wood.*

I am finding finishing *The Code of the Woosters* a ghastly sweat. I don't seem to have the drive and command of words I used to. Towards the end of *Thank You, Jeeves*, at La Fréyère, I wrote twenty-six pages one day! Now I find myself quarrying out the stuff. I imagine the trouble is that I have twice been stopped writing the book for long periods, and this has made me tired of it. Still, the story seems good enough when I get it down.

May 15th, 1938.   *Low Wood.*

It must be about two months since I wrote you. I have been sweating like blazes getting a new novel started. It's about 'Uncle Fred' – I'm calling it *Uncle Fred in the Springtime* – at Blandings Castle. After writing 150 pages, I now have 40 which are right. Every time I write a book, I swear I'll never write another with a complicated plot. In this one – in the first 40 pages – I have either brought on to play a scene or mentioned heavily each of my principal characters – ten including Lord Emsworth's pig. So the going ought to be easier now.

Fancy Paddy Millar turning up at Low Wood!

I wish you had been with him.

How did *Sailors' Women* do?

(Staccato, disjointed style due to fact that this is the 15th letter I've written since tea-time.)

Today is Winky's tenth birthday! Great celebrations. Madge made a sponge cake with 'Happy Birthday' on it in white sugar.

I am hoping to come over on Friday week.

I find the most difficult thing in writing is to describe a character. Appearance, I mean.

Have you sold Reeves Shaw anything lately?

Don't you wish Watt's address was shorter?

Shall we ever get Bradman out in the Tests?

Love to Rene.

June 30th, 1938.   *Low Wood.*

Ethel is going over on Tuesday to look after Norfolk Street, so I shall probably come on Thursday.

Isn't writing in the summer a sweat! I find that my output slows down to about half, and if I can average three pages a day I think I am doing well. I started *Uncle Fred in the Springtime* on May the first and have only got up to near half-way – i.e. about a month behind my schedule. Still, I think the stuff is good. I find it so hard to write in the afternoons. If I go for an exercise walk, I'm too tired to write, and if I don't get any exercise, my brain won't work!

I liked the Gilkes book. I thought Leake had made a good job of it. Though you rather get the impression of Gilkes as a man who was always trying to damp people, to keep them from getting above themselves. ('So you made a century against

Tonbridge, did you, my boy? Well, always remember that you will soon be dead, and in any case, the bowling was probably rotten!'

* * *

The 'Gilkes book' was a sort of history of Dulwich College, featuring A. H. Gilkes, the famous headmaster of our time.

* * *

July 19th, 1938.   *Low Wood.*

I can see what's wrong with that story. You have got a star character – Shuffley – and you don't give him enough to do. He just sits in the background up to page 22, and even then he doesn't really do anything *ingenious*. He just produces fifty quid and hands it over to Brogan. The story is all about the other characters. In fact, you might just as well not have Shuffley in the story at all, except as a mechanism for Brogan getting the money.

The conception of the story is good. What it needs is for Shuffley to do something very funny and ingenious in order to get the money for Brogan – he simply can't say: 'I've got fifty quid, here you are.' I can't think of anything on the spur of the moment, but the sort of thing you need is something like they had in a play called *Turn to the Right*, where the comic crook learns from the old woman who has been kind to him that the local banker (The Menace) is going to sell her up, unless she pays five hundred dollars back rent. The banker comes in, the crook picks his pocket of a wad of money, and then when the banker starts demanding his cash comes forward and says: 'Here you are, paid in full – give me a receipt.'

See what I mean? It shows the principal actor *doing* something. You got the thing absolutely right in *Captain Shuffley's Briar Pipe*, which the *Strand* bought and Illingworth illustrated. In this one, Shuffley somehow ought to fool the two villains and get the money from them. I'm just thinking aloud, now, but if he went to Beigel and said: 'Give me twenty-five quid and I can fool Kirtle out of buying the land, because I know there is going to be a hotel built there,' and then went to Kirtle and told him a similar tale, he could give both sums to Brogan to make up the required fifty.

Of course, this wouldn't work, I suppose. It might, if Kirtle and Beigel – you would call the poor devils names like that – were working secretly from each other. Suppose each had got a private tip that the hotel was to be built and Shuffley demands £25 from each as his price for not telling the other. That looks promising. Shuffley would say he wasn't interested in the thing except as the means of raising a few quid for himself – I mean, he would make it clear that he was not in the market against them.

To work this, I think you would have to conceal it from the reader that he was fooling them *both*. You would have to show him telling Kirtle that he knew what he was up to and that £25 would keep him quiet, and then in the end you would reveal that he had played the same game on Beigel. In fact, the more people you had working against one another, the easier it would be; because you could make Shuffley's silence money smaller. How would it be to have him get £5 from three chaps – or even two, and then run it up to the required sum by gambling?

I think this would work. Its great merit is that it makes Shuffley seem crooked till right at the end when you reveal that his motives were good. That is to say, it gives him character. I think what Rene found wrong, when she said the story was dull, was just what I am criticizing – i.e. that you engage Charles Laughton to play a star part and all the time the audience is saying: 'Hey, but isn't Laughton going to do *anything*?'

* * *

The reason why I have reproduced Plum's letter at such length is that I wished to show his methods of constructing a story or, at least, of turning a thoroughly bad story into quite a good one. Anyone who has ever written fiction or tried to write will understand how difficult a task it is to put right a story by someone else. Here, as so often in the past, Plum saw at a glance where I had gone wrong, and, what was far more profitable, made it possible for me to reconstruct my story on the right lines.

* * *

November 13th, 1938. *Low Wood.*

I'm sorry your novel has stuck, but, boy, you don't know what trouble is! Two weeks ago I got a cable from Reynolds saying:

'*Saturday Evening Post* will buy *Uncle Fred in Springtime*, provided you make certain changes. They like story, but think at present it is difficult to follow week by week. They suggest you might want to eliminate a character or two and clarify relationships.'

You can imagine what it's like, taking two characters out of my sort of story, where a character is put in only because he is needed for at least two big scenes later on in the book!

However, I cabled that I would do it, and for these last two weeks I have been hard at work.

I found that I could simplify the story enormously by dropping the whole of one motive and the two characters it involved, but this meant rewriting practically the whole book. Whenever I came to a spot where I had been hoping to be able just to rip a dozen pages out of the original version and pin them together, I found they were studded with allusions to the vanished characters.

Your troubles must have been pretty bad, but they were part of the first writing, when one expects to encounter a snag or two. But from the tone of Reynolds' cable, I gathered that mine practically got over as it stood, and then some ass in the office said: 'Of course, it wouldn't be a bad thing if there were fewer characters' and the boss editor yawned and said: 'No, that's right. Tell him to cut out a couple of them.'

I am very interested in what you say about *Jill the Reckless*. It's what I always feel about my work – viz. that I go off the rails unless I stay all the time in a sort of artificial world of my own creation. A real character in one of my books sticks out like a sore thumb. You're absolutely right about Freddie Rooke. Just a stage dude – as Bertie Wooster was when I started writing him. If you look at the early Jeeves stories, you'll find Bertie quite a different character now.

The old gentleman blowing the other up with dynamite was in *Money for Nothing*. The burglar on the window-ledge is in *Hot Water*.

November 29th, 1938.   *Low Wood.*

Dear Bill:

Winkie is dead. I can hardly bear to write about it. The usual thing – tick fever. Same as Boo.

I went up to Paris to join Ethel on Monday, taking her with me, and I thought she was more than usually fit. She ran about on the platform at Boulogne Station and seemed splendid. On Tuesday morning Ethel took her and Wonder for a walk and told me that Winkie had refused to run and seemed out of sorts. On Wednesday morning we took her to the vet, and left her there. In the afternoon we went to see him, and he said it was tick fever. We saw her in her cage and she was obviously dying, and that night the vet rang up and said it was all over. We had the body taken down here and she is buried beside Boo in the garden.

On Wednesday, June 21st, 1939, at the Encaenia at Oxford University, Plum – on this occasion Mr Pelham Grenville Wodehouse – received the degree of D.Litt.

In its report of the proceedings in the Sheldonian *The Times* in its issue of June 22nd said:

Last, but in the opinion of the University far from least, came Mr P. G. Wodehouse, whom the Public Orator presented as *festivum caput – Petroniumne dicam an Terentium nostrum?* The Public Orator fittingly marked almost his last public appearance, and delighted his audience by a passage of Horatian hexameters, an exemplum of his own *urbana felicitas*, in which he not only paid tribute to the kindly temper and finished style of Mr Wodehouse's work, but also achieved the difficult task of presenting or suggesting in Latin the familiar figures of Bertie Wooster and Jeeves and Mr Mulliner and Lord Emsworth and the Empress of Blandings and Psmith and even the Honourable Augustus Fink-Nottle and the love-life of the newts.

In the same number of *The Times* there appeared the following verses:

D.LITT, 1939.

Dear Mr Wodehouse, who'll applaud your
D.Litt.? Jeeves, Mr Mulliner, Bertie, Psmith,
Aunt Dahlia, Gussie Fink-Nottle, Tuppy, both
the Freddies,
                    Threepwood and Widgeon,
Sam the Sudden, Ronnie, Empress and
    Lord Emsworth,
Stinker Pinker, Biscuit, Monty, Lotus Blossom,
Beach, Beefy Bingham, gay old Gally Threepwood,
                    Albert E. Peasemarsh.
Who'll look austerely? Lady Constance Keeble,
Baxter, Sir Roderick, all the tribe of Parsloe,
Roderick Blackshorts (Eulalie in Secret),
                    Tilbury, Pilbeam.
Ruler unquestioned of the Land of Laughter,
Scholar, creator, lord of apt quotation,
Master of words, of things yet unattempted,
                    Thanks, Dr. Wodehouse.
                        K.A.E.*

Of Plum, a leader-writer in the June 22nd issue of
The Times said:

—but there is no question that in making Mr P. G.
Wodehouse a doctor of letters the University has done
the right and popular thing. Everyone knows at least
some of his many works and has felt all the better for

* These initials concealed the identity of the late Mrs K. A. Esdaile, the
wife of Dr Arundell Esdaile, C.B.E.

the gaiety of his wit and the freshness of his style. Style goes a long way in Oxford; indeed the purity of Mr Wodehouse's style was singled out for particular praise in the Public Orator's happy Horatian summing up of Mr Wodehouse's qualities and achievements.

Toward the latter end of July Plum was in England once more and my wife and I met him in London; and he took us about with him and was very kind and hospitable. On the Saturday of his short visit he and I went down to Dulwich together to see the school play St Paul's and we sat in the pavilion and met people we had known years before and would have been happy but for the fact this was the dullest cricket match, the slowest and most uneventful, either of us had ever seen.

I said goodbye to Plum at about four o'clock, having arranged to get back to town early, and I left him seated in the pavilion, looking rather bored and rather disconsolate.

That was the last time I saw him.

Six weeks later war was declared. Plum was in Le Touquet. I was in Dover.

And now I feel compelled to discuss at some length the impact of war on one who had never in his life had a really unkind thought concerning any other human being. As the reader will by now have discovered Plum Wodehouse is a man of simple tastes, a hard worker at his chosen occupation, a writer of good English, of far better English than his detractors who sprang up like mushrooms the morning after his first broadcast from Berlin were willing to admit, a writer, too, who chose to depict the absurdities of his fellow countrymen while appreciating their worth. It was, of course, Plum's misfortune that he was capable of finding things to like in the most unlikeable of people, and though loathing the Nazi way of life and their lust for conquest, and their uniforms and posturings, was unwilling to associate the individual German with the excesses and crimes of his Government.

Here is a personal note; one evening when I was working on the ground floor of the little house in Hildenborough where we lived after the Military had requisitioned our house in Dover and before we returned to the Coast, I heard my wife call to me from her bedroom, where she was listening to the radio. I went upstairs and she told me Plum was broadcasting. I listened anxiously and heard a far-away voice, easily recognizable as Plum's, telling of his journey from Loos prison into Germany in a cattle truck without food or water. The broadcast ended with the remark that, so far as I remember, happier days were in store for soon he and his fellow prisoners were to be at Tost. The wave-length was, I believe, 525 medium.

I think it worth while here to put down some of the things said about Plum Wodehouse in the newspapers during and after the War, and in books, and in private letters.

Not everyone who wrote to Plum, sympathizing with him and wishing him well, was known to him. John F. Leeming, the author of a very successful book, *Always Tomorrow*, and a prisoner of war for two and a half years in Italy, wrote:

I would like to tell you that, having read your broadcasts, I cannot see how anyone could possibly see
anything in them the slightest degree pro-German or
anti-British. But I will not give you my own opinion.
I will tell you that of the late Air-Marshal Boyd, R.A.F.
I was his personal assistant and we were prisoners
together in Italy. He read your broadcasts and gave
them to me, saying: 'Why the Germans ever let him say
all this I cannot think. They have either got more sense
of humour than I credited them with or it was just
slipped past the censor. There is some stuff about being
packed in cattle trucks and a thing about Loos jail that
you would think would send a Hun crazy. Wodehouse
has probably been shot by now.'

In his book *Critical Essays*, the late George Orwell had
this to say in his monograph, 'In Defence of P. G.
Wodehouse'.

If my opinion of Wodehouse's mentality is accepted,
the idea that in 1941 he consciously aided the Nazi
propaganda machine becomes untenable and even
ridiculous.

The other thing one must remember is that Wodehouse happened to be taken prisoner at just the moment
when the War reached its desperate phase. We forget
these things now. There was hardly any fighting, the
Chamberlain government was unpopular, eminent
publicists were hinting that we should make a compromise peace as quickly as possible, trade union and

Labour Party branches all over the country were passing anti-war resolutions. Afterwards, of course, things changed. The Army was with difficulty extricated from Dunkirk, France collapsed, Britain was alone, the bombs rained on London, Goebbels announced that Britain was to be 'reduced to degradation and poverty'. By the middle of 1941 the British people knew what they were up against and feelings against the enemy were far fiercer than before. But Wodehouse had spent the intervening year in internment, and his captors seemed to have treated him reasonably well. He had missed the turning-point of the War, and in 1941 he was still reacting in terms of 1939.

George Orwell continued:

In the desperate circumstances of the time, it was excusable to be angry at what Wodehouse did, but to go on denouncing him three or four years later – and more, to let an impression remain that he acted with conscious treachery – is not excusable. Few things in this war have been more morally disgusting than the present hunt after traitors and Quislings. At best it is largely the punishment of the guilty by the guilty. In France, all kinds of petty rats – police officials, penny-a-lining journalists, women who have slept with German soldiers – are hounded down, while almost without exception the big rats escape. In England the fiercest tirades against Quislings are uttered by Conservatives who were practising appeasements in 1938 and Communists who were advocating it in 1940. I have striven to show how Wodehouse – just because success and expatriation had allowed him to remain mentally in the Edwardian age – became the *corpus vile* in a propaganda experiment, and I suggest that it is now time to regard the incident as closed.

In his book *Life With Topsy* Denis Mackail said:

Again the door of a lift was the scene of another parting. It closed. We descended. And the next time I heard those mild and familiar tones was in August, 1941, when Diana suddenly roused me from sleep and rushed me to the radio. She had been twiddling knobs, and Plum's voice, doubly removed, for it was a record that was being played over – was addressing us from Germany, where he had recently emerged from forty-nine weeks of internment. I was much moved, but I can't say that I was indignant. He was being funny; I thought he was being remarkably courageous; he seemed to be making a quiet and almost casual plea against intolerance. But this didn't stop a Minister of Information from overriding the authorities of the B.B.C., and putting up a journalist to blackguard him in another broadcast, to sneer at his Christian names, and to describe him as a 'playboy'. Plum! The most industrious author that I had ever known. But the war couldn't go on without hatred, and Plum hated no one. That was his crime.

Sax Rohmer was one who defended Plum. He wrote:

Mr W. A. Darlington's reference to a claim for £50,000 made by the United States Revenue upon P. G. Wodehouse is calculated to mislead. I would like to point out that a similar claim (in my own case for a less staggering sum) was made upon all English novelists and playwrights, or all of those with whom I am acquainted, who derived any considerable revenue from the U.S.A.

These claims were based upon some obscure paragraph in the Statute book hitherto overlooked even by the lawyers. Never-the-less, assessment was made retrospective. Rafael Sabatini heroically took the matter to Court and fought a losing action which dragged on for more than a year.

In fairness to a man whose good name is at stake on other counts, I think the implication that Wodehouse's misfortune was due to conscious tax-dodging should be disclaimed.

Ethel Mannin wrote:

Since some fellow authors have seen fit to censure P. G. Wodehouse in a 'We-wouldn't-do-that-sort-of-thing' manner, may I suggest that judgment be withheld, since we are none of us in a position to know the facts?

It is always difficult to gauge another person's motives; how can any of us say with certainty what we would do in given circumstances? None of the people so busily censuring Mr Wodehouse has had his experiences. I was always under the impression that part of the Christian ethic was 'Judge not that ye be not judged'.

Not all the letters the *Daily Telegraph* published were from distinguished writers. The one that I thought by far the best was by someone who signed himself 'Disinterested'.

In view of the letters you have received about Mr P. G. Wodehouse, it may be of interest to know the facts surrounding his release from prison camp which have just come into my possession.

Mr Wodehouse was captured last year because he refused to believe that the Germans were approaching his residence where he was working on a book. He wished to finish the last four chapters before leaving France. At that time he was over 58. The Germans are not interning enemy aliens over 60, and Mr Wodehouse will be 60 within a few months.

The camp in which he was imprisoned is one of the best in Germany. A former asylum for the insane, its accommodation is comfortable, and its Commanding Officer, a British prisoner during the last war, moderate and lenient. Although he was offered a room to himself, Mr Wodehouse refused to accept preferential treatment, and shared a room with sixty others. He was, however, given space in which to write. This was a large room in which a tap-dancer, a saxophonist and a pianist were also 'working'.

The Columbia Broadcasting Company and several other American agencies had been in touch with Mr Wodehouse for some time with a view to securing his stories. His broadcasts for Columbia were arranged before he left the prison camp, and set for whatever time he might be released in the normal course of events. This came within a short time of his 60th birthday.

Released prisoners are free to live where they choose, within certain central districts. Mr Wodehouse's considerable royalties from his books published in

Germany undoubtedly decided him to select his greater comfort of the Adlon in preference to more modest accommodation elsewhere in the centre of Berlin.

I have no right or desire to comment or pass judgment on Mr Wodehouse's action, but I would add the remarks made by one who knew him in Berlin. They agree with Mr A. A. Milne that he is politically naïve, and with Miss Dorothy Sayers that he is unconscious of the propaganda value to the Germans of his action. It sprang, they say, from his desire to keep his name before his American reading public. But they do add, most emphatically, that he did not buy his release from prison camp by agreeing to broadcast.

I wrote to Plum regularly while he was in enemy hands: a good many of my letters reached him, some were returned. The last letter I received from him from Le Touquet was dated April 6th, 1940. When I next heard from him, he wrote from Berlin on May 11th, 1942.

* * *

At last I am able to write to you. This is being taken to Lisbon by a German I used to know in Hollywood, who is accompanying the U.S. Embassy crowd. He will mail it there, and I hope it will eventually arrive.

I'm so glad you liked *Money in the Bank*. The only novel, I should imagine, that has ever been written in an internment camp. I did it at the rate of about a page a day in a room with over fifty men playing cards and ping-pong and talking and singing. The first twelve chapters were written in a whirl of ping-pong balls. I suppose on an average morning I would get from fifteen to twenty on the side of the head just as I was searching for the *mot juste*.

As I was starting Chapter Thirteen the Library was opened and I was made President. The President of a Camp Library must not be confused with the Librarian. The Librarian does the rough work like handing out books and entering them in a ledger. The President presides. He stimulates and encourages. I, for instance, used to look in once a day and say 'Everything okay?' and go away again. It was amazing how it helped. Giving the Wodehouse Touch, I used to call it.

Being President of the Library, I became entitled to a padded cell all to myself, and I wrote the rest of the book in a peaceful seclusion disturbed only by the sound of musical gentlemen practising trombones, violoncellos, etc., next door, in the interests of the Entertainment Committee and somebody else lecturing on Chaucer or Beowulf (under the auspices of the Committee for Education). All that I know of Beowulf today I owe to these lectures.

After I had finished *Money in the Bank*, I started a Blandings Castle novel called *Full Moon* and had done about a third of it when I was released. Ethel then joined me in the country, bringing with her the Jeeves novel called *Joy in the Morning*, which I had written at Le Touquet during the occupation.

Those letters in the *Daily Telegraph* about my having found internment so terrible that I bought my release by making a bargain with the German Government were all wrong. I was released because I was on the verge of sixty. When I was in Loos Prison the first week, a dozen of our crowd were released because they were sixty, including my cellmate William Cartmell, the Étaples piano tuner. Of course, he may have made a bargain with the German Government, offering, if set free, to tune its piano half-price, but I don't think so. It all looked pretty genuine to me.

As for finding internment terrible, I didn't at all after the first few months. Loos Prison, Liège Barracks and the Citadel of Huy were on the tough side, but Tost was fine. One thing that helped us enormously there was the presence of the internees from Holland. A good many of them were language-teachers, lecturers and musicians, so we were able to have concerts, shows and so on and brush up on our Beowulf. We also played cricket all through the summer. The prime difficulty in the way of playing cricket was that we had no ball, but the sailors from the *Orama* got round that. They got hold of a nut and wound string round it, and the result was as good a ball as you could want.

The most terrible thing that happened to me as an internee was my shower bath in Loos Prison. Once a week, if you are in the coop at Loos, you all troop up to the top floor and take a tepid shower under the supervision of a warder. You remove your clothes and queue up, and when you reach the head of the line a dab of soft soap is slapped into your hand and you go under the water. And where I went wrong was in making the mistake of supposing that I had lots of time.

I am one of those cautious shower-bathers who put a toe in first and then, if all seems well, another toe, and, in a word, sort of work up to the thing: and it became apparent almost immediately that what the warder wanted to see was something in the nature of an imitation of forked lightning striking a mountain torrent.

The result was that just as I had soft-soaped myself all over, and was hovering on the brink, my feet, as Sir John Suckling beautifully puts it, like little mice stealing in and out, he informed me that my time was up, and told me to put my clothes on and go back to my cell. I don't know if you have ever put your clothes on over a foundation of soft soap, and then gone back to a prison cell, and tried to wash it off at the cold tap without a sponge, but it is one of those experiences that test you. You come out of it a finer, deeper, graver man, not perhaps so fond of French prison warders as you used to be, but with a wonderful feeling of having had your soul tried in the furnace and the realization that life is stern and earnest and that we are not put into this world for pleasure alone.

Did you see a book called – I forget what, but something by one of the American correspondents in Berlin?

If so, I hope you didn't believe the bilge he wrote about me – e.g. that some sinister German had come to the camp to see me and arrange about my being released and speaking on the radio. Nobody ever came near the camp.

The best proof that I did not 'make a bargain' with the German Government is supplied by the Stout–Wodehouse correspondence. Just after the last of the broadcasts I got a cable from Wesley Stout of the *Saturday Evening Post* about *Money in the Bank*. He said he liked it and wanted to buy it, but could do so only on my assurance that I would stop talking on the German radio. I cabled back that I had already stopped, that I had never intended to do more than these five descriptions of camp life, and that he could be perfectly easy in his mind, as I would not speak again on any subject whatsoever.

Now, this cable of mine was written in the presence of an official in the Wilhelmstrasse and sent off by him, and if there had ever been any idea that I had been released because of an agreement on my part to broadcast German propaganda, or, for that matter, to broadcast at all – I hardly think the German authorities would have made no protest when I announced that I intended to go back on the bargain.

Of course I ought to have had the sense to see that it was a loony thing to do to use the German radio for even the most harmless stuff, but I didn't. I suppose prison life saps the intellect.

I remember you saying once how much you liked the men in your regiment in the last war. It was the same with me when I was an internee. I had friends at Tost in every imaginable walk of life, from Calais dock touts upward, and they were one and all the salt of the earth. A patrol of Boy Scouts couldn't have been kinder than they were to me. I was snowed under with obligations. I remember once when I broke the crystal of my watch and seemed likely to have to abandon the thing as a total loss, which would have been a devastating tragedy, one of the fellows gave up the whole afternoon to making a case for it, out of an old tube of tooth paste, while another gave me a bit of string, roughly equivalent in value in camp to a diamond necklace, which I could use as a chain; and a third donated a button, which he could ill spare, to string the string on.

Whenever my bed broke down, somebody always rallied round with wedges. (You drive the wedges in at the end of the planks. Then they don't suddenly shift in the night and let you down with a bump.) When I strained a tendon in my leg, along came Sergeant-Major Fletcher night after night, when he might have been playing darts, to give me massage.

I was so touched by this that I broke into verse on the subject. As follows:

> I used to wobble in my walk
>   Like one who has a jag or bend on;

It caused, of course, a lot of talk,
    But really I had strained a tendon.
And just as I was feeling I
    Would need a crutch or else a stretcher.
A kindly friend said: 'Why not try
    A course of rubs from J. J. Fletcher?'
He gave me massage day by day
    Till I grew lissome, lithe and supple,
And no one now is heard to say,
    'Avoid that man. He's had a couple.'
And so with gratitude profound
    I shout 'Three cheers for good old Fletcher.
He is the man to have around
    When legs get out of joint, you betcher.
Fletcher,
I'm glad I metcher.'

Silly, of course, but that's how it goes.

Let's see. What else? Oh, yes, beards. A lot of us grew
beards. Not me. What I felt was that there is surely enough
sadness in life without going out of one's way to increase it
by sprouting a spade-shaped beard. I found it a melancholy
experience to be compelled to watch the loved features of some
familiar friend becoming day by day less recognizable behind
the undergrowth. A few fungus-fanciers looked about as repul-
sive as it is possible to look, and one felt a gentle pity for the
corporal whose duty it was to wake them in the morning. What
a way to start one's day!

O'Brien, one of the sailors, had a long Assyrian beard, falling
like a cataract down his chest, and it gave me quite a start when
at the beginning of the summer he suddenly shaved, revealing

himself as a spruce young fellow in the early twenties. I had been looking on him all the time as about twenty years my senior, and only my natural breeding had kept me from addressing him as 'Grandpop'.

I shall have to stop now, as the deadline for writing is approaching. Love to Rene. Yours ever, Plum.

P.S. I was very interested to hear about Gilkes taking over Dulwich. I wonder how things will be there after the war. I'm afraid the public schools will have a pretty thin time.

December 30th, 1944.   *Hôtel Lincoln, Rue Bayard, Paris.*

I am not actually at the above address, being at the moment in a hospital (though not ill), but letters sent there will be forwarded.

I am longing to hear how you have been getting on with your novels. I suppose the short story market in England has pretty well vanished, but Denis Mackail in a card which I received yesterday says that all books are selling like hot cakes, so I hope that you are flourishing.

I always think it such a pity that experiences happen to the wrong people. I don't suppose, for instance, I shall ever make anything of life in Paris during the liberation, whereas if you had been here then you would have got a wealth of material. The afternoon of the big parade down the Champs-Élysées, Ethel and I and Wonder went to the park near the Marigny Theatre and Ethel managed to wriggle into the front rank of the crowd, leaving me with Wonder. I was just starting to give Wonder a run on the grass near one of the restaurants which are in the gardens when I saw a policeman coming, so edged away, and at that moment a brisk burst of firing came from the restaurant, which would have outed me had I been on the grass. Then guns began to go off all over the place, and I was in a panic because I thought Ethel was still in the crowd. I rushed about, looking for her, and was swept into the Marigny with the crowd. A dead girl was brought in on a stretcher and laid down beside me. It was all rather ghastly. Eventually, the firing stopped and I was able to get back to the Hôtel Bristol, where we were staying then, and found Ethel there. She had gone back before the firing began, but had run into another battle outside and inside the hotel.

My arrest by the French came as a complete surprise. I have it from what is usually called a 'well-informed source' that an English woman was dining with the Prefect of Police, and said to him: 'Why don't you arrest P. G. Wodehouse?' He thought it a splendid idea and sent out the order over the coffee and liqueurs, with the result that I woke up at one o'clock in the morning of November the twenty-second to find an Inspecteur at my bedside. (Much the same thing, if you remember, happened to the late Abou Ben Adhem.) He took Ethel and me to the Palais de Justice, where we spent sixteen hours without food in a draughty corridor, sleeping on wooden chairs.

Aren't women wonderful? Ethel took the whole thing in her stride without a word of complaint. She was simply magnificent, and the love and admiration which she has inspired in me for the last thirty years hit a new high.

I don't know what was going on behind the scenes, but the news of our arrest apparently caused quite a stir in British official circles. They flew a Home Office representative over, who plunged into a series of talks with the Palais de Justice boys – heated ones, I should imagine, for the whole atmosphere suddenly changed like a flash. We were given beds, and Malcolm

Muggeridge – what a pal that man has been! – arrived loaded with bread, corned beef, champagne and cigars, and we had a banquet.

Next day they released Ethel, and I spent four days in the Inspecteurs' room, getting very matey with them all and resuming work on my novel. (Turn up your copy of *Uncle Dynamite* and read Chapter Nine, the one that begins 'It is a characteristic of England's splendid police force . . .' The whole of that chapter was written in the Inspecteurs' room at the Palais de Justice, with the lads crowding round to see how the stuff was going.)

On the evening of the fourth day I was brought to this hospital, where I have been ever since.

I have a room to myself, quite good food and plenty of tobacco, and Ethel is allowed to come and see me, as are all my friends. So I might be considerably worse off.

I generally wake up at four a.m., lie in bed till six, then get up and boil water on a boiler lent me by one of the doctors and have breakfast. The Concierge arrives with the *Paris Daily Mail* at nine, and after my room has been cleaned, that is by half-past nine, I start writing. Lunch at half-past twelve. At four I get a walk in the garden. In the evening I walk up and down the landing, and then go to bed, never later than eight. Light out at nine-thirty. I get on wonderfully with the Inspecteurs, and am improving my French. When I get visitors, they usually come at three. It isn't a bad sort of life, if you have a novel to write.

Did you happen to see a thing by George Orwell called 'In Defence of P. G. Wodehouse'? He says that my indiscretion (the broadcasts) gave a good propaganda opening to the left-wingers in England because 'it was a chance to expose a wealthy parasite'. Had it ever occurred to you that that is how authors are regarded in England? You, me, Shakespeare, all of us, just parasites. (Have you read any good parasites lately?) It's very different in France. Seeing me hammering out my wholesome fiction, the Inspecteurs treat me with reverence. For two pins (*épingles*) they would call me 'maître'.

When I finish this one, I shall have five novels which have not been published in England, also ten short stories. I wonder if they ever will be published. If England won't have them, I shall have to content myself with appearing in Spain (and Sweden). There is a publisher in Barcelona who is bringing out *eight* of my books a year. He very decently sent me three hundred and fifty thousand francs a year ago, which came in very handy.

I'm afraid this letter is all about me. But I thought you would like to hear details about my life. It's good news to hear that Dulwich is going strong. I wonder if the public schools will survive the war.

By the way, I saw in the *Paris Daily Mail* that Hugh Bartlett and Billy Griffith were in the Arnhem show and got through safely, but since then someone has told me that Bartlett was blown up in a car. I hope it is not true. Have you heard anything? It's awful to think of all those fellows one used to know being in danger all the time.

February 5th, 1945.   *Hôtel Lincoln, Paris.*

Malcolm Muggeridge is leaving for England this week and will post this. He will be in London about ten days, I think, so if you have time to write me a letter you could send it to me care of him. I will add his London address as a postscript, as

I shall not know till I see him this afternoon. I am longing to get a letter from you, telling me all the news.

I was in the hospital when I wrote to you last. (I hope you got the letter all right.) I spent eight weeks there, and then Malcolm drove Ethel and Wonder and me down to Barbizon, about thirty miles from Paris, in the most awful blizzard. We lunched at a marvellous restaurant in the forest in front of a great log fire and thought things were going to be wonderful. But when we got to the hotel at Barbizon, we found it was a strictly summer hotel, no carpets, no heating, and no running water owing to the frost freezing the pipes. However, we settled down and had a very good time for three weeks, though with icicles forming on us, and then the hotel was requisitioned by SHAEF, so we are back in Paris. I think eventually we shall go to Ethel's friends the De Rocquignys at their house near Hesdin; but in the meantime Paris is very pleasant, though living conditions are getting tougher every day and I don't like the look of the Seine, which may burst its banks at any moment. Still, Paris is always Paris, and we are quite happy.

(I was just writing this, when an air raid warning sounded. I thought all that sort of thing was over in Paris. Still, there it is. I will let you know how the matter develops.)

Where was I? Oh yes, Paris. It's all right. Quite a city. La Ville Lumiêre, I have sometimes called it, though it is far from being that these days.

I was thrilled by what you told me about Dulwich winning all its school matches last cricket season, including Harrow and Malvern. It's odd, but I don't find that world cataclysms and my own personal troubles make any difference to my feelings about Dulwich.

The air raid is still apparently in progress, as there has been no 'All Clear', but nothing seems to be happening. We got a scare one night at Barbizon when terrific explosions suddenly shook the hotel. I believe it was some allied plane which had had to jettison its bombs in the neighbourhood.

Do tell me, when you write, about your work since the war started. You mention books you are writing but don't tell me how you're selling these days. I am longing to know the figures. You must have built up a large public by now. Is the *Strand* still going? Have you read ('All Clear' just gone) Hesketh Pearson's life of Conan Doyle? Very interesting. It's curious to think what small prices he got for stories which are world famous. I can't remember off-hand, but I think he got a hundred and twenty-five quid for the complete American rights of *The White Company*.

I have been plugging away at *Uncle Dynamite*. I managed to get a hundred pages done while in the clinic, in spite of constant interruptions. I would start writing at nine in the morning and get a paragraph done when the nurse would come in and sluice water all over the floor. Then the concierge arrived with the morning paper, then the nurse with bread for lunch, then another nurse with wine, then a doctor and finally a couple of Inspecteurs. All the Inspecteurs were very interested in my writing. It was the same thing in camp, where I used to sit on my typewriter case with the machine balanced on a suitcase and work away with two German soldiers standing behind me with rifles, breathing down the back of my neck. They seemed fascinated by this glimpse into the life literary.

February 24th, 1945.   *Hôtel Lincoln.*

There seems to have been some hitch about Malcolm's visit to England, as he is still here. We are meeting him at dinner tomorrow night, so I will give him this letter then. If he is not going over himself, he will probably know of someone who is going.

Meanwhile, your two letters of January 19th and January 30th have arrived, within two days of each other. (So it looks as if letters now take about a month to come, which isn't so bad.) You can imagine how delighted I was to get them.

That story you told me in your letter about someone saying that while I was in camp the German officers talked to me in German amused me. I wonder why people invent these things. All the German I know is 'Es ist schonus wetter' and I mispronounce that. As a matter of fact, they didn't even talk to me in English. It's extraordinary how things get twisted. When I was making my statement in Paris after the liberation to the Home Office representative, he started by questioning me keenly as to whether I had written for a German paper (in English) called *The Camp*, which was circulated among British prisoners. It seemed that somebody had denounced me as having done so, and all that had happened really was that in one number there was a parody of my Jeeves stuff under the title of 'Bertie At The War' or something like that, signed 'P. G. Roadhouse' or some such name.

When I was in camp, I had the most tremendous liking and admiration for the War Graves Commission men. With one of them, Bert Haskins, I formed a friendship which will last all our lives. He was pure gold, and we kept up a correspondence all the time after I left Tost until, a few weeks before the liberation, his letters suddenly ceased and I assumed that he had been repatriated. I hope so. Bert was the chap who, when we were spending that eight hours in the cattle trucks before leaving Loos, suddenly appeared at my side with half a loaf of bread, butter, radishes, a bottle of wine and a slab of potted meat. He didn't know me, but out of sheer goodness of heart he came and gave me the stuff. He was a splendid chap, and I was always so sorry that he was not in my dormitory. It's like being in a house at school. In camp you don't see much of people who aren't in your dormitory. Did I tell you that Lord Uffenham in *Money in the Bank* was drawn from a man in my dormitory? It isn't often that one has the luck to be in daily contact with the model for one's principal character.

I have become very interested in Shakespeare, and am reading books about him, having joined the American Library here. A thing I can never understand is why all the critics seem to assume that his plays are a reflection of his personal moods and dictated by the circumstances of his private life. You know the sort of thing I mean. They say *Timon of Athens* is a pretty gloomy piece of work, which means that Shakespeare must have been having a rotten time when he wrote it. I can't see it. Do you find that your private life affects your work? I don't.

Well, so long. I've probably left out a dozen things I wanted to say, but I will put them in my next.

April 5th, 1945.   *Hôtel Lincoln, Rue Bayard, Paris.*

Will you address all future letters to the Hôtel Lincoln, as the girl at the Consulate is getting a bit sniffy about having to ring me up and tell me there is a letter waiting for me there. (Why she can't just re-address it, I don't know, but she seems to think that would be impossible.) Letters to the Lincoln will always reach me.

I was very interested in your long letter about your books. I wish I could get hold of them, and I suppose that will be possible fairly soon now. The last I read was *Sink and be Damned*, which I thought awfully good. What an infernal nuisance the paper shortage is. It must be maddening to sell out before publication and then not be able to follow it up because there is no paper for another edition. I sympathize with your trouble with the printers and their queries. The American cousins of these birds read the proofs of the *Saturday Evening Post* and I used to spend hours writing sarcastic replies in the margin. I remember in *Quick Service* they queried the grammar of some remark made by a barmaid in a moment of extreme agitation; and I wrote a long essay in the margin pointing out that when an English barmaid is agitated she very often speaks ungrammatically. Futile, of course.

I finished *Uncle Dynamite* last Sunday. What with one thing and another, it has taken me exactly a year to write, but I think the results are good. It was one of those difficult stories where you get everything into a tangle and then straighten it all out in the last chapter, and all the way through I was saying to myself: 'Well, it's all right so far, but that last chapter is going to let the whole thing down.' But, thank goodness, the last chapter came out all right. I now have the following books shuffling their feet nervously in the anteroom, wondering if they will ever get into print: *Money in the Bank*, *Joy in the Morning* (a Jeeves story), *Full Moon* (Blandings Castle Story), *Spring Fever* and this new one, *Uncle Dynamite*. Also ten short stories.

But it's a funny thing about writing. If you are a writer by nature, I don't believe you write for money or fame or even for publication, but simply for the pleasure of turning out the stuff. I really don't care much if these books are published or not. The great thing is that I've got them down on paper, and can read and re-read them and polish them and change an adjective for a better one and cut out dead lines.

A. A. Milne says much the same thing in *Two People*. He says that books ought not to be published. They ought to be written, and then one copy ought to be beautifully printed for the author to read.

This letter will reach you quickly, as Irene Ward, the M.P., is taking it over to England with her tomorrow. I am going to the Consulate today and shall hope to find a letter from you there. All your others have arrived safely, and I have them all pinned together and re-read them continually.

April 22nd, 1945.   *78 Avenue Paul Doumer, Paris.*

The above is now my official address. By an absolute miracle we have been able to get a furnished flat and move in tomorrow. Ethel made friends with the French wife of an Englishman at the Lincoln, who had found a flat and was moving in immediately, and then her plans were all changed by her having to go to the country, so she said we could have the place. I went to see it yesterday and it is just what we want. It is almost impossible to get a flat in Paris now, even people at the Embassy can't do it, so you can imagine how thankful we are. Ethel had managed to keep her room on at the Lincoln, but we never knew when she might not have to move, and there was absolutely nowhere I could go except to this Danish friend of mine, and I felt that he must be getting fed up after five weeks of me. So now we are all right.

Somebody, presumably Slacker, sent me the Dulwich Year Book for 1943 and 1944, which I was delighted to have, though it was saddening to see the Roll of Honour. Most of the names I did not know, but quite a few were of chaps I knew slightly as members of the cricket and football teams. I see Doulton's son and D. G. Donald's have both been killed, and also R. H. Spencer, who played half, and a fellow named Darby who was in the cricket team of 1935 and wrote to thank me for a notice I gave him in my report of the Tonbridge match.

By the way, was 1944 a very wet summer in England? I ask because that was the year we won all our seven school cricket matches and the lad at the head of the batting averages had an average of 25. We seem to have outed the opposition each time for about 83 and then to have made 84 for 8 ourselves. The top score seems to have been 60. Very odd.

Also by the way, I see that in the footer statements the game with Tonbridge is described as 'Abandoned', when we were leading by a goal and a try to nil. How in the name of goodness does a school footer match get abandoned? It can't have been the weather, as one plays through everything. Unless a dense fog suddenly came down.

You never told me if H. T. Bartlett was all right. He got through Arnhem with Billy Griffith, and then I heard a rumour that he had been blown up by a mine. I do hope it wasn't true. I had a message through an R.A.F. man in September from A. C. Shirreff, so he was all right then, but you never know from one day to another, worse luck.

P.S. I have been reading Mark Twain's letters. Very interesting. He thought an enormous lot of W. D. Howells's books. Have you read any of them? I have taken *The Rise of Silas Lapham* out of the American Library here, and it certainly is good. It was written in 1884, but reads quite like a modern book.

May 22nd, 1945.   *78 Avenue Paul Doumer.*

I looked in at the Consulate a day or two ago and found two letters from you, and today your long one of May 2nd was forwarded on from the Lincoln, so I think it is about time I wrote.

I'm like you, I can't remember what I told you in previous letters.

I'm so glad you have got your novel finished. At least, you have done the first draft, and that is always the tough part. Personally, I love rewriting and polishing. Directly I have got something down on paper, however rough it is, I feel the thing is in the bag.

I wish I could get hold of some of Raymond Chandler's stuff. It sounds from what you say just the kind of thing I like. An occasional new book creeps through to Paris, but it is very difficult to get hold of anything except pre-war books. I have just got the new Peter Cheyney, and it makes one realize there has been a war on to look at it. It is about an inch thick and printed on a sort of brown paper and the price is nine and six. Before the war no publisher would have put out a shilling edition like that. I think the paper shortage is worse than the food shortage. Here in Paris the papers don't come out on Monday, which must be maddening for them if something big happens on the previous day. One week the non-appearance day was shifted to Wednesday for some reason, with the result that the papers were not able to report the death of Hitler.

At the present moment I am in a state of suspense, wondering if Billy Griffith is playing for England in the Test at Lord's.

The *Paris Daily Mail* gave the list of the team and said 'Either Griffith or Evans will keep wicket'. The report of the first day's play merely gave the score, and today's paper does the same, plus a description of the Australian innings. I am going down town this afternoon in the hope of finding an English paper. I am hoping that Billy got in all right.

I am having trouble again with the American income-tax people. They have now dug back to 1923 and claim that I made no return that year or in 1924. I have absolutely no means of proving that I did, but I must have done. I was in America both years and left for England, and you can't get on a boat at New York, unless you show that you have paid your income tax. I suppose what will happen is that after I have spent thousands of dollars on lawyer's fees they will drop the thing. But it's an awful nuisance, and I wouldn't have thought that legally they were entitled to go back twenty-two years. But they just make up the rules as they go along. It reminds me of George Ade's story of the man who was in prison and a friend went to see him and asked what he had done. The man told him and the friend said: 'But they can't put you in prison for that,' and the man said: 'I know they can't, but they have.'

I have been meaning to send you a story a man told me some months ago. He was an ex-merchant-navy man, and during the war was in charge of various tough sea assignments. I only put down a hurried note; so I may have got the thing all wrong, but this was what I think he said. He was told off to take a vessel to somewhere off the east coast of England to recover forty tons of nickel which had been sunk in a torpedoed steamer. Right. Well, the sunken ship was in such a position that you had to approach it through E-boat alley. Does that convey anything to you? It didn't to me, though I imagine it must mean some sort of channel where there was a big risk of being attacked by enemy E-boats. The sunk ship was four miles beyond E-boat alley. My next note consists of the words 'Three mines', so I suppose they encountered three mines on their way. Now it gets a bit clearer. When the divers went down, they found on board the sunken ship a lot of unexploded bombs, and also a number of cylinders of poison gas for India. The point is that this made the enterprise very perilous, and you could work it up and invent a lot of stuff. Anyway, the blow-out is that after they had been risking their lives for quite a number of days they were informed by the Admiralty that it was sorry they had been troubled but the Admiralty had just discovered that previous to the sinking of the ship the nickel had been transhipped, and so they needn't bother.

It seems to me that there is a short story for you on the lines of my Hollywood one *The Castaways*, where the entire personnel of the cast sweat their guts out, writing a picture based on a popular novel and then the studio discovers that it doesn't own the rights to the novel. How about it? Do you think you can do anything with it?

June 30th, 1945.   *78 Avenue Paul Doumer, Paris (16).*

Your letter of June 12th reached me about a quarter of an hour ago, when I came in from my afternoon walk. I am sending this by air mail, as they tell me that takes letters to England in a couple of days or so. So note carefully when it arrives. Thanks for sending me the books. I hope I get them all right.

Before I forget. In one of your letters you asked me if I ever had read anything by Trollope. At that time I hadn't, but the other day, reading in Edward Marsh's *A Number of People* that Barrie had been fascinated by a book of his called *Is He Popenjoy?* I took it out of the American Library. I found it almost intolerably slow at first, and then suddenly it gripped me, and now I am devouring it. It is rather like listening to somebody very long-winded telling you a story about real people. The characters live in the most extraordinary way and you feel that the whole thing is true. Of course I read Trollope's *Autobiography* and found it very interesting. But I still don't understand his methods of work. Did he sit down each morning and write exactly fifteen hundred words, without knowing when he sat down how the story was going to develop, or had he a careful scenario on paper? I can't believe that an intricate story like *Popenjoy* could have been written without minute planning. Of course, if he did plan the whole thing out first, there is nothing so very bizarre in the idea of writing so many hundred words of it each day. After all, it is more or less what one does oneself. One sits down to work each morning, no matter whether one feels bright or lethargic, and before one gets up a certain amount of stuff, generally about fifteen hundred words, has emerged. But to sit down before a blank sheet of paper without an idea of how the story is to proceed and just start writing, seems to me impossible.

I'm sorry the short story didn't get over with the *Saturday Evening Post*. How extraordinary that they should be so against war stories. It is a complete change of policy since the last number I read, which was only about a year ago. At that time the synopsis of a *S.E.P.* serial would be something like this. 'Major Dwight van Renasseller, a young American officer in the F.G.I., has fallen in love with a mysterious veiled woman who turns out to be Irma Kraus, assistant Gauleiter of the Gestapo, who is in New York disguised as a Flight Lieutenant of the R.A.F., in order to secure the plans of the P.B.O. One night at a meeting of the I.T.D. he meets "Spud" Murphy, in reality a Colonel in the T.H.B., who is posing as Himmler in the hope of getting a free lunch at a German restaurant on Eighty-fourth Street. They decide to merge the Y.F.S. with the P.X.Q., thus facilitating the operations of W.G.C. Go on from there.'

At present, however, I take but a faint interest in the American market, as the U.S. Government is claiming this large sum of money from me for income tax and would infallibly pouch anything I made over there. My case comes up in September, and I suppose will end, as before, in my paying about a tenth of what they claim. As the year now in dispute is 1921 and all my records have been lost and also, one imagines, all those of the Government, I don't see how any conclusion can be arrived at except a compromise.

I wrote a novel called *Spring Fever* in 1943, and the other day, not being able to get a plot for a novel, decided to make a play of it. It is coming out very well, but as always the agony of telling a story purely in dialogue and having to compress it and keep the action in one spot, is frightful. I have written the first scene of Act I half a dozen times, and it isn't right yet. The curse of a play is that you can't give people thoughts. It all has to be done in the dialogue.

August 1st, 1945.   *78 Avenue Paul Doumer, Paris.*

Well, the books arrived safely and we have been revelling in them.

I'll tell you what's the whole trouble with you, Bill, and that is that you have never done anything except write the stuff and are competing with all these birds who hang around authors' lunches and go about lecturing and presenting prizes at girls' schools. I don't think it matters in the long run, but there's no doubt that all these other fellows who shove themselves forward and suck up to the critics do get a lot of publicity, and it helps them for a while. I always think Hugh Walpole's reputation was two-thirds publicity. He was always endorsing books and speaking at lunches and so on.

I can't remember if I ever told you about meeting Hugh when I was at Oxford getting my D.Litt. I was staying with the Vice-Chancellor at Magdalen and he blew in and spent the day. It was just after Hilaire Belloc had said that I was the best living English writer. It was just a gag, of course, but it worried Hugh terribly. He said to me: 'Did you see what Belloc said about you?' I said I had. 'I wonder why he said that.' 'I wonder,' I said. Long silence. 'I can't imagine why he said that,' said Hugh. I said I couldn't, either. Another long silence. 'It seems such an extraordinary thing to say!' 'Most extraordinary.' Long silence again. 'Ah, well,' said Hugh, having apparently found the solution, 'the old man's getting very old.'

We went for a long walk in the afternoon, and he told me that when somebody wrote a stinker about some book of his, he cried for hours. Can you imagine getting all worked up about a bad notice? I always feel about the critics that there are bound to be quite a number of them who don't like one's stuff and one just has to accept it. They don't get a sob out of me.

I never cared much for Walpole. There was a time when I seemed about to be registered as Number Fourteen or something on his list of friends – did you know that he used to list all his friends in order? – but nothing came of it. He wanted me to come to Majorca with him, but I backed out and this probably shoved me down to number 30 or off the list altogether.

I see in the *Express* that poor Damon Runyon has had an operation which has left him unable to speak. It sounds pretty serious. Do you like his stuff? I have just been reading a book of his stories and I thought they were great.

September 13th, 1945.   *78 Avenue Paul Doumer.*

Thanks for your letter of September 2nd, for sending Watt the clippings, and for *Sabina's Brother*, which arrived yesterday. I am looking forward to revelling in it directly I have cleared off a mass of correspondence which has been hung up.

Your California book sounds as if it would be very good. I remember those movie stories you mention. They were by Charles E. Van Loan, a very nice fellow who lost his right arm and taught himself to play golf with his left so well that he used to go round in the seventies with one arm. The stories were published in book form by George Doran (now Doubleday Doran & Co.). I have them in the archives, but can't possibly get at them, and as to what they were called ... Isn't it extraordinary? I was on the point of saying I hadn't a notion when the title suddenly flashed into my mind. *Buck Parvin and the Movies.* I believe you could get a copy from Doubleday & Co., Rockefeller Center, New York City, though, of course, they may be out of print. Even if you don't need the book for your work, it would be fascinating to read now. Isn't it amazing to think that in 1910 Movies were as primitive as that. As I remember Van Loan's book, you just got a camera and a few pals and went out into the desert and shot some pictures, and that was all.

I'm so sorry Rene is so tired. It must be very hard for her without a maid. We still have one whom Ethel fires on Mondays and Thursdays. On Tuesdays and Fridays she gives her own notice. On Saturdays and Sundays she goes home. So our big day is Wednesday. This is the time to catch us.

I don't know why it is, but I am enjoying life amazingly these days. Thunderclouds fill the sky in every direction, including a demand for $120,000 from the U. S. Income Tax people (case starts on Monday unless they settle in advance); but I continue to be happy.

I don't know what we shall do this winter, but I imagine that we shall probably take on the flat for another three months and dig in. We have laid in a supply of wood big enough to last us through the winter and things seem much better as regards electricity, so that we shall have electric stoves. Last winter was awful. The electricity wasn't turned on till five in the afternoon. The year before it was worse, for as I remember the juice wasn't switched on till about nine. I shall never forget a dinner given us by a friend in a mysterious restaurant, somewhere near here, which was located in a flat. We dined in pitch darkness and there were three black poodles in the room, so that every time anyone moved, they stepped on them, and dinner was punctuated with agonized yelps.

I see in the *Paris Daily Mail* this morning that E. Phillips Oppenheim has managed to get back to his home in Guernsey by getting a lift on a yacht. He is seventy-nine, but must still be pretty fit, if he can dash about like that.

I have always been devoted to Oppy. I saw a lot of him when I was living at La Fréyère. I remember him coming to lunch one day not long after he had had a slight sunstroke, and he was taking no chances of getting another one. There was one of those Riviera trees on the terrace, a dense mass of leaves through which no ray of light could penetrate, and he sat under it with a sun helmet on his head holding a large umbrella over himself. Did you know that he used to dictate all his stuff? I found him in gloomy mood one day. He had had the perfect secretary, who used to squeal with excitement as the story got going on the international spies and mysterious veiled women, which bucked him up enormously, and she had left to get married and in her place had come one of those tall, statuesque, frozen-faced secs who took his dictation in an aloof, revolted sort of way as if the stuff soiled the paper of her note-book. He said it discouraged him.

How *can* anybody dictate? Could you? I should be feeling shy and apologetic all the time. The nearest I ever got to it was when Ethel bought me one of those machines Edgar Wallace used to use, where you talk on to a wax cylinder and then turn back to the beginning to hear how it sounds. I started *Thank You, Jeeves*, on it, and when I played it back I was appalled how unfunny the stuff sounded. I hadn't known it till then but apparently I have a voice like a very pompous clergyman intoning. Either that or the instrument was pulling my leg. Anyway, I sold the damned thing next day.

November 8th, 1945.   *36 Boulevard Suchet, Paris (16).*

Note the above address. We move out of this flat in a day or two and go to this other one, a very ornate joint belonging to Lady Deterding, two doors off the Duke of Windsor. I think we shall be very comfortable. We have a store of wood, and there are fire-places; and also a number of electric heaters. About the only drawback to the place is that it is rather a long way from the shops, and, of course, everything has to be fetched – by me. By the way, the relief of having got rid of bread tickets is tremendous. I have always been O.C. Bread, going out in the morning before breakfast for it and being responsible for seeing that the tickets lasted out, and it was always a very near thing and a great anxiety. One month I had to borrow half a loaf from the concierge on the last day.

I was intending to write to you last night, but I wouldn't have had time to write a long letter, so I put it off till this morning, and at breakfast your letter of November 4th arrived. I'm so glad you managed to fix up the novel so that it did not clash with H. M. Tomlinson's, but what a lot of bother you have had about it and all unnecessary really. I don't think there was ever a chance that Tomlinson would have made a fuss. With the great number of novels published nowadays writers are bound to clash in the way of ideas. Still, it's best, of course, to avoid any possible trouble, as you have done.

I'll tell you what makes life hell for writers, and that is that you meet someone who tells you a story as having happened to himself or a friend, and you work it up and publish it, only to find that the gentleman read the thing in a magazine somewhere. But listen. What is plagiarism? Did you ever see a play by Freddie Lonsdale called *The Last of Mrs Cheyney*? It was about a Society woman who was one of a band of crooks, and this is revealed to the audience at the end of Act I. An exactly similar situation was in an American play called *Cheating Cheaters*. And the big scene of Act II was where the hero gets Mrs Cheyney into his room at night and holds her up for something by saying he is going to keep her there till they are found in the morning, which is exactly the same as Pinero's *Gay Lord Quex*. And yet nobody has ever breathed a word against Freddie for plagiarizing. Quite rightly. The treatment is everything.

I had to break off at this point to take Wonder for her walk. I find it almost impossible to get anything done in the mornings, as I have to suit my time to hers. What I would like would be to hoik her out of bed at 8.30, exercise her and be able to settle down to work at ten. But if I try to do this she curses so much that I desist. It is generally about 11.15 when I am just getting going, that there is a thud on my door, and in she bounds. There is a spaniel who lives at No. 72 and sits inside the front door, which is of thick glass, and every day Wonder toddles up to this door and she and the spaniel start a terrific fight through the glass, which lasts until I haul her away. The other day the spaniel nipped away and suddenly appeared at the open ground-floor window, whereupon scene of perfect camaraderie ensued, both dogs immediately becoming bosom friends. But next day the fight started again.

Back to the subject of plagiarism. The best plagiarism story I know was the one Guy Bolton told me about Owen Davis, the American playwright. He had a show on in New York, a melodrama, and a tailor claimed that it was stolen from a play which he – the tailor – had dashed off in the intervals of tailoring. Davis got together with him, and asked him just what he based the accusation on. The tailor said his play was about a man accused of murder and all the time he was innocent, and so was Davis's. Davis then took him round to some of the other plays running on Broadway at the moment – *The Crimson Alibi*, *At 9.45*, *The Sign on the Door*, etc. – and pointed out that these too were about men accused of murder and by golly in the end they turn out not to have done it after all. But you can't down an author with evidence of that sort. 'They've ALL stolen my play!' was his only comment.

Frank Sullivan wrote a very funny article at the time when a Miss Georges Lewis sued Eugene O'Neill, charging him with stealing *Strange Interlude* from a play of hers called *The Temple of Pallas Athene*. Asked for the examples of similarity between her play and his, she cited these:

> I have been sadly disillusioned.   (Lewis)
> You have been sadly disillusioned?   (O'Neill)

> Old fox.   (Lewis)
> Old fox.   (O'Neill)

> My goodness.   (Lewis)
> My goodness.   (O'Neill)

'I shall sue O'Neill, too!' Frank wrote. 'And I may even sue Georges as well, because, strangely enough, in my play *The Forgotten Galosh*, there occurs not only the line "*He* has been sadly disillusioned" but also the line "My goodness". This, to my mind, makes it look very very bad for Georges and Eugene. Even if great minds do jump, three of us would never have thought of that pearl. It looks fishy to me.'

He ends:

'I have plenty more evidence, which I propose to produce at the proper time unless the playwrights mentioned above see fit to settle out of court. I'll take ten dollars.

Well, five.

Not a cent under three. I'd be losing money.

Well, don't go, hold on a minute, I'll take a dollar.

A half-dollar I'll take.

Could you spare a nickel for a cup of coffee?'

Which is about how most of these plagiarism suits end.

December 7th, 1945.   *36 Boulevard Suchet.*

The new flat is a great success. It is like living in the country with all the advantages of town. I go out into the Bois every morning before breakfast in a sweater and golf knickers and do my exercises, and I wear golf clothes all day. The great merit of this part of Paris – up in Auteuil – is that nobody stares at you no matter what you do or wear. We have hot water here all the time, which is wonderful, and we can keep one room warm with wood fires, so we are well off. So far we have been able to get food, though at a terrific cost. Butter is £1.5 a pound.

We have a female Pole who comes each morning at nine (or is supposed to) and leaves after getting us lunch, but there is so much to do that Ethel generally does all the cleaning of the flat. We have a very simple meal at night. I wonder when things will get easier. The effect it has on me is to mess up my work pretty completely. Whenever I try to settle down, there is always something to do like going to the cellar for wood or going out and buying vegetables.

I had a letter from Denis Mackail the other day, drawing a very gloomy picture of the short story situation in England. He says there is now practically no market, and if you do write a short story it mustn't be over 2,000 words. Bobbie Denby, writing from America, says that over there you mustn't exceed 5,000. This dishes me completely, as I can't keep under 7,000.

January 11th, 1946.   *36 Boulevard Suchet.*

It shows the advantage of putting things off. I meant to write this letter yesterday, but postponed it because I hadn't time to write a really long one, and this morning yours of January 6th arrived, so I can answer that as well as yours of December 11th.

You've got me stumped on those things in the California book. Who the dickens were the motion picture stars of 1911? Mary Pickford, of course, but not Douglas Fairbanks, because in 1911 he was an actor on the stage and incidentally playing the part of Jimmy in my *Gentleman of Leisure*, at the Playhouse in New York. It must have been at least two years after that before he went into pictures. Ha! Something Bunny and Flora Finch. Was Barbara La Marr going in 1911? Wallace Reid? Fatty Arbuckle? It's darned hard to remember. But surely any motion picture magazine would tell you. Theda Bara. Sidney Drew.

Life continues very pleasant here. I am getting fonder and fonder of Paris. It was a blow when they started rationing bread again, but in actual practice it doesn't affect us much. We now have a cook who buys the stuff and there always seems enough. There is some sort of row on just now between the wholesale and retail butchers, which has resulted in no meat for the populace for about two weeks. But something always seems to turn up. There is a mysterious Arab gentleman who calls from time to time with offerings. He has just come and fixed us up with a rabbit. Also a Dane (a stranger to me) has sent me an enormous parcel from Copenhagen, the only trouble being that all the contents are labelled in Danish, so we don't know what they are. There are three large tins which I hold contain bacon, but Ethel, who is in pessimistic mood today, says that they are floor polish. But surely even the most erratic Dane wouldn't send hungry Britons stuff for polishing floors. The only way I can think of solving the mystery is to ring up our Danish friend at Neuilly and spell the labels over the phone to him, and ask him to translate.

March 7th, 1946.   *36 Boulevard Suchet.*

I wrote to you yesterday and today got yours of March 4th.

It must be a great relief to you getting the new book off. I hope they won't make you cut it, but 200,000 words does seem a lot for these shortage-of-paper days. They'll probably print it all in smaller type than *MacRann*, in which case I shall have to use a magnifying glass.

Odd about the shortage of reviews of *MacRann*. Denis Mackail tells me he has seen none at all of *Huddleston House*. I can't understand the reviewing situation in England. Ethel brought me home an *Observer* and a *Sunday Times* yesterday and the books they reviewed seemed the sort that nobody could possibly want to read. (With the exception of *George Brown's School Days*, by Bruce Marshall, which looks as if it might be interesting, though apparently the same old anti-public-school stuff. I often wonder if you and I were unusually fortunate in our schooldays. To me the years between 1896 and 1900 seem like Heaven. Was the average man really unhappy at school? Or was Dulwich in our time an exceptionally good school?)

Back to the subject of reviews. I believe the only thing that matters to an author is word-of-mouth advertising. My experience has been that the ordinary member of the public, like myself when I am not a writer but a reader, is always on the look-out for authors that he can read but is very wary about taking on new ones. Quite by accident, generally, he dips into a book by someone who has been writing for years, likes it and says to himself: 'Here's a chap to keep an eye on. I'll read the rest of his stuff.' When a sufficient number of people have done that, the author has a public. I think this is what is happening to you. All the time single readers all over the country have been coming across stray books of yours in seaside libraries and so on, and have put you on their list. As an instance of this, the other day, browsing in the American library, I picked up a book by Naomi Jacob, saw that it was about music-hall performers, was interested in music-hall performers, decided that after all I wasn't taking such a big chance, as I could change it next day, took it home, liked it and now am resolved to read all her others. Have you ever read any of her stuff, by the way? This book *Straws in Amber* was good.

April 29th, 1946.   *36 Boulevard Suchet.*

A rush of correspondence prevented me answering your April 3rd letter, and this morning yours of April 26th arrived with the good news about *South of Forty-Five* and the bad news about *Fool's Gold*.

First, congratulations on the 12,000 sale. Terrific! This must have done a lot to offset the other knock.

Of course I shall be delighted to read *Fool's Gold*. I may be able to suggest cuts. Reading the two readers' reports, I got the impression that the length was all that was wrong with it. I mean to say, dash it, 215,000 words! At a time when they've probably only got about half a dozen bits of paper in the office.

Did you read Kipling's autobiography? In that he maintains that the principal thing in writing is to cut. Somerset Maugham says the same. Kipling says it's like raking slag out of a fire to make the fire burn brighter. I know just what he means. You can skip as you read, but if the superfluous stuff is there, it affects you just the same. The trouble is to know what to cut. I generally find with my own stuff that it's unnecessary lines in the dialogue that are wrong, but then my books are principally dialogue. I should say at a guess that in *Fool's Gold*, in the effort to put down all you knew, you had rambled a bit.

I can't make out what's happening in the book world these days. Someone sent me a copy of the *New York Sunday Times* the other day, and I see that Daphne du Maurier's new book has sold over a million already. I suppose it's all these book clubs they have in America. If you have the luck to be selected by one of the big ones, that means a 600,000 sale right away.

Here's another odd thing. Almost without exception these enormous sellers are historical novels. It's curious, the passion for historical stuff in America. When I first went there in 1904, all the big sellers were historical novels, and now they are at it again. I suppose they are entitled to read what they like, but it does seem strange that, when we are living in about as interesting a period as the world has known, what people want is all that stuff about plain John Blunt following his dear lord to the wars and bigger and better hussies at the court of Charles the Second.

Probably it won't be till around A.D. 2500 that the boys will start writing about the glamorous days of 1946.

We have had so many parcels from America that the food situation is much better now. My trouble is that the shortage of bread in the prison camp has left me with a yearning for the stuff, and the present rations are pretty small. We just get through the month. Luckily there is a shop around the corner where you can get biscottes, so we manage. But what I want to know is what has become of the potato? I had always supposed that in times of food shortage you just lived on potatoes, but they are like jewellery in Paris.

I've just read Raymond Chandler's *Farewell, My Lovely*. It's good. But a thing I've never been able to understand is how detectives in fiction drink so much and yet remain in the hardest physical condition. And how do Peter Cheyney's detectives manage to get all that whisky in London in war-time? They must be millionaires, as I believe the stuff is at about four quid a bottle. Do you ever read Rex Stout's Nero Wolfe stories? A good many of them came out in the *Saturday Evening Post*. They're good. He has rather ingeniously made his tough detective drink milk.

George Orwell. I wish I could get hold of that book of his, as it's just the sort of thing I like reading nowadays. He is a friend of my friend Malcolm Muggeridge and about a year ago or more came over to Paris and gave us a very good lunch at a place down by Les Halles (the Markets to you). I liked him very much indeed.

May 22nd, 1946.   *36 Boulevard Suchet.*

I started *Fool's Gold* last night and have just reached Page 136, and my opinion so far is that it is the most fascinating thing I have ever read. The idea of cutting a line of it revolts me. And at the same time I am saying to myself 'Am I all wrong about this book? I mean, is my mind so constituted that I am the only person who would enjoy it?' – this, of course, being due to the two publisher's readers' criticisms. (This, I gather from your letter is exactly the impression it makes on you. You say, 'I do not believe anyone would be interested in the book save myself.')

I think the reception of the book depends entirely on what the reader is led to expect. I mean, if he thinks he is going to get a quick-moving, dramatic story of the old West, then I suppose he would be disappointed. But I can't imagine anyone in the right mental attitude not liking it.

Anyway, I love the thing! Which reminds me of the story of the actress's sister who telegraphed her on the opening night of her new show, 'Whatever happens, always remember that Mother and I love you.'

Money in the Bank appears on Monday, when I expect you will get your copy. Jenkins assure me that 25,000 copies at least will be sold, which will be nice.

June 3rd, 1946.   *36 Boulevard Suchet.*

My pleasure in reading your kind words about *Money in the Bank* was slightly marred by the sudden arrival of a spectacled Frenchman with a bill for thirteen mille for electricity, this including nine mille penalty for over-indulgence during the winter. Ethel nearly fainted, and I, though a strong man, was shaken. I always knew we were for it, as we went in freely for hot water and heaters during those cold months, but I had supposed that they would just shake a playful finger at us and fine us about a quid. Still, it's better than being cold.

August 27th, 1946.   *36 Boulevard Suchet.*

Thanks for your letters. I would have written to you a long time ago, but have been tensely occupied with a rush job which started on August 8th and finished last night, viz. the dramatization of *Leave it to Psmith* for America.

The effect of this has been to give me eye trouble, and it was a great comfort to read what you said in your letter of July 29th about paying no attention to those floating specks. If they don't matter, that's fine. But now when I move my right eye a sort of black thing swings across it. If it is only a blood vessel, right ho, but, like you, I was brought up on *The Light that Failed* and suspect any funny business along those lines.

Incidentally, why do all these critics – George Orwell, for instance – assume that *The Light that Failed* was a flop and is recognized as such by the reading world? It certainly didn't flop in the sense of not making money, as it probably sold several hundred thousand in the ordinary edition and was also serialized and successfully dramatized. And if they mean that it's a failure because it doesn't grip you, they are simply talking through their hats.

It's odd, this hostility to Kipling. How the intelligentsia do seem to loathe the poor blighter, and how we of the *canaille* revel in his stuff. One thing I do think is pretty unjust – when they tick him off for not having spotted the future of the India Movement and all that sort of thing. I mean, considering that he left India for ever at the age of about twenty-two.

I wish these critics wouldn't distort facts in order to make a point. George Orwell calls my stuff Edwardian (which God knows it is. No argument about that, George) and says the reason for it being Edwardian is that I did not set foot in England for sixteen years and so lost touch with conditions there. Sixteen years, mark you, during most of which I was living in London and was known as Beau Wodehouse of Norfolk Street. He is also apt to take some book which I wrote in 1907 and draw all sorts of portentous conclusions from it. Dash it, in 1907 I was practically in swaddling clothes, and it was extremely creditable to me that I was able to write at all. Still, a thoroughly nice chap, and we correspond regularly. In his latest he says he has taken a house twenty-six miles from anywhere, up in the north of Scotland.

We are now making arrangements for going to America. I don't want to fly, and if one goes by boat it will mean sharing a cabin with about thirty other men on a 10,000-ton Liberty ship. Though I am not sure if on the Liberty ships the number of passengers isn't limited. Are they really cargo boats? What I would like would be to get a passage on one of your tramp steamers, but how is this managed? Anyway, I expect I shall leave somehow towards the middle of September. We have to give up this flat on October 15th, and Ethel wants me out of the way during the move. I am hoping that she will clean everything up and join me in New York in about a month.

The news about my books is good. Jenkins writes that they have about 4,000 left of the 30,000 they printed of *Money in the Bank* and are preparing a new edition, and Doubleday in New York sold 15,000 in advance of *Joy in the Morning*, which came out in America on August 22nd, and are very pleased about it and expect to sell a lot more.

Since I wrote last, we have had a short holiday at Le Touquet, where I ran into several men from my camp. I went several times to see Low Wood. It isn't in such bad shape as I had feared. The walls, ceilings, staircases and mantelpieces are still there. It would apparently cost about two thousand quid to put it right, and Ethel has given a man an option till next Monday to buy at four thousand. Our trouble is that, until they relax this rule about not being able to touch our English money, we simply can't raise two thousand, and four thousand paid over in cash would be the salvation of us. At present we are living on driblets from America, just enough to keep us going.

I met Madge at Le Touquet, looking just the same. She has taken over Mrs Miffen, the Peke, the one we had in 1940. I met Mrs Miffen – now called Poppy, of all ghastly names – and of course she didn't know me from Adam. She is one of those square, ugly Pekes, but very nice.

You say you tend to get tired nowadays. Me, too. After all, we're both heading for 70. Silver threads amongst the gold, laddie! (Extract from book I was reading the other day:

'Latterly his mind had been going to seed rather. He was getting on toward seventy, you see.')

August 30th, 1946.   *36 Boulevard Suchet.*

I sent you a copy of *Joy in the Morning* yesterday. I hope you will like it. I don't think it's bad, considering that it was written during the German occupation of Le Touquet, with German soldiers prowling about under my window, plus necessity of having to walk to Paris Plage every morning to report to the Kommandant.

When you say you liked Priestley's book, do you mean *Bright Day*? I read that and liked it, and I also liked *Daylight on Saturday*. I haven't seen any others by him. I am now reading Evelyn Waugh's *Put Out More Flags*, and am absolutely stunned by his brilliance. As a comic satiric writer he stands alone. That interview between Basil Seal and the Guards Colonel is simply marvellous. And what a masterpiece *Decline and Fall* was.

September 11th, 1946.   *36 Boulevard Suchet.*

I ought to be working, I suppose, but I feel I must write to you, as it may relieve the gloom which has come upon me strongly this morning, due principally to the problem of where we go from here.

I envy you having a place of your own where you can dig in. The only thing to do these days is to follow Voltaire's advice and cultivate your garden. If only Low Wood were habitable.

We have to move from here in October, and then what? I feel I ought to go to America and make some money, but against this is the fact that I would be separated from Ethel, added to the fact that I should have to doss in with three or four other men on the boat. As you say, when you get to 65, you want sleeping accommodation to yourself. Here's an odd thing, though. When I was in camp, I slept in a dormitory with sixty-six other men and loved it. I don't think I would mind mucking in with twenty or thirty men on board a liner. The trouble would be, though, where would I get a place to write in? Incidentally, when I first went to America in 1904, I travelled second-class with three other men in the cabin, so the wheel has come full circle, as you might say.

I shall sail for America directly I can get a passage on something. When that will be, with all these shipping strikes raging, I don't know, but soon, I hope. I hear these Liberty ships are quite comfortable. Talking of which, I met a woman the other day and mentioned that I was thinking of sailing on a Liberty ship, and she said: 'Oh, did you hear that one broke in half not long ago outside Dieppe?'

Pavillon Henri Quatre,
November 1st, 1946.   *St Germain-en-Laye.*

After booking my passage on the *America*, supposed to be sailing on October 26th but, owing to strikes, not likely to leave before the middle of November, I thought it over and decided to postpone my visit to the U.S.A. I suddenly realized how impossible it would be to leave Ethel for probably months, and there was really no immediate need for me to be in New York. I don't suppose I shall sail now until the Spring. I want to get the novel I'm doing, *The Mating Season*, finished before I leave.

This is a heavenly place. Nine miles out of Paris, but right in the country. This hotel is on the edge of a terrace a mile and a half long which looks all over Paris, and to the left of the terrace there is a forest. Trains to Paris every quarter of an hour do the journey in twenty-five minutes, so that I am really just as near to the American Library as I was at Boulevard Suchet. This is the house where Louis the Fourteenth was born, if that interests you.

I am following the doings of the Dulwich team this season with interest. So far they have won their first four school matches, running up a total of 91 points to 17. I wonder if it is going to turn out one of the big sides, like 1909?

How is the novel going? And what do Rich and Cowan think of the revised version of *Fool's Gold*? And again, Bill, I have to say that Kipling was right about cutting. I think one has to be ruthless with one's books. I find I have a tendency to write a funny line and then add another, elaborating it when there is no necessity for the second bit. I keep coming on such bits in the thing I'm doing now. I go through the story every day and hack them out.

Do you find you write more slowly than you used to? I don't know if it is because *The Mating Season* is a Jeeves story, and in a Jeeves story every line has to have some entertainment value, but I consider it a good day's work if I get three pages done. I remember I used to do eight a day regularly. This present thing is growing like a coral reef. I am only up to page 130 after months of work. Still, the consolation is that the stuff seems good, and there is no hurry, as I am so much ahead of the game. But I wish now and then that I could strike one of those spots where the thing really flows.

The manageress here has a Peke called Ming, which I take for walks. Have you ever considered how odd it is that female Pekes don't like male Pekes? Just as chorus girls don't like chorus boys. If Wonder sees another dog miles away on the horizon, she races up to fraternize, but she takes no notice of Ming whatsoever, though he is a most attractive dog. On their walks together they never exchange a word.

Things seem pretty gloomy in England. Here they are distinctly better. For one thing, we find we can get ham, which makes an enormous difference to the budget. It means that instead of getting soaked in the restaurant downstairs, we can dine for practically nothing in our room. Paris in the summer was full of fruit and vegetables. Meat was off the ration. In fact, I think France is picking up, though, of course, everything is terribly expensive.

Do you ever read John O'Hara? I have got his last book, *Pipe Night*. What curious stuff the modern American short story is. The reader has to do all the work. The writer just shoves down something that seems to have no meaning whatever, and it is up to you to puzzle out what is between the lines.

It must be quite a job, though, writing anything for the American magazines these days. Here is a cautionary manifesto which one of them has sent out to its contributors. The editor says he won't consider any of the following:

Stories about gangsters, politics, regional problems. Stories with historical settings. Military stories, World War Two. Stories with a college background. Sex stories. Stories with smart-alec dialogue. Stories in which characters drink. Stories with a newspaper background. Dialect stories. Stories about writers or editors or advertising men. Radio stories. Stories about religion. Stories concerning insanity. Crime stories. Mistaken identity stories. Stories of the First World War. Stories about adolescent characters.

Apart from that, you're as free as the birds in the tree tops and can write anything you like.

What about that England team in Australia? I don't like the look of it. I don't think we shall ever get them out in a Test match. They were crazy not to take Billy Griffith along.

Pavillon Henri Quatre,
St Germain-en-Laye.

November 20th, 1946.

Isn't it odd, when one ought to be worrying about the state of the world and one's troubles generally, that the only thing I can think of nowadays is that Dulwich looks like winning all its school matches and surpassing the 1909 record (because now they play nine schools, and in 1909 it was only five). There are no papers published here on Sundays, so I had to wait till yesterday to go to Paris and get hold of a *Sunday Times* and learn the result of the Bedford match. It must have been a close thing. But I repeat, isn't it odd that after all these years one can still be as keen as ever on school football?

What you said about laughing immoderately over the prize-giving scene in *Right Ho, Jeeves*, made me wince a bit, as I am headed for a similar scene in *The Mating Season*, and I'm haunted with an awful feeling that it is going to fall flat. The set-up is that Bertie has got to recite A. A. Milne's 'Christopher Robin' poems at a village concert, and I shall have to try to make the village concert a big scene. And at the moment I can't see how I am going to make it funny. Still, I suppose it will be all right when I get to it. It generally happens that after I have got momentum on in a story the various hurdles come easily. I haven't got down to thinking of the scene yet. Meanwhile, the story is coming out very well, though, as I told you in my last letter, slowly.

December 24th, 1946.   *St Germain-en-Laye.*

It was a great relief to get your letter of December 8th and to hear that Rene was better. I was very worried after getting your first letter. I do hope that now she will be all right and that she won't find the conditions of life too much of a strain. Life is really terrible for women these days. (Wonder has just insisted on jumping on my lap, so I am finding it hard to type!)

It's curious how life nowadays has got down to simplicities. All that matters is three meals a day and light and warmth. Here we are all right for food, in fact extremely well off, but every Monday and Friday there is no electric light till six in the evening, which means that the heating subsides to nothing.

These last few days have been frightful, as I suppose they have been in England. The only person who seems to like the cold spell is the manageress's Peke. I take it out for a three-mile walk every day, and it races about like a greyhound, revelling in the cold.

I return the Rich & Cowan letter. Publishers do think up the darnedest objections to an author's book. As you say, how could David Copperfield possibly have remembered word for word the conversations he had with Mr Micawber, at the age of ten or thereabouts. They might just as well argue that in real life, when a man says 'I am Hawkshaw, the detective!' or 'So, Maria, it was really you, after all,' a curtain doesn't fall and cut off the reply. If you are going to bar all conventions in novels and plays; why should a novel or a play ever end?

I, too, have had my troubles. In *Joy in the Morning*, Bertie speaks of himself as eating a steak and Boko is described as having fried eggs for breakfast, and Grimsdick of Jenkins is very agitated about this, because he says the English public is so touchy about food that stuff like this will probably cause an uproar. I have changed the fried egg to a sardine and cut out the steak, so I hope the situation is saved. But I was reading Agatha Christie's *The Hollow*, just now, presumably a 1946 story, and the people in it simply gorge roast duck and soufflés and caramel cream and so on, besides having a butler, several parlour-maids, a kitchen-maid and a cook. I must say it encouraged me to read *The Hollow* and to see that Agatha was ignoring present conditions in England.

Do you ever write a book knowing that it will stand or fall by some chapter near the end? I'm up against that in *The Mating Season*. It's fine as far as I've got – about two-thirds of the way – but unless I can make the village concert chapter as funny as the prize-giving one in *Right Ho, Jeeves*, the thing will flop. At least, it won't exactly flop, because I pick up immediately after the concert with a lot of good stuff, but it needs a solid punch at that spot to make it perfect.

February 14th, 1947.   *St Germain.*

I agree with you absolutely about cut-backs. I hate the type of novel which starts off in childhood, so that you don't get to the interesting stuff till about page 234. There is something, too, about the cut-back in itself which is valuable. It gives the reader a sort of double angle. I mean, he has become absorbed with the story of old Jones as a grown-up and then suddenly he gets a glimpse of him as a kid, and the fact that he has been absorbed with him as a grown-up makes the kid stuff twice as vivid as it would have been if simply dished up as kid stuff at the start of the book. Rottenly put, but you know what I mean. Denis Mackail works the thing in his new book, *Our Hero*, but there he does it in alternate chapters. He gives you a scene with his hero as of today, then the next chapter is back in the fellow's childhood. It's very effective.

And now let us speak of parcels. As far as I can gather, the entire postal service of the world has gone cock-eyed, though I may be wronging the rest of the world and the fault may lie entirely in France. If you sent me the second script last Saturday, why haven't I had it yet, today being Friday? And if Nelson Doubleday sent me a parcel on November 27th, why did it reach me on February 10th? And why hasn't another parcel sent from England got here at all? My bet is that your first script will eventually arrive. I hope you registered the second one, as I believe they really do take a certain amount of trouble over registered parcels.

Ethel came back from Paris yesterday bringing a book called *Night and the City* by Gerald Kersh. Do you know his work? I have seen his name about in literary papers, but the only thing of his I had read was a short serial in *Collier's*. This book is terrific. Sordid to a degree, with only one moderately decent character in it, but tremendously gripping. An odd thing is that the book was published originally in 1938 by Michael Joseph and is now issued by Heinemann. I should imagine that what happened was this. M. Joseph sold about two thousand copies, and then called it a day and the plates or whatever they call them returned to the author. Then there were six years of war, ending with a general coarsening – or at any rate a toughening – of the public taste, and what was too sordid for them in 1938 is now just their dish. (For I gather that Kersh is the big noise of the moment.)

Ethel and I have our passage booked on the *America*, sailing April 18th.

Since I last wrote, things have been moving on the Low Wood front. Ethel has now decided to rebuild, so that we can live there. (We expect the French Government to chip in with something pretty good in the way of footing the bills, but we have to pay out first and then they pay us back.)

The catch is that the French Government is cagey. It says, 'Oh, so you lost all your baths, did you? Well, okay, here are some to replace them,' but whereas your baths were expensive jobs in pink and mauve and so on, the Government take the line that a bath is a bath and give you the cheapest available. Same with chairs. You lose your posh chair for which you paid a fortune, and they give you a kitchen chair, and when you kick, they say, 'Well, it's a chair, isn't it?' (Or, more probably, 'C'est une chaise, hein?') So we shall have to dig down and pay the difference if we want the good stuff. Still, it'll be worth it, to have a home.

Wonder has just been discovered chewing tobacco on the floor.

April 1st, 1947.   *St Germain.*

I found your letter on my desk when I came in just now after taking Wonder for her walk, and am answering it two minutes after finishing reading it, which is quick service.

I shall be writing to you again before I leave, but meanwhile an address which will always find me in America is care of my lawyers (Perkins, Malone and Washburn) at 36 West 44th Street, New York City, 18. Of course, the moment I'm settled, I will let you know my address, but Washburn's last letter said that he was having some difficulty in finding a hotel.

The latest news, which will make you laugh, is this: Inquiries have revealed that throughout the war the American War Department was using my broadcasts in its Intelligence School at Camp Ritchie as models of anti-Nazi propaganda for the instruction of the lads they were teaching how to do it. Washburn in his last letter said that on March 24th he wrote to the War Department for further particulars, so I shall know more when he next writes. But it's funny, isn't it?

I'm so glad the new book is going well, but what bad news about the paper shortage crisis! It does seem a shame that when the public is snapping up books as they are the publishers can't produce them. Did I tell you that I broke off *The Mating Season* in order to rewrite that play which George Abbott turned down in 1945? I sweated blood over the play, and Marcel Bernard, the French Davis Cup player, took it over with him to New York. I have now got a letter from Abbott saying it is greatly improved, but I can't write plays without Guy.

Meanwhile, I have just had a letter from a New York manager saying he is putting on a piece by Molnár and Molnár thinks I am the only person capable of doing a decent adaptation of his stuff, and can I possibly get over in time to attend rehearsals and fix the thing up? They have just gone into rehearsal, so, of course, I shall arrive as they are finishing, but I have written saying that I shall be delighted to come on the road and do anything I can. So perhaps when I land in New York I shall have to go straight to Boston or somewhere. My adaptation in 1926 of Molnár's *The Play's the Thing* was a great success, and apparently he has never forgotten it. I met him once at the Casino in Cannes and he stopped the play at the table for about five minutes while he delivered a long speech in praise of me – in French, unfortunately, so I couldn't understand it, not being the linguist then that I am today.

About not being able to realize that other people have grown older. Yes. I saw in the paper this morning something about Ivor Novello: 'a lean Welshman of 54'. It seems incredible that he can be that age. I thought he was about thirty. It's worse with actresses. You do a play and think 'the *ingénue* will be a great part for Jane Jones', and you suddenly realize that Jane is now in the late fifties. I remember some years ago a grey-haired matron accosting me in a restaurant, and she turned out to be a girl who had been in the chorus of one of the shows which I did with Guy Bolton and Jerry Kern at the Princess Theatre.

I say, are you sure those specks that dance in front of one's eyes are all right? Mine are pretty bad now, and I view them with concern.

April 12th, 1947.

My address in New York will probably be Savoy Plaza Hotel, Fifth Avenue. At any rate to start with. The Savoy Plaza has the enormous advantage that it is just opposite the Park, so that airing Wonder (which is after all the most important thing in life) will be simple.

Thank goodness my American income-tax trouble has been settled after dead silence on the part of the Tax Court since October, 1945! What happened was that the tax people suddenly got the idea that I had not paid taxes for 1921–1924, if you can imagine it. They impounded all my money over there. The Court now decides that I did pay tax in the years mentioned (as of course I did, only naturally all records have been destroyed years ago). The net result of all the various cases is that they will stick to about $20,000 and I shall get a refund of about $19,000, and the extraordinary thing is that instead of mourning over the lost $20,000 I am feeling frightfully rich, as if I had just been left $19,000 by an uncle in Australia. I find nowadays that any cash these Governments allow one to keep seems like money for jam. Anyway, my whole financial position in America has changed overnight, and instead of landing without a penny and having to make a quick touch from Doubleday or someone, I have become self-supporting. Great relief.

What a business it is, making this trip to America. Poor Ethel stayed up till six o'clock this morning, packing. The unfortunate thing is that she is buying some new clothes, not having had any for six years, and so has had to go to Paris every day. We have to get the heavy trunks off on Tuesday, and after that the situation ought to become simpler. I have just found that the train journey to Cherbourg takes six hours. Thank goodness we have a good stateroom. It would have been awful to have got on the boat all tired out and had to pig it. The great question now is can we by tipping right and left smuggle Wonder into our stateroom? I can't see her turning in for the night in a cage on a lower deck!

I wonder if you would like T. H. White's stuff. I love it. He started off with a beauty, *The Sword in the Stone*, and has just got one out called *Mistress Masham's Repose*, which I liked very much. They are sort of fairy stories, full of charm and lots of humour.

I find the only way to get anything to read nowadays is to go to a public library and browse round the shelves and get the sort of books nobody has ever heard of.

I have now completed *The Mating Season* all but the final chapter, which should be only three or four pages, but I can't seem to get the right kick-off for it. Do you have the same trouble with your stuff? I find the opening words of each chapter more difficult than anything. I shall probably have to wait and write it on board ship.

May 15th, 1947.   *Hotel Weylin, East 54th Street, New York.*

Well, as you will have deduced from the above address, here I am in New York and still feeling a bit dizzy.

We had one of those rough voyages that the sailors in your books are always having on the western ocean, which seems unjust at this time of year. But the worst part was before it started. We arrived at Cherbourg and got on the tender and then we had a five hours' wait before the *America* turned up, it having been delayed by fog in the Channel. I've never felt so hungry in my life, not even at the Citadel of Huy. We just sat there, hour after hour, starving. We finally got aboard at ten o'clock at night and had a belated dinner, which was worth waiting for. Poor Wonder was carried off to a cage on the boat-deck, but next day we managed to sneak her down to our stateroom, where she was as good as gold for the rest of the trip.

It's just ten years since I was last in New York. Scott Meredith, my agent, has sold a couple of my short stories, so I am hoping gradually to get back into the swim of things, though there are very few markets now for my type of work. Everything in the magazines has to be American nowadays and – as far as I can tell from a cursory glance – pretty bloody awful.

Did I ever tell you about Scott? An amazing chap. Only about twenty-five years old, but already one of the leading literary agents in New York. He started off as a writer at the age of fourteen, and by the time he was twenty had sold over four hundred things to the *Saturday Evening Post* and other magazines. He then was in the army, and on coming out got a job with a moribund lit. agency which he and his brother subsequently bought with the bit of money they had been able to save. From then on he went steadily ahead, first with a tiny business and now with one that employs a whole squad of assistants. I don't know anyone I admire more. When I think how utterly incompetent I was at his age...! I suppose the sort of life he has had develops one quickly. He told me that he was in a school in Brooklyn when he was a boy, the personnel of which consisted almost entirely of negroes, and he had a fight with someone every day for four years. That kind of thing must toughen a chap!

It's quite a business arriving in New York now. In the old days the only newspaper man one saw was the ship reporter of the *N.Y. Times*, who sauntered up as one was seeing one's stuff through the Customs and asked if one had had a pleasant voyage, but now a whole gang of reporters flock aboard at Quarantine and a steward comes to you and tells you that the gentlemen of the Press are in the saloon and request your presence. It's like being summoned before a Senate Committee.

I always get on well with reporters, and I found them very pleasant, especially the man from *P.M.*, one of the evening papers. We became inseparable and last Monday he gave a big dinner for Ethel and me at his house down in Greenwich Village.

My second morning I held a formal 'Press Conference' at the Doubleday offices, with a candid camera man taking surreptitious photographs all the time. These were the literary columnists. I am going to a cocktail-party at the house of one of them next week.

Next day I was interviewed on the radio, reaching three hundred and fifty stations, and the day after that on television. All this sounds as if I were a hell of a celebrity, but the explanation is that Doubleday's publicity hound arranges it all in the hope that it will lead to the sale of a copy or two of *Joy in the Morning*. I don't suppose it helps a bit, really. I don't imagine the great public sits listening spellbound while I answer questions from the interlocutor, and says: 'My God! So that's Wodehouse! How intelligent he looks! What a noble brow!

I must certainly buy that last book of his!' Much more probably they reach out and twiddle the knob and get another station.

Guy Bolton tells me that *Sally* is going to be revived with lyrics by me extracted from other Bolton-Wodehouse-Kern shows, and another management is doing *The Play's the Thing* with Louis Calhern in the Holbrook Blinn part, but apart from that I don't think there is much chance of theatrical work. The whole situation has altered completely since I was here last. There don't seem to be any regular managers now, the sort who used to put on their three or four shows every season. Today what happens is that some complete novice decides that he would like to have a pop, and he gets hold of a play and then passes the hat round in the hope of raising enough money to produce it. When it fails, he goes back into the suit and cloak trade.

How anybody ever does raise the money beats me, for today you need a minimum of $50,000 for a straight play with only one set and for a big musical anything from $250,000 up. Of course, if you get a colossal smash like *Oklahoma*, it doesn't take very long to get your money back at six or seven dollars per ticket, but with even a fairly successful show the position seems to me hopeless. A man who had put up some money for a musical that's running now showed me the week's balance sheet the other day. The gross box office receipts were $36,442.90 and the profit on the week was $3,697.83. In other words they will have to go on doing nearly $37,000 a week for about seventy weeks before they can begin making anything. They start off by coughing up $10,000 for the rent of the theatre, then the company's salaries are another $10,000, the 'crew' takes $1,700, the extra musicians $2,200 and the authors and composer another $2,200. You have to do $50,000 a week, like *Oklahoma*, if you're going to get anywhere.

The story of *Oklahoma* is quite a romance. Oscar Hammerstein, who adapted it from Lynn Riggs' *Green Grow the Lilacs*, had had no great success since he wrote *Show Boat* twelve years ago. The thing looked like a flop out of town and the Theatre Guild, which produced it, needed another $20,000 and couldn't raise it. They were about reconciled to calling it a day and closing, when someone thought of S. H. Behrman, the playwright. He had had some hits in the past with the Theatre Guild, so they went to him and pleaded with him for the sake of Auld Lang Syne to come to the rescue. Moved by their anguish, he wrote a cheque for $20,000 and got in return ten per cent of the show. Then they opened in New York and were a sensation and have played to capacity ever since. Difficult to say how much Behrman will make out of it, but somewhere around half a million dollars, I suppose, which isn't bad on a $20,000 investment.

But the really romantic figure to me is Lynn Riggs. His original play was one of those sixty-or-seventy-performances things, and he must have written it off as a complete loss. And then out of a blue sky it becomes a gold mine, for he can't be getting less than one per cent of the gross, more probably two.

Talking of raising money in the theatre, there's a manager here who got a rich man to back a show by reading him Eugene O'Neill's *Hairy Ape*. The millionaire thought it sounded pretty good, and gladly coughed up. The manager then used the money to finance a bedroom farce he had written. The backer, seeing it on the first night, complained 'But this isn't the show I originally heard'. 'Oh, well,' said the manager, 'you know how these things always get changed around a bit at rehearsals.'

New York is simply incredible. About five times larger than when I last saw it. I said in my radio talk that every time I came back to New York it was like meeting an old sweetheart and finding she had put on a lot of weight. The prosperity stuns one after being in France so long. There is nothing in the way of food and drink you can't get here. And that brings me to a most important point. I want to start sending you food parcels, but before I do I should like to know what you and Rene are most in need of. I could put in a standing order with the British Food Parcels people, but the trouble with the British Food Parcels people is that they don't use their intelligence. When I was in France, I asked for tobacco, and they sent me a pound of it and a box of fifty cigars. Right. The happy ending, you would say. But mark the sequel. The following week another pound of tobacco and another box of fifty cigars arrived, and so on week after week, with the result that among my effects in storage in Paris are ten one-pound tins of tobacco and a ton of cigars. So I don't want to go wrong with your parcels. Just write and tell me what you particularly need.

(I'm glad the flannel bags arrived all right. Do you really mean to say they weren't long enough? They came up round my neck.)

January 15th, 1949.   *2 East 86th Street, New York.*

I have sent you – at enormous expense, four dollars, no less – a book that has headed the American best-seller list for months, *The Naked and the Dead.* I can't give you a better idea of how things have changed over here than by submitting that novel to your notice. It's good, mind you – in fact, I found it absorbing – but isn't it incredible that you can print in a book nowadays stuff which when we were young was found only on the walls of public lavatories. One thing which struck me about it – you'll get this letter weeks before you get the book, so all this won't make sense to you – is how little formal discipline there seems to be in the American Army. A Lieutenant talking to a General never seems to call him 'Sir', and so on. But whatever you think about the book, I'm sure it will interest you.

I have just received from the U.S. Treasury a cheque for $4,500. What it is and why they sent it, I simply can't imagine. My lawyer says it's something to do with repaid interest on my 1941 tax. But the thing doesn't make sense. The Government put a lien on my money and won't let Doubleday pay me what they owe me till the last of the cases is settled, and at the same time they send me these doubloons. The more I have to do with Governments, the less I understand them. The result of my case before the Supreme Court isn't out yet, but I can't see why there should have been a case at all. The point at issue was, Does the money I got for *Saturday Evening Post* serials count as income? Any normal person would say 'Yes, of course it does, what else do you think it was?' But the Government is solemnly deliberating the point and it's quite possible that they will refund me all the money I have paid in taxes on those serials. . . .

Practically all Governments ought to be in Colney Hatch.

March 30th, 1949.

The more I try to cope with the modern American magazine, the more I realize that if you are English it is terribly difficult to pretend in a story that you are American. I find that if I try to, I get self-conscious. I realize now what stupendous luck

I had, being able to get away with English stories in the old days. There are a few English writers whom the magazines will accept, like Gerald Kersh and Evelyn Waugh, but as a general rule they seem to insist on American stuff.

But what asses editors are! I met one at a cocktail-party the other day, and he asked me if I had any short stories that would suit him. I said I had a couple lying around and I sent them to him next day. He accepted them with enthusiasm, and it then turned out that Scott Meredith had offered them to him a month or two previously and he had refused them. They were the same stories – not a word changed – so how do you explain it? My considered opinion, after a careful study of today's American magazines, is that ninety per cent of the editors are cuckoo. I think that when one of them applies for a job on a magazine, they ask him 'Any insanity in your family?', and if he says, 'You bet there is. My father thought he was Napoleon and nothing would convince my mother that she was not a tea-pot', they engage him at a large salary.

The odd thing nowadays is that – except for Clarence Budington Kelland – there seem to be no regular professional writers in the American magazine world. You never see a name you know. All the stories seem to be the work of amateurs who do one story and then are never heard of again.

I see that English nurses are protesting against the movie, *The Snake Pit*, because it represents nurses as hard and unsympathetic. The curse of today is the Pressure Group, especially in America. You can't take a step without getting picketed by someone. One odd aspect of it is that you can no longer put a negro on the stage unless you make him very dignified. Owing to the activities of the Negro pressure group, comic negro characters are absolutely taboo. The result is that all the negro actors are out of work, because the playwrights won't write parts for them.

May 2nd, 1949.   *2 East 86th Street, New York.*

Did I tell you that we were housing Guy Bolton's Peke, Squeaky, while Guy is in England? She is an enormous success, and Wonder gets on splendidly with her. She is an angel and loves everybody. She is pure white, and her way of expressing affection and joy is to scream like a lost soul, or partly like a lost soul and partly like a scalded cat. When the Boltons were in Hollywood, the neighbours on each side reported them to the authorities, saying that they had a small dog which they were torturing. They said its cries were heartrending. So a policeman came round to investigate, and Squeaky fortunately took a fancy to him and started screaming at the top of her voice, so all was well.

June 20th, 1949.   *1000 Park Avenue, New York.*

Note new address. We now have what the licentious New York clubman has in the movies, a duplex Park Avenue penthouse. There is a room downstairs where I work, and upstairs a long gallery with French windows opening out on to our terrace, which is about the size of a small suburban garden. At the end of the terrace is a fence with a door in it, through which you get on the public roof of the building, invaluable for airing Wonder and Squeaky. We have fitted the terrace up with a big hedge, trees, geraniums, etc., and it looks wonderful. We have all our meals there, and at night I sit out there and read. We are very lucky in that there are no high buildings within two blocks, so we get a fine view of the park and perfect quiet. We are on the thirteenth floor, and at night we don't hear a sound. I never want to go away from the place, even in the summer.

We are only two blocks away from the best part of Central Park, where the reservoir is. I had never been up in the Eighties before – we are on 84th Street – and it is extraordinary how different it is from the rest of New York. It's almost like being in the country.

Squeaky refuses to leave me for an instant. She is under my desk now and has just shoved her head up, which means that I shall have to pick her up and try to write with her on my lap. She really is the most amiable dog in the world.

Great excitement yesterday. Ethel had left a melon to ripen on the terrace, and Wonder, apparently suspecting its intentions, started a fierce fight with it. She kept rushing at it, barking furiously, and then losing her nerve and jumping back ten feet. The melon preserved an unmoved calm throughout.

Story in the paper this morning. Wealthy-looking woman in mink coat gets on a Fifth Avenue bus, and looks about her amusedly. 'Goodness!' she says to the conductor as she gives him her fare. 'It does seem strange to be riding in a bus instead of in my car. I haven't ridden in a bus in two years.' 'You don't know how we missed you,' the conductor assured her.

December 13th, 1949.   *1000 Park Avenue, New York.*

Sad bit of news in the *Herald Tribune* this morning.

FAMED BRITISH MAGAZINE
GOES OUT OF BUSINESS

is the headline, and it goes on to say that the final number of the *Strand* will be published in March. As practically everything I have written since July, 1905, appeared in the *Strand*, I drop a silent tear, but I can't say I'm much surprised, for anything sicker-looking than the little midget it had shrunk to I never saw. Inevitable, I suppose, because of paper shortage. And in my opinion never anything worth reading in it, either, the last year or two.

How on earth does a young writer of light fiction get going these days? Where can he sell his stories? When you and I were breaking in, we might get turned down by the *Strand* and *Pearson's*, but there was always the hope of landing with *Nash's*, the *Story-teller*, the *London*, the *Royal*, the *Red*, the *Yellow*, *Cassell's*, the *New*, the *Novel*, the *Grand*, the *Pall Mall* and the *Windsor*, not to mention *Blackwood*, *Cornhill*, *Chambers's* and probably about a dozen more I've forgotten. I was looking at the book of acceptances and payments which I kept for the first five years of my literary career, and I note that in July, 1901, I sold a story to something called the *Universal and Ludgate Magazine* and got a guinea for it. Where nowadays can the eager beginner pick up one pound like that?

People wag their heads and tell you that what killed the English magazine was the competition of movies, motors, radio and so on, but, dash it, laddie, these things are not unknown in America, and American magazines still go merrily along with circulations of three and four million. My view is that the English magazine died of 'names' and what is known over here as 'slanting'.

The slanter, in case you don't know, is a bird who studies what editors want. He reads the magazines carefully, and slings in a story as like the stories they are publishing as he can manage without actual plagiarism. And the editors, if they are fatheads – and they nearly always were in the days I'm thinking of, say 'Fine!' and accept the things, with the result that after a while the public begin to find it a bit monotonous and stop buying.

Names, though, were almost as deadly as poison. The *Strand* was better than most of them, but practically every English magazine would buy any sort of bilge, provided it was by somebody with a big name as a novelist. The reason the *Saturday Evening Post* was always so darned good was that Lorimer never fell into this trap. Have you read *George Horace Lorimer and the 'Saturday Evening Post'* by a man named John Tebbel? Probably not, as I don't think it has been published in England. But here's what Tebbel says on p. 241.

> No writer was bigger than the *Post*. If one chose to leave, there were always others to succeed him. Nor could he give any less than his best for the *Post*, because Lorimer would not hesitate to turn down the work of the highest-paid writers if he thought it fell below standard. He read every contribution as though it were the first piece the writer had submitted.

That's absolutely true. Mary Roberts Rinehart in her *My Story* says: 'I once saw him turn down some stories by Rudyard Kipling, with the brief comment "Not good enough".' And Ben Ames Williams sold a hundred and sixty-two stories to the *Post* between 1917 and 1936, but several of his things were rejected during that time. The Boss was an autocrat, all right, but my God, what an editor to work for. He kept you up on your toes. I had twenty-one serials in the *Post*, but I never felt safe till I got the cable saying each had got over with Lorimer.

December 16th, 1949.   *1000 Park Avenue, New York.*

I returned this morning from Niagara Falls, where I crossed to the Canadian side, spent a couple of nights and came back into the U.S.A. on the quota, thus stabilizing my position and avoiding having to keep getting renewals of my visitor's visa. (I got three altogether, each for six months.)

What a business it is doing this sort of thing nowadays. I had to make three trips to Ellis Island, and I had to be there at nine in the morning, which meant that I woke myself up at 4 a.m. and stayed awake so as not to be late. The boats to Ellis Island run every hour. If you miss the return boat, you have to wait for another hour, and I always did miss it by a couple of minutes. And nowhere to go except the corridor and nothing to do except pace up and down it. If I never see Ellis Island again, it will be all right with me.

I also had to have X-rays done of my chest, I suppose to prove that there was nothing deleterious inside it. I took the X-rays home and stored them in a cupboard, and on arrival at the American Consul's at Niagara Falls found that I ought to have brought them with me and couldn't get my visa without them. It seemed for a moment what we French call an *impasse*, but fortunately the Consul was a splendid fellow and let me wire to the Ellis Island doctor, asking him to wire back that I was O.K. When the doc's wire arrived, saying that my chest was the talk of New York and had five stars in Baedeker, I was given my visa. Next day the Consul drove me in his car to Buffalo, which saved me some tedious railway travelling, and I am now back home on the quota, so unless I plot to upset the American Government by violence – which I doubt if I shall do; you know how busy one is – I can't be taken by the seat of the trousers and slung out.

But, gosh, what a lot of red tape, as the man said when they tried him for murdering his wife. I remember the time when I would be strolling along Piccadilly on a Tuesday morning and suddenly say to myself: 'I think I'll go to America', and at noon on the Wednesday I would be on the boat en route for New York. No passports, no visas, nothing. Just like that.

I always find a great charm in Canada, and sometimes toy with the idea of settling there. The last time I was there was when I came back from Hollywood, in 1931, and spent a very pleasant day with Stephen Leacock. I liked him enormously, and felt sad to think that in all probability two such kindred spirits would never set eyes on each other again. (We didn't.)

May 2nd, 1950.   *1000 Park Avenue, New York.*

Two interesting lunches this week. The first was with Michael Arlen, whom I had run into one day when I was having a bite at the Colony with Evelyn Waugh. Talking of Alien, I always remember the time when we were out on the road with one of the Princess shows and one of those small-town know-it-alls fastened on to Guy and me in Utica, I think it was, and started gassing about how he was just like that with all the celebrities in the literary world. I asked him if he knew Michael Arlen, and he said 'Michael Arlen? Do *I* know Michael Arlen? I should say I do. Wild Irishman. Nice fellow, but like so many of these Irish, too belligerently patriotic.'

The reason I bring M.A. up is that, if you'll believe me, he hasn't written a line in the last fifteen (I think he said) years.

He says business men retire, so why shouldn't an author retire? How he fills in his time, I don't know. Can you imagine yourself not writing for fifteen years?

The other lunch I had was with Molnár, if you could call it having lunch with Molnár. When I arrived at one o'clock at the little Italian restaurant on 58th Street, he was there all right, but he had done his stoking-up at eleven, so I tucked in by myself with him looking on and encouraging me with word and gesture. For the last few years he has lived at the Plaza Hotel on 59th Street, and he never moves off the block where the Plaza is. He goes to bed at nine, gets up at five, has a cup of coffee and writes till eleven, when he toddles round to this Italian restaurant – never going off the pavement which runs to Sixth Avenue and down to 58th – has his lunch and then toddles back and is in for the night. Central Park is just across from the Plaza, but he never sets foot inside it. As I say, he doesn't move off the pavement – ever. An old friend of his from Buda-Pesth had trouble with his wife the other day, and as it was in all the papers and he knew Molnár must have heard about it, he was hurt that Molnár didn't come to see him and console him, and wrote him a stiff letter, reproaching him. 'My dear fellow,' Molnár wrote back, 'I am a very nervous man. I fear this New York traffic. You cannot expect me to risk driving through it in a cab every time your wife deceives you.'

Well, there's one thing to be said for being in the New York theatre world – you meet such interesting people.

I am always terribly sorry for Molnár. What he wants is the *café* life of Buda-Pesth – it no longer exists, of course – and I can see he is miserable in New York. He is homesick all the time, and nothing to be done about it. Also, these modern managers look on him as a back number and won't do his plays.

I have adapted two of them – *Arthur* and *A Game of Hearts* – and I don't think there is an earthly chance of them being put on. *Arthur* has a different (and elaborate) set for each of the three acts, and the cost of producing it would be prohibitive.

September 24th, 1950.   *1000 Park Avenue.*

Long silence on my part due to the fact that I have only just got back from my travels. I can't remember if I told you that I had written a play. (Not the one I sent to George Abbott, another one.) Anyway, I had, and a management decided to try it out on what they call the 'straw hat circuit' here – i.e. the summer resorts. A good many of these summer resorts have theatres now, and it is a good way of trying out a new play. You go from spot to spot, playing a week at each.

We went first to Skowhegan, Maine, rehearsed eleven days and opened at the wonderful theatre they have there. But before proceeding I must tell you a story a Maine man I met at Skowhegan, Maine, told me about a Maine farmer. The farmer's wife, it seems, was subject to fits, and the farmer used to get very fed up because people were always calling him in from his work when they came on, and by the time he reached the house she would be all right again. So time went on, and one day he was busy ploughing, when someone shouted to him 'Go to the house quick, Joe, your wife is in a bad way'. And this time, when he got to the house, he found her lying dead on the kitchen floor. 'Well,' he said, 'that's more like it.'

Right. Where were we? Skowhegan, Maine. We did our eight performances, and on the Saturday the management informed us that our next port of call would be Watkins Glen, New York. We would drive there in a couple of station wagons.

No one seemed to know anything about Watkins Glen. 'Somewhere near here?' we asked. 'Oh, pretty near,' said the management. About six hundred and fifty miles, they thought. Or it might be seven hundred.

So on the Sunday morning we started off. We got up at five-thirty, stopped in Skowhegan for a bite of breakfast, and then off through New Hampshire, Vermont and Massachusetts. It was a great moment when we crossed the Massachusetts border into New York state, because there we could get a drink, a thing barred elsewhere on Sundays. (By the way, in Maine you may drink sitting down, but you mustn't drink standing up. If you are having a snifter and start to your feet to welcome an old friend who has entered the bar, you must be careful that you aren't holding your glass as you do so, because if you are, you're breaking the law and rendering yourself liable to a big fine.)

So picture us, *mon vieux*, tooling on and on through the long summer day on a journey about the equivalent in England of starting at Land's End and finishing up somewhere near the Hebrides. I enjoy my little bit of motoring as a rule, but it's a pretty gruesome experience to realize, after you have gone three hundred miles, that you have scarcely scratched the surface, so to speak, and there are still another four hundred to go. Even assuming, mind you, that there was such a place as Watkins Glen. We only had the management's word for it, and they might quite easily have made a mistake.

Years ago, when I had a penthouse apartment on the twenty-second floor of an office building on East 41st Street, I became temporary host to an alley cat which I had found on the front doorstep resting up after what must have been the battle of the century. I took him in, and for a few days he was a docile and appreciative guest, seeming to have settled down snugly to bourgeois respectability and to be contented with regular meals and a spacious roof for purposes of exercise. There, you would have said, was a cat that had dug in for the duration.

But all the while, it appeared, the old wild life had been calling to him, and one morning he nipped out of the door and headed for the open spaces. And not having the intelligence to ring for the lift, he started to walk downstairs.

I stood above and watched him with a heavy heart, for I knew that he was asking for it and that remorse must inevitably creep in. And so it proved. For the first few floors he was jauntiness itself. He walked with an air, carrying his tail like a banner. And then suddenly – it must have been on floor twelve – I could see the thought strike him like a bullet that this was going on for ever and that he had got to Hell and was being heavily penalized for not having been a better cat. He sat down and stared bleakly into an eternity of going on and on and arriving nowhere. If ever a cat regretted that he had not stayed put, this cat was that cat.

After three hundred miles in that station wagon, I could understand just how he had felt.

Well, sir, it turned out that there really was a place called Watkins Glen, and we reached it at four in the morning. We stayed there a week, playing in the High School Auditorium with an enormous basketball arena behind the stage. This rendered the show completely inaudible. We then went on to Bradford, a journey of a hundred and fifty miles, where we got a theatre but ran into Old Home Week, with the entire population dancing in the streets and refusing to come anywhere near our little entertainment, with the result that we played to about eleven dollars on eight performances. The management then announced that on the Sunday we would be leaving for Chicago. 'Isn't that rather far?' we asked. 'Far?' they said. 'What do you mean, far? It's only about a thousand miles.'

At this point I put the old foot down firmly. I said I wished them well and would follow their future career with considerable interest, but I was going back to New York. Which I did. The unfortunate company went off in an aeroplane, and I never saw them again, for from Chicago they went to Easthampton, Long Island – twelve hundred miles – and when I motored to Easthampton the Friday before Labour Day, I found there wasn't a bed to be had in the place, so twenty minutes after arrival I motored back again.

I was told later that I hadn't missed much. Our star had laryngitis and was inaudible, and the principal comic character started drinking, became violent, wrecked the house where he was staying and was taken to prison. The police let him out each night to play his part and on Saturday for the matinée, and then took him back to the jug again.

The net result is that unless I can find another management to put on the show – say one that was dropped on its head as a baby and is not too bright – it may be considered dead. I see now that the trouble with it was the same that James Thurber found in a play of his when he analysed it.

'It had only one fault,' he said; 'it was kind of lousy.'

October 30th, 1950.   *1000 Park Avenue, New York.*

The night before last I was interviewed on the radio by none other than Mrs Franklin D. Roosevelt. A charming woman, and I would have liked to have lolled back in my chair afterwards and had a long and interesting conversation about life in the White House. Unfortunately she threw me out on my ear the moment the thing was over – we did it on a record for release in a couple of weeks – because John Steinbeck had come in to do his interview. I think my performance was adequate. We kidded back and forth with quite a bit of *élan* and *espièglerie*, and I wound up by telling that story about the woman who sat next to me at dinner and said how much her family admired my work, my invariable procedure when interviewed on the radio.

Why does one always say the wrong thing? Just to put him at his ease and to show him that my heart was in the right place, I said to John Steinbeck, 'And how is your play going, Mr Steinbeck?' he having had one produced a day or two before. He gave me a long, wan, sad look and made no reply. I then remembered reading in the paper that it had come off after four performances.

How did you like Raymond Chandler's book? Denis Mackail sent me his new one, which I liked very much. The other day I got hold of a book called *Brimstone in the Garden*, by Elizabeth Cadell, which I liked so much that I bought everything she has written. They are gentle English character stuff with lots of comedy, rather like Margery Sharp. (Making four times in five lines that I've used the word 'like'. Thank goodness one doesn't have to polish a letter.)

It's hard to say whether what you say – there I go again – about the English being disliked in New York is exaggerated or not. I fancy someone like one of your sailors, mixing with the tougher elements of the community, would have unpleasant experiences which someone like the Marquis of Milford Haven, mixing with the rich, wouldn't. Living as I do in the Eighties, which is a sort of village where one knows everybody, I find everyone very friendly. You find a lot of anti-British sentiment in some of the papers. On the other hand, you get a book like *Assignment to Austerity*, by the London correspondent of the *New York Times*, and it raves about the English character and virtues. It's all very puzzling. But don't you think that everybody except you and me hates everybody else's guts nowadays? I don't imagine Americans dislike Englishmen any more than they dislike Americans.

By the way, I have just heard from Watt that the B.B.C. want to do my *Damsel in Distress* on their Light Programme. Always up to now they have told him that nothing by P. G. Wodehouse would even be considered. Well, what I'm driving at is that I had always said to myself: 'One of these days the B.B.C. will come asking for something of mine, and then won't I just draw myself up to my full height and write them a stinker saying that after what has occurred I am amazed – nay, astounded – at their crust – etc. etc.' Of course what actually happened was that I wrote to Watt saying Okay, go ahead.

* * *

The story to which Plum refers was of a nice old lady who sat next to him at dinner one night and raved about his work. She said that her sons had great masses of his books piled on their tables, and never missed reading each new one as it came out. 'And when I tell them,' she concluded, 'that I have actually been sitting at dinner next to Edgar Wallace, I don't know what they will say.'

* * *

March 8th, 1951.   *1000 Park Avenue, New York.*

Do you remember a year or so ago my telling you about a giddy attack I had? I got all right in a day and had no more trouble. But about three weeks ago I suddenly got another. This was on a Sunday. On the Monday I felt fine, went for a five-mile walk and went to the dentist and so on. Then on the Tuesday after lunch, still feeling all right, I started to walk down town to change my library books, and I had got to 82nd Street and Park Avenue when without any warning, I suddenly felt giddy again. (At least, it's not exactly giddiness. The scenery doesn't get blurred or jump about. It's just that I lose control of my legs.) Well, Park Avenue fortunately is full of doctors, and I groped my way to the nearest, about half a dozen yards. I had great luck, as I happened to hit on one of the best doctors in New York, quite a celebrated man who attends Gertrude Lawrence, Oscar Hammerstein and other nibs.

Since then I have been taking every known form of test, and the general view is that I have got a tumour on the brain. If this is correct, it is presumably the finish, as I don't suppose I can survive a brain operation at my time of life.

March 14th, 1951.   *1000 Park Avenue, New York.*

After a great many consultations and more tests, including that ghastly job of taking fluid out of the spine, the docs have decided that I have not got a tumour on the brain. (And, I have been feeling recently, not much brain for it to be on.) Nobody seems actually to know what is the matter, and there is a school of thought which says it's probably my eyes. I never know what oculists mean when they talk technical language, but mine says my eyes are 'off' fifteen points or degrees or something. This, I take it, is not so hot, and I'm wishing I had never read *The Light that Failed*. The score, then, to date is that I am deaf in the left ear, bald, subject to mysterious giddy fits and practically cock-eyed. I suppose the moral of the whole thing is that I have simply got to realize that I am a few months off being seventy. I had been going along as if I were in the forties, eating and drinking everything I wanted to and smoking far too much. I had always looked on myself as a sort of freak whom age could not touch, which was where I made my ruddy error, because I'm really a senile wreck with about one and a half feet in the grave.

(My doctor, by the way, summing up on the subject of the giddy fits and confessing his inability to explain them, said, 'Well, if you have any more, you'd better just *have* them.' I said I would.)

We now come to the subject of basketball, a game unknown in England – hence the term 'Merrie England' – but played throughout America in schools and colleges between the football and baseball seasons. At each end of the arena is a basket, perched high up on the wall, and the object of the game is to throw the ball into these. It sounds silly, and it is silly. Well, obviously, then, the taller you are, the easier it is for you to basket the ball, and the various teams scour the country for human giraffes, who can just walk up and drop it in. And now the gamblers have turned their attention to the game and basketball scandals are popping up all over the place.

All of which is leading up to an article John Lardner has in one of the weekly papers this week. Apparently the head man of the Littlewood pools stated in an interview that England has been shocked by the news of these basketball 'fixes'.

'We don't fix amateur sports in England,' he said.

Lardner writes:

To summarize conditions to date, then, England is (1) honest, but, (2) shocked. But I would like to tell the story of a college basketball game that was not fixed, some years ago. It seems that there was a fellow who went out on the street and met a tall man. The fellow stuck $500 in the man's pocket, which he could just reach, and whispered hoarsely, through a megaphone:

'The spread tonight against Kansas City is eight points.'

'Oh, is it?' said the tall man politely. 'Well, so long,' and he went down to the railroad station, bought a ticket to Albany, settled in that city as part owner of a coal and ice business, and lived happily ever afterwards.

Basketball would be wholly honest if more people worked like that, because it is the wrong way to fix a game. For textbook purposes, the principle might be stated thus: You cannot assume that every tall man you see is a basketball player. Some of them are deadbeats, some are taxidermists, and some are wearing elevator shoes.

John Lardner is the son of Ring Lardner, one of the most formidable blokes I ever met. He was at least eight feet high, with a grim, poker face, like Buster Keaton's. When you spoke to him, he never uttered but just stood staring coldly over your head. I sometimes think he must have been the hero of the story I once heard Clarence Budington Kelland tell. Late one night this fellow rang the bell of a neighbour's house, and the neighbour, donning bathrobe and slippers, went downstairs and let him in, and it was apparent to him right away that the visitor had recently been hoisting a few.

'Hello,' said the householder. 'Nice evening.' No answer. 'What keeps you out so late?' No answer. 'Have a drink?' No answer. 'Have a cigar?' No answer.

The belated guest then sat down and stared at his host for two hours without saying a word, and the host finally went to sleep in an arm-chair. He awoke as dawn was breaking, to find his guest still sitting and staring at him. Finally the guest broke his long silence.

'Say, why the hell don't you go home and let a man go to bed?' he said.

The only thing that makes me doubtful about it being Ring Lardner is that final speech. I don't believe Ring ever said as many words as that at one time in his life.

John Lardner is quite different, very genial and pleasant. I had lunch with him the other day and was dying to ask him if his father had ever spoken to him, but hadn't the nerve.

May 11th, 1952.   *1000 Park Avenue, New York.*

Life in New York continues jolly, but it would be much jollier if it wasn't for the ruddy Crime Wave. Practically everyone you meet is either coming away from sticking up a bank or just setting out to stick up a bank. Which reminds me of a story I saw in the paper the other day. Young man went into a bank, and asked to see the manager. Conducted into the manager's office, he said he wanted a loan. 'Ah, yes?' said the manager. 'A loan, eh? Yes, yes, to be sure. And what is your occupation?' 'I stick up banks,' said the young man, producing a gun. The manager handed over $204 without collateral or argument.

The liquor store a few blocks up from where we are was held up a few days ago, also a hotel which is even nearer, and last week

Ethel was held up at a dressmaker's on Madison Avenue. She was in the middle of being fitted, when a man came in brandishing a large knife and asked for contributions. He got eighteen dollars off Ethel and disappeared into the void. Wonder, who had accompanied Ethel, slept peacefully throughout.

This seems to have been one of those routine business transactions, conducted – like conferences between statesmen – in a spirit of the utmost cordiality, but the binge at the hotel was very stirring. At half-past five in the morning a gang of six ankled in with the idea of cracking the hotel safe, unaware that there was a cop on the premises having a wash and brush-up in the basement. He emerged just as the intruders were telling the night clerk at the desk to put his hands up, and started shooting in all directions. The gang started shooting back, and things were getting brisk, when more policemen arrived and eventually three of the blokes were captured on the roof and the other three in the beauty parlour.

'There was about a million bucks in the place, the way we had it figured,' one of the bandits said, as they loaded him into the wagon. 'It's too bad,' he added, probably clicking his tongue a bit, 'that this young cop went and ruined everything.'

They are very strong over here for what is known as the parole system. Some enterprising person is caught burgling a bank and sentenced to seven years in the coop. After about six months he is released on parole and immediately goes off and burgles another bank. He then gets ten years and six months later is again released on parole, when he immediately . . . But you get the idea. It must be a dog's life running a bank in these parts. Never a peaceful moment.

Listen, Bill. If you want to make a pot of money, come over here and go into domestic service. You can't fail to clean up.

A man and his wife came here from England some years ago and got a job as butler and cook at $200 a month plus their board and lodging. They were able to salt away a hundred and fifty bucks each pay day. After they had been in this place for a while they accepted an offer from a wealthier family at $300. They had two rooms and bath and everything they wanted in the way of food and wines and were able to put away $250 a month.

About a year later their employer made the mistake of entertaining a Hollywood producer for the week-end, and the producer was so struck by the couple's virtuosity that he lured them away with an offer of $400, to include all expenses plus a car. They now banked three hundred and fifty a month. And when a rival producer tried to snatch them, the original producer raised their salary to $500, at which figure it remains at moment of going to press. They now own an apartment house in Los Angeles.

We have had a series of blisters – both white and black – in our little home, each more incompetent than the last and each getting into our ribs for sixty dollars a week – which tots up to something over a thousand quid a year – in spite of the fact that Ethel does all the real work with some slight assistance from me. Ninety per cent of them have been fiends in human shape, our star exhibit being dear old Horace, a coloured gentleman of lethargic disposition who scarcely moved except to pinch our whisky when we were out. We had laid in a stock of Haig and Haig Five Star for guests and an inferior brand for ourselves, and after it had been melting away for a week or two, we confronted Horace. 'Horace,' we said, 'you've been stealing our Haig and Haig and, what's more, you've also been stealing our . . .' He gave us a look of contempt and disgust. 'Me?' he said. 'I wouldn't touch that stuff. I only drink Haig and Haig Five Star.' Well, nice to think that we had something he liked.

I heard of some people here who engaged a maid who had just come over from Finland. She seemed a nice girl and willing, but it turned out that there were chinks in her armour. 'How is your cooking?' they asked. She said she couldn't cook. At home her mother had always done all the cooking. 'How about house work?' No, she couldn't do house work – back in Finland her aunt had attended to all that sort of thing – nor could she look after children, her eldest sister's speciality. 'Well, what *can* you do?' they asked. She thought for a moment. 'I can milk reindeer,' she said brightly.

So if you can milk reindeer, come along. Wealth and fame await you.

June 20th, 1952.   *Remsenburg, Long Island.*

The above is where we have just bought a house. When writing, address the letter 'Remsenburg, L.I,' because it's one of those primitive hamlets where you don't have a postman, but go and fetch your mail from the post office.

Guy Bolton has a house here, and Ethel and I have been staying with him and Virginia, as Guy and I were writing a play together. While we were working, Ethel explored the neighbourhood and came back one evening to say that she had bought this house. It's at the end of what is picturesquely known as Basket Neck Lane, and has five acres of ground which lead down, through a wood, to a very attractive creek. Unfortunately one can't bathe in the creek, as it is full of houses. Which sounds peculiar, but what happened was that when that hurricane hit Long Island a few years ago it uprooted all the houses on the shore and blew them into the bay, whence they drifted into our creek and sank. So if I dived in, I would probably bump my head on a kitchen or a master's bedroom. I do my bathing at Westhampton, about four miles away, where one gets the ocean.

The play looks good. We wrote it with London in mind, not New York, and Klift and Rea are going to put it on next year some time. I am now turning it into a novel called *Ring for Jeeves*. Our original title was *Derby Day*, but someone has told us that that was used for a film. It's too English to have a chance here, I think. It's about a hard-up young peer who becomes a Silver Ring bookie.

Guy, who always likes to have something to occupy his time, is also writing two musicals and a straight play, and weird collaborators keep turning up here to confer with him. One of them used to be a taxi-driver. He was always thinking of funny gags and when one day Eddie Cantor happened to take his cab, he sprang a dozen or so of his best ones on him, and Cantor was so impressed that he engaged him as one of his official gag writers. Since when this chap – Eddie Davis his name is – has never looked back. During the war he had an idea for a musical comedy, but was, of course, incapable of writing it by himself, so the management called Guy in and the thing ran two years. Eddie has the invaluable gift of being able to raise money. He belongs to some strange club in the heart of Broadway where he is always meeting men who are eager to put a hundred thousand dollars into a show. So they have collected the two or three hundred thousand they need for this one, and it is now simply a matter of waiting till they can get a satisfactory cast.

I say 'simply', but, my gosh, there's nothing simple about

casting a play for Broadway nowadays. Everybody you want is either in Hollywood or has a television contract he can't break. I can't remember if I told you about that play of mine, the one I made into my novel, *The Old Reliable*. I wrote about six versions of it, but couldn't get it right, and finally handed it over to Guy, who wrote almost a completely new play, which was wonderful. We have a manager, and he has the money, and Joe E. Brown wants to star in it, but everything has been held up because Brown has this television show of his. So we shall have to wait till the autumn of 1953. It makes one sigh for the old days when actors needed jobs.

August 11th, 1952.   *Remsenburg, L.I.*

We are down here till the cold weather starts, when we shall return to 1000 Park Avenue with Squeaky, two kittens and a foxhound.

I went up to New York for a few days while Ethel stayed here to see the furniture put in. I rang her up one night and asked how things were going, and she said everything looked pretty smooth. 'But,' she added in a melancholy voice, 'a foxhound has turned up.' It seems that she was just warming to her work when she looked round and there was this foxhound. It came into the garden and sat down, looking on. It was in an advanced state of starvation, and so covered with ticks that it took two hours to get them off. These beastly ticks get on the dogs and swell to the size of marbles. The poor animal had hardly any blood left in him, and had to be taken to the vet for transfusions.

When I came down, he was quite restored and full of beans. We can't imagine where he came from. He is a beautiful dog and an expert here tells us that he is one of the famous Colonel

Whacker hounds from Kentucky. There are one or two packs on Long Island, and I suppose he must have strayed. He had evidently been wandering in the woods for days, getting nothing to eat and accumulating ticks.

The next thing that happened was that we went to a man's birthday party in Quogue and somebody had given him two guinea hens as a present. Ethel asked him what he was going to do with them, and he said 'Eat 'em'. Ethel was horrified, and asked if she could have them. So we took them away and built a large run for them in the garden; and they settled down very happily.

A few nights later we heard something crying in the dark and went out and there was a tiny white kitten. This was added to the strength.

About a week after that I was walking to get the mail when I saw a car ahead of me suddenly swerve and it seemed to me that there was a small dark object in the middle of the road. I went up, and it was a black kitten. I picked it up and put it on my shoulder, and it sang to me all the way to the post office and back, shoving its nose against my face. It, too, has been added to the menagerie, so the score now is one foxhound, two guinea hens, Squeaky, and two kittens, and we are hourly expecting more cats and dogs to arrive. I think the word must have gone round the animal kingdom that if you want a home, just drop in at Basket Neck Lane, where the Wodehouses keep open house.

The bright side is that all our animals get along together like sailors on shore leave. Bill, the foxhound, has the most angelic disposition and lets the kittens run all over him, while Squeaky of course would never dream of hurting anything. A very united family, thank goodness.

As soon as I have got this novel out of the way, Guy and I are going to start writing our reminiscences of the New York theatre. It is now just forty years since we started working on Broadway, during which time we wrote twenty-three shows together and met every freak that ever squeaked and gibbered along the Great White Way, so it ought to make an interesting book. It may turn out something which we can publish only in America, but I don't think so, as there will be a lot of London stuff in it, so many of our shows having been produced in England.

The drawback to Remsenburg is the mosquitoes and the ticks. We have had a very hot summer and the mosquitoes have rolled up in droves. Fortunately, the tick season isn't a very long one – it ought to be over by next month – but while it lasts things are very strenuous. Everybody tells me that these ticks don't fasten on to human beings, but they seem to be saying 'Who made that rule?', because twice this week I have been horrified by finding them glued to my person, enlarged to bursting point.

September 10th, 1952.   *1000 Park Avenue, New York.*

Up in New York for a few days, then back to Remsenburg.

Have you a television set? I always swore I would never get one, but finally yielded, so now I am in a position to see all the films of 1930, each of which seems to have been shot through a blinding snowstorm. What a loathsome invention it is. You hear people say it's going to wipe out books, theatres, radio and motion pictures, but I wonder. I don't see how they can help running out of material eventually. The stuff they dish out is bad enough now, and will presumably get worse. (Not that you can go by what I predict. I was the man who told David Graham Bell not to expect too much of that thing he had invented called the telephone or some such name, as it could never be more than an amusing toy.)

There's only one thing worth watching on television – even when I am appearing on it – and that's the fights. Those are superb. They have them every Friday, and you get a much better view than if you were in a ringside seat. The second Joe Louis–Jersey Joe Walcott fight cured me of attending these binges in person. Ethel and I bought a couple of seats for some enormous price, and found that they were about a mile and a quarter away from the ring. (This was an open-air bout at the Yankee Stadium.)

Talking of fights, is there a short story for you in this thing I read in the paper the other day? It was very long, but I'll try to condense it.

College Inn, Chicago, the year Jack Johnson beat Jeffries. (In case you've forgotten, Johnson was the negro who had won the heavy-weight championship by knocking out Tommy Burns, and Jeffries was the White Hope, who was coming back to the ring to regain the supremacy for the Caucasian race, and all that sort of thing.) Well, anyway, there was a gang of news-paper men who lunched at the College Inn every day, among them a chap called Lou Housman who was going to Jeffries' training camp to report on his progress till the day of the fight. He said as he was leaving: 'Don't any of you bet a dollar till you hear from me. As soon as I decide how the thing's going to go, I'll wire Billy Aaronson.' Billy Aaronson was the head waiter at the College Inn.

Well, Housman went off to Nevada to the Jeffries camp, and a week later Aaronson suddenly dropped dead. A new man,

Marcel, succeeded him. And one night Marcel came in with a telegram.

'I don't get this,' he said. 'I open all wires addressed to Aaronson, because they keep coming to him from people wanting reservations who don't know he's dead. But this one is different.'

He showed them the telegram. It ran:

> Aaronson
> College Inn,
> Sherman Hotel,
> Chicago.
> Black. – Lou.

Well, of course, the newspaper men knew that it meant that Housman was sure Johnson was going to win, and they had complete faith in his judgment, so they went out and put their shirts on Johnson. And they also made up a pool and betted it for Aaronson's widow. The fight came off. Johnson knocked Jeffries out. They all cleaned up big.

Days went by. They knew Housman must be back in Chicago, but nobody saw him. He didn't come to the College Inn. And then, about two weeks later, one of them bumped into him and he confessed.

'I hadn't the nerve to face you fellows,' he said. 'I was so sure. I thought I knew it all. I shouldn't have dragged you boys in with me!'

'What do you mean?' his friend said. 'We were all set to bet on Jeffries, when your wire switched us. We made a killing on Johnson.'

'On Johnson? Didn't Aaronson explain?'

His friend told him of Aaronson's death, and said that the wire had reached them and they had bet accordingly.

Housman nearly swooned.

'When I said goodbye to Billy that night,' he said, 'I gave him a code. I didn't want the telegraph office there or here to know my pick. So we arranged that "white" would mean Johnson and "black" would mean Jeffries. I didn't think Johnson had a chance.'

Can you do anything with that? Wouldn't O. Henry have jumped at it!

November 18th, 1952.   *1000 Park Avenue, New York.*

Life, always difficult, has been much complicated of late by the eccentricities of Bill the foxhound. We brought him up from Remsenburg, having nobody to leave him with down there, and he decided right away that city life was not for him. Alighting from the car, he flatly refused to enter our apartment house, evidently suspecting a trap. With a terrific expenditure of energy I dragged him as far as the lift, and again he jibbed. I finally got him in, and he then refused to emerge. Assisted by the lift man, I got him out, and he then stoutly declined to go through our door, which he obviously assumed led to the Den of the Secret Nine. When the time came to take him for an airing, he refused to go out of the door, into the lift, out of the lift, across the lobby and out of the front door, and on returning from our stroll showed the same disinclination to go through the front door, across the lobby, into the lift, out of the lift and through our door.

This went on for about a week, when he suddenly decided that his fears had been ill-founded and that there were no plots against his person. The only trouble is that he now wants to be taken for a walk every quarter of an hour or so, and I see no prospect of ever doing any more work. I take him for a mile hike before breakfast, a three miler in the afternoon and perhaps another mile after dinner. It's doing wonders for my figure, of course, but it has made me practically a spent force as a writer.

Though I sometimes wonder if I really am a writer. When I look at the sixty-odd books in the shelf with my name on them, and reflect that ten million of them have been sold, it amazes me that I can have done it. I don't know anything, and I seem incapable of learning … I feel I've been fooling the public for fifty years.

I mean, take that prison camp, for instance. I was cooped up for a year with thirteen hundred men of all trades and professions and nothing to do all day but talk to them and find out about their jobs, and I didn't bring a thing away with me. You in a similar position would have collected material enough for twenty novels. There is this, of course, to be said in excuse for me, that it takes a steam drill to extract anything of any interest from anyone. I tried to get some inside stuff from a man who ran a hotel in Boulogne – just my dish, I thought – and all he could tell me was that sometimes a customer asked him to have a drink. You can't make a powerful eighty-thousand-word novel out of that.

I met a woman the other day whom I used to know back in 1912 or thereabouts, and she said: 'Why don't you write about *real* things?' 'Such as?' I asked. 'Well, my life, for instance.' 'Tell me all about your life,' I said. And she thought for a while and came up with the hot news that when in Singapore during the war she had gone about with a tin helmet on her head. I explained to her that that would be terrific for – say – the first twenty thousand words, but that after that one would be stuck.

Talking of war and prison camps, I am sending you the script of my Camp book. I ought to have let you have it years ago, but in some mysterious way all the copies disappeared. I have now found one *chez* my lawyer. It will never be published, but I hope it will amuse you. I wrote it at Tost after I had finished *Money in the Bank*, except of course for the diary stuff about my life at the Citadel of Huy, which was jotted down day by day during my stay there.

* * *

I naturally read the Camp book – Plum had given it the title of *Wodehouse in Wonderland* – with intense interest. If the book is never to be published, that, of course, is that. But I propose to give here some extracts from it, beginning with – what he calls 'the diary stuff' about life at the Citadel of Huy.

August 3rd.

First night at Huy. Arrived four-thirty. Glad to be out of our cattle trucks, but things don't look too good. They have put forty of us in a room large enough for about fifteen. No beds. Not even straw on the floor. I am writing this at 8.30, half an hour before lights out, and it looks as if we should have to sit up all night.

August 4th.

Our first night was not so bad as I had thought it was going to be. At the last moment we were moved into a larger room, and somebody suddenly remembered that there was straw in the cellars, so we went and fetched it – a hundred and ten steps down and ditto up. There was only enough to form a very thin deposit on the floor, and it stank to heaven. Still, it was straw. No blankets. I slept in flannel trousers, shirt, sweater and my red cardigan, using my other trousers, my grey cardigan and my suitcase as a pillow.

Parade was at eight-thirty on the first morning. The morning was given up to cleaning. We cleaned passages and wash-rooms. It is gradually borne in on me that we are a ruddy peripatetic fatigue party. We cleaned up Liège barracks and they moved us on, and now we shall presumably clean up the

Citadel of Huy and move on again. By the time we have finished, you will be able to eat your dinner off Belgium.

A nasty jolt for our sensibilities today. We hear that all the Germans have been able to get for us in the way of food tomorrow is fourteen kilos of macaroni.

August 6th.

Rumour proved true. Our buckets contained a sort of sweet hot water with prunes floating in it. I have seldom tasted anything so loathsome, but it was really rather a *tour de force* on the part of our cook, for it is not easy to brew soup for eight hundred men on a foundation of twenty-eight pounds of macaroni. In adding prunes I think he overstressed the bizarre note, but I suppose he had to add something. A less conscientious man might have put in a couple of small Belgians.

August 7th.

Big day. Just after breakfast the rumour spread through the camp that one of the Belgian boys had escaped, and unlike most of our rumours turned out to be true. He had got out through one of the window slits in the wall at the end of the passage, leaving rope behind him tied to the water pipe.

Atmosphere rather like Dotheboys Hall after escape of Smike. At 11.30 Kommandant is heard bellowing orders outside. We are all told to go to our rooms and stay there. Presently four soldiers with bayonets enter our dormitory. They take away our washing cords and even small bits of string which we were saving up for shoe laces. There is a moment when it seems as if our belts will go, too, but this final disaster does not happen. No doubt it would be embarrassing for all concerned to have eight hundred internees parading with their trousers hanging round their ankles. Prevent smartness and snap.

Old Scotch windjammer sailor comes and sits on our window-sill and discusses the affair in a broad Glasgow drawl. He also touches on conditions here, which he thinks might be worse. Says he was in prison in Glasgow for five days and this is luxury in comparison. 'Ye had a wooden pillow, and ye didn't need to turn it over, 'cos it was the same both sides.' He doesn't like the Belgian boy who escaped, says he was in his room at Liège and they couldn't get him to wash! 'A greasy young ——' he says, which explains how he managed to slide through that slit in the wall.

Opinion is divided between appreciation of the lad's enterprise and the feeling that he showed a lack of public spirit in getting away and leaving us to receive the kick-back. God knows what the reaction will be. We had just got all set to ask the Kommandant if we couldn't have a little more bread, but when we heard his voice outside commenting on the big news, we felt that this was not the moment.

August 9th.

Horrible shock today. The bread ration failed and we each got thirty biscuits instead, about the size of those which restaurants used to give you to go with your order of oysters. Felt like a tiger which has been offered a cheese straw. The great problem is how to split up one's ration, i.e. whether to gorge half your biscuits for breakfast, or hold off at breakfast, relying on the heat of the coffee to give you the illusion of having fed, and go a buster at supper.

August 13th.

I have now been sleeping for ten nights without a blanket, and it gets bitterly cold at night at this height. Today I went to the Sergeant, accompanied by Enke, our linguist, and complained. The Sergeant was apologetic, but it seems there are no blankets. His attitude seemed to be that you can't have everything.

Parade this morning at 7.30. Further parades at 9, 10, and 11, and again in the afternoon. Sandy Youl says – apropos of this constant parading – that if he has enough money after the war, he is going to buy a German soldier and keep him in the garden and count him six times a day.

I have a theory about these parades. They have dug this blighted Kommandant out after years of obscurity and given him this fairly important job, and it has gone to his head. He loves the feeling of strutting up and down, giving out orders. He is a man of sixty-two and used to be an inspector of police. The German soldiers assure us – through Enke – that he is a pain in the neck to them. They call him the Thief-Catcher.

The German soldiers themselves are all right. Being cooped up with them in this small place, we see a lot of them and they are always friendly. They are all elderly reservists longing to get home to their wives and children, whose photographs they constantly show us, and they sympathize with us. One of them gave Arthur Grant and me his soup yesterday. Full of rice with bits of meat in it.

There is one particularly genial sergeant, whose only fault is that he has got entirely the wrong angle on these damned parades. He wants us to go through the motions smartly, with lots of snap. 'Come on, boys,' he seems to be saying. 'Get the Carnival spirit. Switch on the charm. Give us the old personality.'

He actually suggested the other day that we should come on parade at the double. When we were convinced that we had really heard what we thought we had heard, we looked at one another with raised eyebrows and asked Enke to explain to this visionary that in order to attend parade we had to climb twenty-seven steep stone steps. It was unreasonable, we felt, to expect us to behave like mountain goats on a diet of biscuits about the size of aspirin tablets and one small mug of thin soup a day.

'Try to make him understand,' we urged Enke, 'that it is pretty dashed creditable of us getting on parade at all. Tell him he has sized us up all wrong. We are elderly internees, most of us with corns and swollen joints, not Alpine climbers. If we are supposed to be youths who bear 'mid snow and ice a banner with the strange device "Excelsior", there ought to be Saint Bernard dogs stationed here and there, dispensing free brandy. Ask him if he expects us to yodel.'

Enke put these points, and the man saw reason. Only once has our iron front broken down. That was the day before yesterday, when a spruce young lieutenant, a stranger to us, took over and electrified us by suddenly shouting 'Achtung!' in a voice like someone calling the cattle home across the Sands of Dee. It startled us so much that we sprang to attention like a Guards regiment.

But we were waiting for him in the evening. He shouted 'Achtung' again, and didn't get a ripple.

August 16th.

Met cook today and congratulated him on yesterday's soup. He was grateful for my kind words, for his professional pride had been wounded by grumblers who criticized the quantity. He said he could have produced more soup by adding water, but that would have weakened it, and he refused to prostitute his art. I said he was quite right and that it was the same in my business. A short story is a short story. Try to pad it out into a novel, and you lose the flavour.

August 17th.

A 'Camp incident' today. Extra parade is called, and Sergeant and three Privates go down the ranks with a spectacled internee, the man we call the Snake, who looks after the electric lights. They seem to be chasing something, and it gradually develops that the Snake has been 'insulted' by a boy who said that he would throw him into the river ... whereby, as lawyers say, our client goes in fear of his life.

To us the idea of this as a threat seems a bit comic because (a) it would require a super hurler to perform the feat, as the party of the second part would have to be lofted over a high wall, after which there would be a carry of several hundred yards, and (b) because there is nothing the majority of us would welcome more than being thrown into the river. Give us a couple of days' rations and a little money for railway expenses and then throw us into the river, and leave the rest to us ... that is our view.

We stand on parade for about three-quarters of an hour while the Snake seeks vainly for the villain of the piece. After a while, in order to narrow the search down, all those under the age of thirty are lined up apart. But does that mean that we who are in the middle and late fifties are allowed to dismiss? Not a bit of it! The Snake has distinctly stated that the Menace was a 'boy', which ought to let out at least the grandfathers. But no, we go on standing there while the Snake potters hither and thither with a questing look on his face, like a witch-doctor from one of Rider Haggard's early African romances smelling out the evil-minded, but still with no result.

Things are getting difficult. We are told that if the criminal does not confess pretty soon, we shall all be confined to barracks.

Our intelligent minds instantly spot the flaw in this. The snag in the way of confining internees to barracks is that they are jolly well confined to barracks already. About the only way you could confine us to barracks any more would be to put us in the cellar. We saw the thing was going to be a wash-out and it was. About twenty minutes later, the Sergeant, who is presumably as sick of it as we are, offers to settle it out of court if we all promise not to do it again. We do, enthusiastically, and go off to rest our feet.

Two hours later there is another parade. A strange new big pot arrives, inspects us, goes through the dormitories and disappears. We never see him again. Probably just someone slumming.

August 18th.

The coming of the biscuit has made us all more and more obsessed with the subject of food. There is a man here with whom I got friendly at Liège. A very earnest sort of bloke. He was always telling me what a wonderful spiritual experience this is and how altruistic it is bound to make us all. This morning he came to me frothing at the mouth because – so he says – other dormitories are getting more potatoes in their soup than his. I never saw a man so bitter.

The windjammer sailor tells me that all this is nothing compared with what he has been through in his time. He says his first voyage lasted three hundred and forty-five days, and that they had been living for weeks on one weevily biscuit and an inch of water a day, when they eventually fetched up at Pitcairn Island. He didn't actually say so, but I got the impression that he rather disapproved of the high living at Huy and was wondering what it was going to do to his figure.

Still no bread. We get nothing but biscuits now, thirty per man and only just visible to the naked eye. It seems to date from the day when we complained to the Kommandant that we were not getting enough bread. He took the statesmanlike course of giving us no bread at all. ('Bread?' says the windjammer sailor. 'Why, on my third voyage . . .' And then we get some revolting anecdote about biscuits and weevils.)

August 24th.

A genuine General arrived today to inspect the camp. Our spirits soared when the word went round that he was making inquiries about the food, but unfortunately the two men he asked if we were getting enough to eat were Enke and the Snake. Enke, the stoutest man in the place, said we were being starved, and the General glanced sceptically at his tummy. Enke endeavoured by waggling his waistcoat to show that there had been a lot of wastage and that the tummy was nothing to what it had been, but there was such a lot still left that the demonstration achieved nothing. The General then button-holed the Snake, who let the side down by saying that he had plenty to eat, omitting – blast him! – to add that he was getting double rations for looking after the electric light.

August 25th.

The General's visit was a wash-out. Biscuits again today. A man tells me that one of the coloured internees, who describes himself as having been in peace-time a 'dancer and bottlewasher in a circus', has been able to put by a reserve of a hundred and twenty-eight biscuits. This must be the fellow I have noticed dancing about in front of the guard-room. Apparently he amuses the German soldiers with his comedy act, and they give him bread, thus enabling him to save his biscuit ration.

All one's values change in a place like this. This revelation makes me look on the bottlewasher as a millionaire. It is like hearing someone talk of Henry Ford or the Aga Khan. As Emerson said, 'Give me health and a hundred and twenty-eight biscuits, and I will make the pomp of Emperors ridiculous.'

My friend tells me that this morning the bottlewasher's comedy fell flat with a new lot of German soldiers who have just arrived. It seems that in the recent fighting a Senegambian killed one of their crowd by biting him in the throat, and this has prejudiced them against gentlemen of colour. In fact, when they saw our coloured contingent, they recoiled and asked, 'Are they dangerous?'

This new lot of Germans are simply baffled as to who on earth we are. One of them took an internee to the dentist's this morning, and the dentist asked him if we were prisoners of war. He said he didn't think so. 'Civil prisoners?' 'No.' 'Then who are they?' The soldier said he didn't know. He seemed to look on us as just Acts of God.

I'm bound to say the whole thing puzzles me a bit, too. Why Germany should think it worth its while to round up and corral a bunch of spavined old deadbeats like myself and the rest of us it is beyond me to imagine. Silly horseplay is the way I look at it.

The idea, I suppose, is that if left at large, we would go about selling the plans of forts. But one would have thought that a single glance at me would have been enough to tell them that if somebody handed me a fort on a plate with watercress round it, I wouldn't know what to do with it.

I wouldn't even know what price to charge.

August 27th.

We were given forms to fill out today – questionnaires regarding age, health, etc. In the space allotted to Health Max Enke wrote, 'Tolerably sound but with some weakness. Reduced girth, skeletal construction more apparent,' and had to write it over again.

A great experiment is being tried. Two men have clubbed together and taken their biscuit ration to the cookhouse to be baked. They hope to get a cake, but they are running an awful risk of wasting good biscuits.

August 28th.

The cake turned out a sensational success and has revolutionized thought throughout the camp. Everybody's doing it now. One great talking point for cake is the fact that if you have false teeth you don't have to chew. Algy, soaring above mere cakes, has argued our little group into subscribing to a pudding. We all donated biscuits, and I had a tin of condensed milk and Arthur Grant a pot of jam and somebody else some sugar, so we threw it all into the venture. The result was wonderful. I have never tasted anything so good. But, as in all good things, there is a catch ... One's bit of pudding just slides down one's throat and is gone, and a man with good teeth, like myself, can make a biscuit last out half the morning with careful nibbling.

Terrible disaster at lunch today. I put my mug of soup on my suitcase and upset it. Practically all the soup went west, most of it seeping through into the interior of the suitcase. Amazing how soup can spread itself. Life seemed to become for a moment all soup. I was able to lick some of it off my shirts, but I should have fed sparingly if Algy had not given me a couple of bits of potato from his ration.

September 1st.

The pudding problem is becoming acute. Today I gave up fifteen biscuits, and I am wondering if it is worth it. By careful chewing, I could have made fifteen biscuits last out all day.

September 2nd.

Reluctantly decide to stand out of pudding quartette.

September 3rd.

Jeff went to the town to oculist's this morning and came back with a chunk of bread, given to him by sympathizer in street. He very sportingly divided it up among dormitory. Split twenty ways, it ran to about a mouthful apiece. Very welcome.

About this going to town. Internees are let out with a guard to go to dentist, oculist, etc. At first they used to smuggle in food with great caution and secrecy, one man coming back with a jam tart wrapped round his chest. Then they got bold and went out with bags and sacks, egged on by the guards, who were all for it. Jeff tells me his guard was a married man with children and hadn't been home for two years. He spoke a little English, and they became very friendly. Offered a drink, he told Jeff not to spend his money on him, but to save it for food for himself.

This golden age lasted about a week, and then men got too reckless. An unexpected Colonel found them roaming about the shops, buying up everything in sight, and the order has now gone out that no one is to be allowed down town! We are hoping that this is only temporary, as most of these *verboten* orders are.

September 4th.

Canteen started again today, after having been *verboten* for some unknown reason for quite a time. Jock got quite a lot of cheese, but we hear that the Dutch frontier has been closed, so this is probably the last cheese we shall get. (The windjammer sailor says we ought to have been with him on his fifth voyage. They made half a pound of gorgonzola last from Liverpool to

San Francisco, and towards the end, it kept escaping into the top-gallants, and had to be brought back by search parties. The more I listen to this man's conversation, the gladder I am that I did not adopt the merchant marine as a profession in my youth. It never seems to have occurred to anyone to victual the ship properly at the start of the voyage. Apparently they just bought a cheese and a few biscuits and trusted to luck. And then the breeze failed two days out, and there they were.)

September 8th.

We are suddenly told at 2.30 that we are to parade and be ready to leave. I had just washed my clothes and had to pack them all wet. We parade for two hours, and there is an issue of half a loaf of bread per man and half a sausage. We then march down the hill to the station. I am faced with the problem of how to tote my baggage. I have the suitcase I came away with, a briefcase full of papers (including copious notes for *Money in the Bank*) and the enormous suitcase which Bunny sent me, weighing a ton. Fortunately I manage to get hold of a stick and Joe McCandless, always a friend in need, shoves this through the handle of the suitcase and I take one end and he takes the other, and somehow we get it to the station. And so off into the unknown.

*　　*　　*

The next chapter, 'Journey's End', describes the arrival at Tost in Upper Silesia, where the internees from Huy were housed in the local lunatic asylum.

*　　*　　*

A man I was always very sorry for at Tost was Internee Bob Shepherd. His was quite a sad case. If we had got to Tost in 1926, instead of 1940, we should have been in Poland, for it was in that year that a plebiscite was held to decide whether this slice of territory should be German or Polish and the Poles drew the short straw.

To assist in keeping order during this plebiscite a contingent of English soldiers was sent over, and one day about a week after our arrival Internee Bob Shepherd, the camp trombonist, was seen wandering to and fro with a puzzled look on his face, like a dog confronted with some lamp-post of its puppyhood, muttering 'I have been here before'. It turned out that he had been one of the English soldiers who, like us, were quartered at the local lunatic asylum. It was the barbed wire that had prevented Bob recognizing the old place at first. It confused him, he said.

What the emotions are of a man who comes to stay at Tost Lunatic Asylum twice I cannot say, for Bob was always reticent on the point. If you asked him, he just blew his trombone in a thoughtful sort of way. But I should imagine they are pretty poignant.

Tost is no beauty spot. It lies in the heart of the sugar-beet country, and if you are going in for growing sugar-beets on a large scale, you have to make up your mind to dispense with wild, romantic scenery. There is a flat dullness about the countryside which has led many a visitor to say, 'If this is Upper Silesia, what must Lower Silesia be like?' And the charm of any lunatic asylum never strikes you immediately. You have to let it grow on you.

I came in time to be very contented in this Upper Silesian loony bin, but I was always aware that what I liked was the pleasant society rather than the actual surroundings. These screwball repositories are built for utility, not comfort. There is a bleakness about their interiors which might exercise a depressing effect if you had not the conversation of dormitory 309 to divert your thoughts. The walls are bare and the floors are bare, and when you go in or out you climb or descend echoing stone stairs. And the bars on the windows lower your spirits till you stop noticing them.

All the windows at Tost were heavily barred, even those of the dining-room, though why the most unbalanced lunatic should want to get out of a dining-room by the window when the door was at his disposal I cannot say. The gratifying result of this was to cause me to take a step up in the animal kingdom. At Huy I had felt like a water beetle. At Tost my emotions were more those of one of the residents of a monkey house at the Zoo. If I had had a perch to swing on and somebody outside pushing nuts through the bars, the illusion would have been perfect.

At first sight Tost looks as if it were near nothing, except possibly the North Pole, but actually it is but a stone's throw from Slupska, Koppienitz, Peiskretscham and Pnibw. It was not immediately that I discovered this, but when I did the lyrist in me awoke and I sat down at a table in the upper dining-room and wrote a song hit.

As follows:

A young man was sipping soda in a gilded cabaret,
When a song of home sweet home the orches*rah* did start
   to play:
And he thought he'd ought to tie a can to dreams of wealth
   and fame

And go right back to the simple shack from which he once
    had came.
    And as for his soda he did pay,
To the head waiter these words he then did say:
    'Goodbye, Broadway'.

There's a choo-choo leaving for dear old Pnibw
Where the black-eyed susans grow
    (I wanna go, I wanna go).
There's a girl who's waiting in dear old Pnibw
    (Oh, vo-de-o-de-o-de-o)
      Tender and dreamy,
      Yearning to see me.

There are girls in Koppienitz and girls in Peiskretscham
And possibly in Slupska too,
But the honey for my money is the one who's sitting
    knitting
Underneath the magnolias in dear old Pnibw.
America, I love you with your eyes of blue,
But I'm going back, back, back to the land where dreams
    come true.
P-n-i-b-w spells Pnibw,
And, as Ogden Nash would say, what the hell did you
    think it was going to do?

It is a little rough at present, as I have not had time to polish
it, but the stuff is there. It has the mucus.

The journey to Tost took three days and three nights, and it
was rendered more trying than it need have been by the fact
that we were not given the slightest clue as to how long it was

going to last. We just sat and sat and sat and the train rolled on and on and on.

It was rather like being on the ship of the dead in *Outward Bound*.

A little trying the whole thing was. The Citadel of Huy had had its defects, but at least when there we had known where we were. Now we did not know where we were or where we were going, if anywhere. It seemed to us quite possible that the engine-driver had been told just to keep on taking us about the countryside until Headquarters had cleaned up a heavy lot of outstanding business on its desk and was at leisure to get around to deciding where it wanted us dumped.

And even if the man had received definite instructions as to our destination, he might have forgotten them. The conviction to which we came on the second day was that he had lost his way and was too proud to make inquiries. Sometimes he would stop at a siding for an hour or two, and we knew that he was thinking things out.

'Now let me see,' we could hear him saying, an elbow on his knee and his chin supported by his hand, like Rodin's "Penseur". 'They told me at Huy to go straight on till I came to the church and then bear to the left. Or was it to the right? And was it the church or the duck-pond? Well, anyway, I'm pretty sure I'm going in the right *direction*, because I'm in Germany and if I'd been going the wrong way I should be in France. I suppose I *am* in Germany? There's a thing one wants to get straight about before going any further. Hey, mister, I'm looking for a place called Tost.'

The passer-by pauses and stands listening to the hiss of the steam in the boiler.

'I don't like the sound of that engine,' he says. 'Sort of wheezy noise it's making. I'd say your sprockets weren't running true with the differential gear.'

This offends the driver.

'Never mind about my engine,' he retorts, nettled. 'You leave my engine alone and it'll leave you alone. I want to go to Tost.'

'Where?'

'Tost.'

'All right. Don't be long.'

'Do you know the way there?'

'Where?'

'Tost.'

'How do you spell it?'

'T-o-s-t.'

'Oh, *Tost*? I thought you said Vienna.'

'You know Tost?'

'Never heard of it.'

'Well, anyway, is this Germany?'

'I'm afraid I couldn't tell you,' says the passer-by. 'I'm a stranger in these parts myself.'

He saunters on, and the engine-driver rises to his feet with a weary grunt.

'Well,' he reflects, 'I suppose the only thing is to keep going on. Must get somewhere, if you keep going on. Stands to reason. Ho hum, back to the old grind.'

And when we did get to Tost he passed it without a glance and took us on to Gleiwitz, where we remained at a siding for six hours before somebody happened along and told him to go back till he came to Farmer Schmidt's barn and then left as far as the old mill and after that he'd better ask somebody.

For several days after our arrival I had a private yard to myself; not through any special dispensation on the part of the authorities, but because I was the only man with the quick intelligence to realize that we were allowed there. It lay in the angle formed by the main building and was fenced in with wire, and its whole aspect was of a place that is *verboten*. You would see men staring wistfully into it, and you knew that they were saying 'Boy! What a place to go and spit', but they never got any further than peering in.

I was the first who took a chance on it. I felt a little breathless the first day when soldiers passed, but I heard no raucous cry of 'Raus' and decided that all was well. And so for quite a time it was. For some reason the story went through the camp that I had been allotted this haven by the Lagerführer as a special tribute to my general worth, and though faces continued to peer in, nobody ventured to crash the gate. I basked there in the sunshine alone, and very pleasant it was. For the artist soul loves to muse, and it is much easier musing in solitude than when you are rubbing elbows with thirteen hundred of your fellow men.

It could not last. Came a day when a venturous Dutchman faltered in and finding that nothing happened stayed in. He was followed by others. Presently the spitters began to arrive, and one morning, seeking my favourite corner, I found it occupied by my old friend Spotty, the camp's champion spitter, playing like a Versailles fountain. I knew then that the end had come.

Spotty, by the way, was the only man I have ever met who could express his every emotion by spitting. Where you or I would have rapped out an oath or thrown off an epigram, Spotty spat. It was constant association with him that inspired me to begin a poem which, if I ever get it finished, will be in all the anthologies. These were the opening lines:

> This is my case
> Against the human race:
> It
> Has a tendency to spit
> On mountain, vale and lea
> And frequently on me ...

But here, I must confess, I wronged Spotty. He always avoided what Shakespeare would call the Spit Direct. The Spit Courteous, the Spit Modest, the Spit Churlish, the Spit Quarrelsome and the Spit with circumstance, yes, but never the Spit Direct. He would shoot all round you till you felt like a knife-thrower's assistant, but you were really quite safe. His control was perfect, and there was nothing you could teach him about allowing for windage. (Young spitters *must* remember to allow for windage. On several occasions at Tost members of the crew of the *Orama*, operating from their window on the fourth floor, very nearly missed me as I sat in the yard below through overlooking this.)

The windjammer sailor says that there has been no real spitting since the days of sail. Precision in the true sense of the word, what they would have called precision in the fo'c'sle of the *Bertha May*, in which he made his eighth voyage, vanished with the coming of steam. Naturally almost anybody can hit a sitting author, but let them try to pick off a passing albatross in a high gale, said the windjammer sailor. That is where Class tells.

Checking in at an Ilag where you may be going to stay for several years is a much more elaborate affair than taking up a temporary abode in a prison or a barracks. There is about it a certain ceremonial pomp which, if you have just come from a three-days' and three-nights' trip on a train, you find a little trying. By the time the formalities had been concluded, we were in rather weary mood and the general feeling was that after all this Tost had better be good.

When we actually arrived at Tost station, we felt more lenient towards that engine-driver and less inclined to blame him for having experienced a little difficulty in finding the place. It consists of some planks dumped down in the middle of the woods, and it was not surprising that the man at the controls should have failed to recognize it for what it was. Only when we observed that the platform was filled with steel-helmeted soldiers and the compartment doors began to be unlocked did we ourselves suspect that this was where we got off.

We could have betted what would happen next. Yes, there was a parade. Then the baggage which looked too heavy to be carried was sorted out from the lighter stuff and loaded on trucks. We then started to march to the village, distant about two miles, and eventually found ourselves parading again outside the White House.

Here there was a restful pause of about an hour and three-quarters, pleasantly occupied in shifting from one leg to the other and wondering when we were going to eat. It was so long since we had done so that we were afraid we might have forgotten the technique. Then, at long last, soldiers appeared carrying large wicker-work baskets, and from these, like benevolent Santa Clauses, the Corporals produced porcelain bowls, tin mugs, spoons, knives and forks, which they proceeded to distribute – to each man

A bowl
A mug

A spoon
A knife
and
A fork.

They passed these out in a careless, off-hand way, as if there was nothing unusual about it all, but gasps of amazement escaped us and we looked at one another with rising eyebrows, awed by such lavishness. This, we felt, was stepping high. At Huy we had had no forks or spoons and the tin mug which we used for coffee in the morning had to serve for soup at midday. And at Liège we had been obliged to get along with what we could dig out of the dustbin. It was rather like coming to stay with a millionaire uncle after living for years on the wrong side of the railroad tracks. One regretted not having brought one's white *piqué* waistcoat and one's copy of *Manners and Rules of Good Society*.

I mentioned this to Spotty, who was next to me in the ranks, and he spat twice. I knew what he meant. He was saying '*And* one's gold toothpick'.

As we numbered eight hundred, the distribution took a considerable time, as did the subsequent march to the cookhouse, and the filling of the porcelain bowls with soup. But we were so proud of having porcelain bowls and it was so jolly seeing soup again that our spirits rose, and we looked forward gaily to the prospect of collecting our mattresses and turning in for the night.

It was, accordingly, something of a shock to discover that there weren't going to be any mattresses. When we returned to the White House, we found that we had got to sleep on the floor. And if anybody wants a testing experience, let him travel for three days and three nights on hard wooden seats in a crowded compartment of a train and then turn in for the night on a cold stone floor. In the little brochure which I am preparing, entitled 'Stone Floors I Have Slept On', this one at the White House at Tost will be singled out for special mention. I do not accuse the German Authorities of having deliberately iced it, but the illusion of being a pound of butter in a refrigerator was extraordinarily strong and grew during the night. A philosopher, I suppose, would have consoled himself with the thought that he was not going bad.

In the morning we were paraded and marched off in batches to the laundry above the cookhouse, where we found a number of enormous wooden tubs and were enabled to scour off the geological strata which had accumulated during our journey. To save time, three men used a tub simultaneously, and I remember thinking that a word of apology was owing to the two who were going to share mine. I felt that I ought really to have been sent to the cleaner's.

I need not have worried. I drew Spotty and the windjammer sailor, who were even more deeply encrusted than I was. But even we, it seemed, could not claim the European record. The windjammer sailor said we ought to have seen Joe Purkiss at the conclusion of the voyage of the *Saucy Sally* from Pernambuco to Hull. They had to dig him out with spades.

After that, all pink and rosy, we took our baggage to the lower dining-room, where it was closely examined, everything of a suspicious nature being pounced on and removed. I can still recall the agony with which I watched the notes for *Money in the Bank* being trousered by a stern official, who plainly thought that he had got hold of something hot in the way of espionage codes and could hardly wait to pop it into the incinerator.

In this connection, I would point out the curious fact that from the German view-point there is something fishy about Tennyson's poems but not about Shakespeare's plays. They impounded my Tennyson, returning it to me some weeks later after it had presumably been gone through for subversive matter, but Shakespeare got by without a hitch. It just shows – I don't know what, but something.

We were then given our numbers and the metal discs which we were told must never leave our necks. And I must admit that my sensitive spirit, which had been keeping its end up nicely until now, winced at this point, as if it had bitten into a bad oyster. I had the unpleasant feeling of having sunk in the social scale. In Loos Prison I had at least been Widhorse. Here I was merely Number 796.

After that we were sent off to find our dormitories. Upon the choice of these hung our future happiness or discomfort. The internee's social life centres in his dormitory, and it is essential, accordingly, that he gets into the right one. I cannot imagine a more delightful one than mine – Number 309, the Pride of the Ilag. Presided over by George Travers and his lieutenant Sam Mayo and containing such rare souls as Arthur Grant, Sandy Youl, George Pickard, Smyth, Czarny, Tom Sarginsson, Max Enke, Charlie Webb, Mackenzie, the Moores, father and son, and Joe McCandless, it was an earthly paradise. Its only flaw was that old Bert Haskins was not a member of it.

None of us snored: and if Arthur Grant sometimes started giving a golf lesson in his sleep and somebody else dreamed that he was watching a football match and suddenly sprang from between the blankets at two in the morning with yells of advice and encouragement, these were small things and did nothing to mar the general harmony.

This leads into a chapter entitled 'The Dormitory'.

What its slice of gorgonzola is to the cheesemite, his dormitory is to the internee. It is the only place where he can really nestle and invite his soul, the only spot where he can find something moderately soft to sit on. Elsewhere throughout the establishment there are nothing but benches of an indescribable hardness, very wearing on the fleshy parts, but in the dormitory he has his bed.

Dormitories at Tost were of all sizes, ranging from Number 302, the Belgian room, with its hundred and ten occupants, to the luxury suite which the Camp Captain shared with the Camp Adjutant. Number 309 was a long room with two doors, three large tables with benches, a small table where George Travers worked, three electric lights and seven windows. It also contained three wooden chairs and a stool. Its floor was of wood, its walls distempered. There were no cupboards and no hooks. When you went to bed, you dropped your clothes on the floor or slept in them.

The window-sills were used as storage depots for tin cans, cardboard boxes, cold potatoes and other properties. When you wanted to open a window you dropped these on the floor. The space between the double windows served as a frigidaire. That was where you put your butter and what was left of your potted meat. There were two radiators, useful for heating potatoes in the winter.

The population of Dormitory 309 fluctuated between a high of 68 and a low of 57. (But that was in the very early days, before there were any new arrivals.) During most of my time at Tost we stayed firm at 66, and our constant endeavour was to prevent our numbers being added to. It was not that we were unsociable; we just wanted to be able to breathe. The room had originally been designed to accommodate thirty, which made sixty-six a nice cosy number by internee standards. Sixty-seven, we felt, would have been a squash.

Every time a fresh bunch of internees filtered into the camp we sat bristling and defiant, prepared to resist to the utmost all attempts to ring them in on us.

I have the following entry in my diary for December 11th, 1940:

Today was one of our fractious days, when we become more like small boys than ever. Word was brought by the Corporal that a man from the sailors' room was to be moved to our dormitory. Apparently he had asked the authorities if he might join us, as he was getting on in years and disliked the boisterousness of the younger set in his room.

We appreciated the compliment implied in his desire to be with us, but regretted that we were compelled to reject this contribution owing to lack of space. We pointed out to the Corporal that we were wedged into a solid mass already and that the addition of a sailor would make life impossible.

The Corporal, speaking through Max Enke as interpreter, pleaded that it was a very small sailor. We stood firm. We all admired the Merchant Navy enormously, and only a couple of days before had made up a collection of clothes for the *Orama* boys, who had had to go overboard without stopping to pack, but we insisted that even a powder-monkey or a midshipmite would ruin our comfort irretrievably.

Unfortunately we had to say all this in English, which didn't register, and Enke, who has one of those ingenious minds and loves trying to solve problems, he being the Camp's chess champion, started to demonstrate to the Corporal that by squeezing the beds on our side of the room together space could be made for one more bed.

Charlie Webb thereupon flatly refused to move his bed an inch, saying that by international law he was entitled to the present amount of space between beds. Enke, swiftly changing his strategy of attack, said that Charlie's chair wasn't really Charlie's chair but a communal chair, and that Charlie had a nerve treating as a private chair what was in fact a chair provided for the use of the entire dormitory, and Charlie said he wasn't talking about the bloody chair but about the bloody space between the bloody beds.

I thought his point well taken. It so often happens in these arguments of ours that people wander from the main issue. I have known a discussion on the Life to Come, inspired by one of the Salvation Army Colonel's sermons, to change in the space of a quarter of a minute into an inquiry as to who put their potted meat on somebody else's butter.

Arthur Grant then urged Enke to listen to the voice of his better self, accusing him of being jealous of us single-bedders just because he, Enke, happened to be sleeping in a double-decker. These things, he pointed out, were simply the luck of the draw.

Charlie Webb said that the whole question of space between beds had been thoroughly thrashed out at the Hague Convention.

Enke, coming back strongly, accused Arthur of treating the radiator as a private radiator, when it was really a communal radiator. I said Arthur didn't treat the radiator as a private radiator, but Enke had his answer to this. He said: 'Well, you keep your suitcase between your bed and the wall, which makes your bed stand out six inches from the wall, and it ought to be up against the wall.' McCandless, coming to my rescue, said: 'Well, you upset my coffee last night.'

Charlie Webb said if we didn't believe him, go to the Hague. Just go to the Hague, mention his name and ask them.

Enke was starting what promised to be a longish speech about McCandless inviting friends from other dormitories to come and sit on his bed, when somebody told him to put a sock in it, and he said: 'I won't put a sock in it. Can't I talk?' To which Smyth, who has a simple dignity which we all respect, said: 'Oh, for God's sake go and boil your damned head. The trouble with you is that you're always talking. When you're not talking about chess, you're talking rot', this closing the debate.

It was exactly like the sort of squabble one used to have in a junior dormitory at school, and when you consider that nobody taking part in it was under the age of fifty, I think it does us credit. Internment may have its drawbacks, but it certainly restores one's youth.

I don't know how we managed it, but we didn't get the sailor. It was one of our notable victories.

When sixty-six men lounge all day and sleep all night in a room designed for thirty, the problem of ventilation is bound to arise; and it was unfortunate for those of us who had always been accustomed to breathe at night that many of our companions had for years been married to French wives and had imbibed from them those strong views on the closed window which are so characteristic of French wives. A Frenchwoman of the sturdy lower middle class considers that to inhale air in which a spoon will not stand upright is to court pneumonia.

From the moment of our arrival a silent war – and not always so silent, at that – had broken out between the fresh air brigade and the fug lovers, causing the only jarring note that ever disturbed the pleasant harmony of Dormitory 309 for more than a passing moment. The forces ranged in opposition were numerically unequal, but we fresh airers, though heavily outnumbered, enjoyed an important strategical advantage. Five of the seven windows in the room were always kept hermetically sealed, but the other two were commanded by the beds of Arthur Grant, myself, McCandless and Smyth, and we usually managed to sneak one open for a while.

This sometimes led to complications, as witness the entry in my diary for February 27th, 1941:

> Dormitory row this morning. Last night McCandless opened his window after Lights Out and got away with it till about midnight. Then Enke across the way became aware of coolness and feeling that he was entitled by international law to frowst at night lumbered over and shut it.
>
> In the morning Mac discovered that his cold coffee had been upset, either by Enke or by the breeze. The row arose from a desire on the part of all to fix the responsibility. Enke stoutly denied having upset the coffee, and Mac said he must have done it. High words and black looks.
>
> What makes the thing so dramatic and lifts it to the level

of a crisis is that this is the fourth time Mac's coffee has been upset; once by me, once by George Travers, and twice by Enke. He puts the stuff on the window-sill in a cloth-covered jam-pot, which nobody would recognize for what it is. I know that on the occasion when I was the guilty party, I thought there must be hairbrushes or something inside, and nobody more surprised than myself when I found cold coffee gushing out.

Charlie Webb made the best suggestion for the avoidance of further disasters of the sort. 'Why don't you drink your blasted coffee at the proper time?' he asked. 'Nobody but you would be able to swallow the muck cold, let alone hoard it up as a treat for the morning.' I must say I thought he was right. Mac is a man of strange pleasures.

Yet in spite of the difficulty of keeping the atmosphere from resembling that which makes the French provincial home so memorable to all who have had to experience it, I loved my dormitory dearly. It was not too good, perhaps, at six o'clock on a cold winter morning, when the steam and electric light had not been turned on and we were all getting up simultaneously and tramping over each other in the dark as we groped for our clothes, but from seven onward it was as jolly and cosy a place as you could wish for.

It is difficult to say when it was actually at its best – at nine in the morning, when we brewed our cup of tea; between two and four in the afternoon, when we took our siesta; between seven and eight in the evening, with the harmonicas going; or at nine at night, when the lights went out and one lay in bed staring drowsily at the barred window and listening to the raconteurs at the top end telling their stories.

I have never slept better in my life than on that plank bed, and I am convinced that the secret of health and well-being is to turn in at nine and get up at six.

To make a really luxurious plank bed you need four planks. Owing to a shortage of wood, we got only three. We could arrange these as we liked – a solid mass of planks in the middle, if we pleased, or, if we preferred it, a plank here, a plank there and a plank there. The great thing was to get the springy one in the middle.

Getting the pillow just the right height was always a difficulty. Some men used suitcases for bolsters, but I found that I obtained the best results with a sweater, a cardigan, a pair of trousers, a Red Cross parcel and the Complete Works of William Shakespeare. Shakespeare, who wrote not for an age but for all time, produced exactly the right amount of stuff to make him an ideal foundation on which to build.

Internees for the most part sleep in layers. There were only seven single beds in Dormitory 309, and it may surprise people that a dreamy artist like myself was able to secure one. The explanation is that when the rush began I had the shrewdness to stick close to Algy, whom I had recognized from the very beginning of my internment as one of those men who always manage to get things. He had been a Quartermaster-Sergeant in the first world war, and once a Quartermaster-Sergeant, always a Quartermaster-Sergeant.

'Algy,' I said to him, as I surveyed the milling mob, 'I place my affairs unreservedly in your hands. Consider yourself my accredited agent.'

And when all the tumult and the shouting had died, there he was with a single bed for himself and a single bed for me in the best spot in the room, right under the window.

I had become so used at Huy to burrowing into straw at night like a rat in a barn that when I found myself with a bed, and not only a bed but a pillow (stuffed with straw), a mattress (the same) and a cotton sheet and two blankets, I received an impression of almost Oriental magnificence, which never quite left me during my stay at Tost. You might say that the place had me dazzled from the start.

When I came to mingle with the internees from Holland, I found that they judged their surroundings by different standards, and were inclined to be captious. It appeared that they had been brought to Tost from a camp near the Hague where the conditions, to hear them tell it, must have been rather like those prevailing in a Sultan's palace of the better class. To them Tost was a distinct come-down. To me, who had come up from the slums, it seemed staggering in its luxury.

'But we've got *beds*!' I used to say.

'Plank beds,' sneered the Dutchmen with a wistful look in their eyes as they recalled the swansdown on which they had slept in their last place. (If you didn't like swansdown, you could have rose petals.)

Well, after Huy, any Ilag that gave me a bed, plank or otherwise, was Claridge's to me, and I was prepared to write in the visitors' book to that effect.

And here is a chapter entitled:

LAGERFÜHRERS, LANDESCHÜTZEN AND WHAT NOT

Two things about a regular internment camp impress themselves upon you very soon after your arrival there. The first is

274

the ingenuity with which privacy has been guarded against, the second the smooth efficiency with which the place functions. There was at Tost none of the casual sloppiness which had been the keynote of Liège and Huy. Everything had been organized. Shortly after we clocked in a manifesto was issued from up top and passed round the dormitories.

It ran thus:

ILAG VIII (TOST)

Ilag Tost consists of—
1. (a) The outer camp with headquarters, Administration Offices, Barracks of the Landeschützen.
   (b) Internee camp with barbed wire fence.
2.   Kommandant of Camp and Deputy.
3. (a) All contact between the internees and headquarters goes through the Lagerführer.
   (b) Internees have been detailed into four companies and those subdivided into platoons. German N.C.O.s will act as Company Commanders. The platoons are commanded by suitable internees.
   (c) Internee Officers:

Camp Captain	Floor Wardens
Deputy Camp Captains (2)	Room Wardens
Camp Adjutant	

   The duty of the Camp Captain is to put into force the orders of the Kommandant and his Deputy and supervise their carrying out. He also reports to the Kommandant through his Deputy, all complaints, if he considers them justified.

(d) In each company a Room Warden is to be appointed by the Lagerführer on the recommendation of the Camp Captain. The Room Wardens have the same duties to their Companies as Camp Captains to the Camp as a whole.

Now I can see, of course, that in getting the stuff down on paper for our benefit the authorities meant well, and I could see it at the time. But the trouble about a document like this is that it suffers from the same defect as the Plan of House, showing Squire's room, Aunt Isobel's room, Lord jasper's room, Cyril's room, Mabel's room, cupboard on landing and bloodstained section at foot of stairs (marked X) where body of masked dancer was found with dagger between third and fourth ribs, which writers of detective stories always insert at about Page 20. It is intended to be helpful, but isn't.

You look at this manifesto, but you don't take it in. I still find my mind skidding off it as I read, just as it did when I read it for the first time over a mug of tea and a cheese sandwich in the dormitory.

'George,' I said to George Travers, 'what the hell is all this about?'

He confessed himself baffled. And when a thing baffles George Travers, it may be written off as beyond the scope of human ingenuity.

It will be best, therefore, if you don't give it another thought. Just forget you ever saw the thing and preserve an open mind while I tell you in a few simple words exactly:

How An Internment Camp Is Run

First Get Your Internees:

These are indispensable, for nothing looks sillier than a prison camp without prisoners. Internees of all sorts and sizes may be readily obtained at little cost and trouble. They come in every shade from midnight black to primrose yellow, or, like me, a pretty pink. Having stocked up with internees,

Buy Plenty Of Barbed Wire:

You can have lots of fun decorating the place with this. It will bring back old memories of the days when you used to hang up the mistletoe at Christmas.

Lice:

These may be provided, but probably the internees will bring their own.

You are now all set to begin, and you start off with a Lagerführer, some Captains, some Lieutenants, as many Sergeants and Corporals as you wish and a couple of hundred privates, and you put them in barracks outside the barbed wire.

To these, however, we need pay no attention, for they do not enter into the internee's life. It is nice to know they are there, in case of burglars, but apart from that they don't mean a thing to the internee. The only members of the crowd he ever sees are the Sentries, who are always getting relieved. I have been in the grounds of Ilag Tost at every hour of the day, and whenever I was there somebody was relieving the Sentries. German soldiers earn their money easily.

Practically, then, you need not let this Outer Camp worry you at all. Just dismiss it from your mind. All that interests you is:

The Inner Camp

comprising the buildings and all that portion of the grounds and messuages which is enclosed in the barbed wire.

The inner camp is a seething mass of internees presided over by the Lagerführer and four German Corporals, one to each floor. You also find Sergeants drifting about occasionally, and I have seen a Captain and a German dog, but the great thing is to avoid elaboration of detail, so forget everything except

The Lagerführer

and

The Corporals

and then we shall really get somewhere.

I cannot impress it too strongly upon the young internee that the great thing, when he is starting out in business, is to have a good Lagerführer. Get a bad one, and you're sunk. An outstanding example of the bad Lagerführer was the marble-eyed old dug-out who was in charge of us at Huy. It was not that he was actually hostile, oppressing us and grinding us under the iron heel. It was just that he was one of Nature's stinkers, and for the comfort of internees a complete absence of stinkers in the outer camp is essential.

At Tost we were lucky. Oberleutnant Buchelt, to whom the Kommandant had 'delegated the supervision of the inner camp', was nothing less than the answer to an internee's prayer. He might have been constructed from our own blueprints. There is no actual obligation binding a Lagerführer to do any-thing more than see that order is maintained and appear once a day on parade, but Buchelt was working all the time in our

interests; not, it was rumoured, without a good deal of opposition on the part of the men higher up, who held the view that
when you have given internees a nice lunatic asylum to live in
you have done all that can be expected of you.

He had the White House thrown open, started the library
and the *Tost Times*, encouraged education and entertainments,
procured for us beer, boiling water and cook stoves, got us permission to go to the sports field in the village, held the parades
indoors instead of out in the yard, allowed smoking in the
corridors and got the ban against looking out of the corridor
windows lifted.

This last concession may not sound much, but it made all
the difference to our comfort. The corridor is the internee's
club, and a clubman's whole enjoyment of a club depends on
his being allowed to sit in the window goggling out like a fish
in an aquarium. In the beginning it was *streng verboten* so much
as to glance sideways when passing a corridor window, and
scarcely a day passed without the Sentry on the path below
reporting members who had been unable to resist the urge.

It was not that there was anything much to see when you did
look out; just a village street with a deserted beer garden across
the way; but that mattered little to us. We did not ask for the
Grand Canyon or the Taj Mahal. What we wanted was to
stand there and goggle. And this, thanks to Oberleutnant
Buchelt, we were finally permitted to do. I am happy to say that
the privilege was only once abused, when the Sentry reported
that some internees on the second floor had been blowing
kisses at him. But this was in the Spring, when that sort of
thing is always liable to happen.

So much for the Lagerführer. As for the Corporals – Ginger,
Rosebud, Pluto and Donald Duck – they gave us no cause for

complaint. It was their job to see that we were counted before the Lagerführer came on parade and to pop up unexpectedly out of traps and catch us smoking in the corridor during prohibited hours, and they performed these duties with reasonable courtliness and suavity.

On the third floor we had Rosebud – of whom our only criticism was that he used to burst into the dormitory like the Charge of the Light Brigade at six a.m. and shout 'Auf!' at the top of his voice. And this was remedied later. Internee Mackenzie, who spoke German fluently, took him aside and told him that 'Auf!' was a little abrupt and hurt our feelings, besides making us think that a bomb had hit the building.

A few days later he had got him saying 'Git opp', but even this did not satisfy Mackenzie. He was a man who before becoming an internee had run a school for problem children in Warsaw, and he had infinite patience in training the budding mind. With gentle persistence he kept at it, and one morning we were all enchanted by a musical 'Git opp, gentlemen, if you please'. It was amazing what a difference it made.

Co-operating with the Lagerführer and the Corporals, we have, as the manifesto informed us,

> The Camp Captain,
> The Camp Adjutant,
> The Deputy Camp Captains (2),
> The Floor Wardens and the Room Wardens.

Of these the Room Wardens rank lowest in the social scale – a Deputy Camp Captain, for instance, would go into dinner before a Room Warden – but they are able to console themselves with the thought that it is they who do all the real work about the place.

Let us turn the searchlight on the activities of their colleagues, beginning with those almost inanimate objects, the Floor Wardens.

The Floor Wardens may try to make us think that they earn the double rations which go with their job by sweating themselves to the bone warding the floors, but we are too astute to be fooled. One simple question is enough to unmask their pretentions. If a Floor Warden's duties had involved even the merest suggestion of work, would Jock Monaghan and Algy have become Floor Wardens? We rather fancy we need say no more.

None of these living corpses ever did a stroke of honest toil. There were eight of them in a room at the end of our corridor, and they used to lie on their beds all day eating their double rations and dropping cigarette ashes on the floor which was their sacred charge. A fat lot of warding they did. I don't suppose the floor knew they were there. Lilies of the field, that's what they were, just lilies of the field. I said as much to Spotty one day.

'Spotty,' I said, 'they're simply lilies of the field, nothing more.'

And Spotty spat at a passing fly, and I knew that what he was saying in his peculiar way was 'How right you are, my dear fellow'.

(The story that I tried to become a Floor Warden and was rejected has, I admit, a certain substance in fact. That is to say, there were informal conversations on the subject, in the course of which – with no thought of double rations in my mind but purely out of public spirit, because I thought they ought to have a good man – I indicated my willingness to take office. But the fact that I was not chosen has nothing to do with the heat of the above remarks, which are dictated entirely by a civic conscience.)

So much for the Floor Wardens. Let us leave a distasteful subject. What of the Deputy Camp Captains (2)? Slightly more active than the human sloths to whom I have been alluding (with their double rations, forsooth), they bustle about, trying to look as if the whole welfare of the Ilag depended on them, but, coming right down to it, what do they *do*? They follow the Lagerführer up and down the ranks at morning parade, and that is all.

They don't even try to make a race of it. Many a time, standing at attention in the corridor and watching the Lagerführer round into the straight with Deputy Camp Captains Greenways and Tom Sarginsson lying a couple of lengths behind, I have felt that all that was required on the part of the last-named (my Selection for the Day), was a sudden spurt and a quick challenge and have muttered under my breath 'Come on, Tom'. But when the numbers went up on the board, it was always the same story.

1. Lagerführer.
2. First Deputy Camp Captain.
3. Second Deputy Camp Captain.
   Also Ran, Corporal.

My private belief is that the thing was fixed.

The Camp Adjutant's existence was even more languorous. He just didn't do *anything*. Picture in your mind a Turkish odalisque on a warm day in Stamboul, and you will have the Camp Adjutant.

Nor was the Camp Captain's daily task of a nature to tax an able-bodied man. He acted as a connecting link between the internees and the Lagerführer, going to see the latter in his office once a week with hard-luck stories gleaned from the rabble – that is to say me and the rest of the boys.

If, for instance, the coffee had been cold two days in succession, we of the proletariat told the Camp Captain, who told the Lagerführer, who told the Kommandant, who presumably cursed the cook, and if the cook excused himself on the plea that the boiler had burst, made him sacrifice his chewing-gum to mend it.

It was also the Camp Captain's duty to come to us on parade after the Lagerführer's departure and say 'Gentlemen, one moment, please', and then scold us for our sins and threaten frightful penalties, like a short-tempered nurse with a family of children who are not too strong in the head. He would appear and announce that if we looked out of the corridor windows we would be deprived for a month of the privilege of writing letters; that if we smoked in the corridor, we would be forbidden to smoke anywhere in the building; that if we shuffled our feet on parade we would be dragged out of bed and made to parade again. We would stare at him in an owlish way, gently shuffling our feet, and then light our pipes and go and look out of the corridor windows.

Occasionally he would get things mixed. One night he informed us that from tomorrow on we must move our heads as the Lagerführer passed on parade and follow him with our eyes. It was, he said, a special order that had gone out, and the penalty for not obeying it was – I forget what, but something lingering with boiling oil in it. It was only after a blushing Lagerführer had hurried coyly up and down the ranks next morning under the penetrating scrutiny of two hundred men, each with his eyes bulging like a snail's and performing the motion picture gesture known as the slow double take, that the

Camp Captain returned and explained that there had been a slight error. What he had meant to say was that we must *not* move our heads as the Lagerführer passed on parade and follow him with our eyes.

It straightened out the whole thing.

Well, that is what a Camp Captain's job is, and you can't say that it is very strenuous or makes any great demand on the intelligence. I possess few of the qualities which go to make an executive, but I have always felt that I could have been a Camp Captain without straining a sinew. But I wouldn't have become a Room Warden to please a dying grandmother.

Each dormitory, as soon as it has fixed up the distribution of beds and put its potted meat on the window-sill, elects a Room Warden and points at him with pride ... and also with that gentle pity which the kind-hearted always feel when they regard the fellow whom Fate has called upon to be the Patsy, the Squidge or, putting it another way, the man who has been left holding the baby. They know what he has let himself in for.

In Dormitory 309 the People's Choice was good old George Travers, in private life the proprietor of a *café* at Arras, as fine a man as ever worked like a beaver all day and said 'Well, good night all' a quarter of an hour after Lights Out.

You take George, now. Never idle for a moment. He improved each shining hour and perspired at every pore. He was a kind of combination of Postmaster-General, nursemaid, laundry van and messenger boy. He had to sort out and distribute incoming mail, see that outgoing mail was properly addressed, supply us with letter cards, collect letter cards when written, give out clean towels, collect dirty towels, distribute clean sheets, collect dirty sheets, put up the parcels list on the board, fill up forms, represent the dormitory at the canteen and hound us out of the room before morning and evening parade and line us up and count us, remembering who were absent in hospital, getting parcels, on fatigue and so on.

And when he had done all this, the Floor Warden would saunter along, bulging with his double rations, and say 'Everything Okay, George?' and that completed the Floor Warden's duties.

High up on the list of World's Workers I Have Met comes the name of George Travers. The canteen aspect of his job alone was enough to intimidate anyone but a man of chilled steel.

Fairly early in our sojourn at Tost it was discovered that if thirteen hundred men go to a canteen in a body and try to get served simultaneously, confusion results, so it was decreed that all orders must be placed through the Room Wardens. You went to George Travers and said: 'George, I want six of beer, a pair of shoelaces, some salt, some saccharine, half a dozen pencils, as much paper as you can get and one of those little gadgets, I forget what they're called, but you know what I mean,' and he would say, 'Rightyho'.

And then fifty other men would come to him with their commissions, and he would say 'Rightyho'. And before you knew where you were he was back in the room, having carried the stuff across the yard and up three flights of stairs, and nothing forgotten or left behind.

Only the fact that I am writing this bare-headed prevents me at this point raising my hat to George ('What a man') Travers.

And finally a chapter entitled 'The Eats'.

Food!

That magic word, at whose sound the internee starts like a war-horse hearing the bugle.

It may seem rather gross of me to devote a whole chapter to the subject of food. Already there has been quite a good deal about it in this book, and I can hear spiritual-minded critics asking disgustedly: 'Did this man never think of anything but his stomach?'

The answer is 'Never' – or, at least, 'Very seldom'.

Under certain conditions the mind is bound to dwell on food. Shackleton once told me that when he was in the Polar seas, he used to dream every night that he was running about a field chasing those three-cornered jam tarts which were such a feature of life at our mutual school. And if that was how Shackleton felt, I am not ashamed of having felt that way myself.

It is not as if I had been the only one to give food priority in my mind. We were thirteen hundred internees with but a single thought. A bevy of tapeworms could not have been more pre-occupied with the matter of nourishment than the inmates of Ilag VIII. Some of us played darts, and some of us sang hymns to the accompaniment of a piano which would have been the better for half an hour with William Cartmell. Some of us walked in the park of an afternoon, and some of us took off our boots and slept. Some of us crouched over the chessboard, and some of us studied Spanish. But whether we were hurling the dart or bellowing the hymn, saying 'Check' or whatever it is that people say when they are learning Spanish, subconsciously we were all thinking of food.

At the sight of it, even if it was only barley soup, our hearts leaped up as if we had beheld a rainbow in the sky. We sprang at the black pudding like wolves at a Russian peasant. Even the windjammer sailor, a man who, having passed his formative years in the society of weevily biscuits, might have been supposed to be above human weakness, never failed to show visible emotion when the whistle blew for meals.

Before lunch we would speculate as to what we were going to have for lunch. After lunch we would discuss what we had had for lunch, generally in a derogatory spirit, for we were not easy critics. You may take it as a fact that no matter how apparently absorbed an internee may be in some passing task or recreation, his thoughts are really on his last or his next meal. And when he talks, he talks of little else.

A man told me once that, sickening of the universal topic, he followed Father Reeves, the Roman Catholic priest, and myself round the park one morning, hoping to get a bit of mental and spiritual uplift. What he actually drew was a discussion of the respective merits of sauerkraut and those peculiar slices of sausage which we used to call 'rubber heels' and some rather strong remarks on my part on swedes, criticizing sharply the habit of these vegetables of swimming in a curious black juice which looks like swamp water.

This, I should mention, was in the early days of our stay, before parcels started coming in and we were at liberty to turn our thoughts into broader fields. If he had caught me a few weeks later, he might have heard something good about neo-post-vorticist poetry or the influence of James Joyce on the younger English novelists. But I'm not sure. Even when we were living highest my conversation was always a little apt to touch on the browsing and sluicing.

With me, during the lean times at Huy and through the first few weeks at Tost, the obsession took the form of a wild regret that when I had been in the midst of plenty, I had not made better use of my opportunities. I used to sit and marvel at the thought that I had walked the streets of New York and passed lightly by candy-shop windows, full from end to end of assorted chocolates; that in London I had often lunched at Simpson's in the Strand and taken only one helping of the juicy joints the high priests wheel around there; that in Paris I had frequently been satisfied with a mere omelette. I felt like a prodigal who had thrown away all his chances in life.

What I craved for principally was bread. It is a curious thing about bread. As Compton Mackenzie points out in one of his books, nobody ever eats bread for pleasure. There is nothing in bread as bread that offers the least attraction. It is really used as a kind of anæsthetic for all other food. But how I longed for it at Tost. There was never a moment when I would not have traded the finest tin of sardines or even a slab of chocolate for bread.

And when I say bread, I mean the stuff the authorities laughingly called bread, made of leather substitute and sawdust.

The only time when we were in possession of enough bread was on Saturday nights, when a double ration was issued. But then we were compelled to force ourselves to hold back from it, for it had to see us through Sunday and breakfast on Monday. It was splendid moral exercise to peep into one's suitcase and see all that bread lying there and to know that only one's will-power prevented one swooping on it, but what I felt, and others have told me they felt the same, was, 'To Hell with moral exercise!' What I wanted was bread. Sometimes I would gladly have been back in Loos prison where, though conditions were cramped and I had had to sleep on the floor with my head up against the family one-holer, I had been given a whole loaf to myself every morning.

But one was not hidebound. One did not insist on bread. Any sort of food would have been welcome. And what aggravated the agony of having to get along on the diet of a banting canary was that nearly every book one read went into such close particulars about food. It was not pleasant, when one had just supped on three small biscuits and a mug of sewage overflow, to come upon the passage in an Agatha Christie thriller where Monsieur Poirot and Scotland Yard are discussing the contents of the corpse and to read:

> As for what he ate at dinner, it was the same as everybody else had. Soup, grilled sole, pheasant and chipped potatoes, chocolate *soufflé*, soft roes on toast.

Give me one blow-out like that, I used to feel, and you wouldn't find me making a fuss if somebody added a dose of some little-known Asiatic poison as a chaser.

But corpses in detective stories always have all the luck. It seems to me sometimes that they live for pleasure alone. I have never known one that had fewer than five courses inside it, not counting the arsenic.

An internee's diet is carefully thought out by committees of experienced German medical men, so they tell me. I don't believe it. I see behind it the hand of some foul vegetarian society. Nobody else would be capable of so stressing the vegetable note. These men had apparently never heard of such things as chops and steaks and cuts off the joint. And here is the final damning proof – they looked on swedes as human food.

If any of my readers, by the way, is reading this aloud to the tots, I should like him to make it quite clear that when I say swedes I don't mean Swedes, I mean swedes. Between the Swede who comes from Sweden and the swede which tries to mask its malevolence by hiding in black juice there is a great gulf fixed. I yield to no man in my respect for Swedes, but swedes give me a pain in the neck, and elsewhere.

'In reading the books of explorers,' says Somerset Maugham in his *Gentleman in the Parlour*, 'I have been very much struck by the fact that they never tell you what they eat and drink unless they are driven to extremities and shoot a deer or a buffalo that replenishes their larder when they have drawn their belts to the last hole. But I am no explorer and my food and drink are sufficiently important matters to me to persuade me in these pages to dwell on them at some length.'

I am glad to have the moral support of a writer whom I admire so much as I do Mr Maugham. Following his firm policy, I will now give details of what we got to eat at Tost.

At supper two loaves of brunette bread were deposited on each of the tables and divided up among the nine men who sat there. And when I say divided, I mean divided. There was none of that casual business of saying 'Help yourself, George; and pass it along'. At my table Tom Sarginsson got out his slide rule and started measuring, and the rest of us watched him like hawks to see that his hand didn't slip. For our share had to last us till supper-time the next day.

If you divide two regulation German army loaves among nine men, each reveller gets a chunk about so thick and about so long – well, say about as thick as what reviewers call 'this slim volume of verse' and about as long as a pipe with a shortish stem. About the amount which in times of peace you would eat while waiting for the waiter to bring the smoked salmon.

With the bread came a small piece of margarine, a minute spoonful of grease, an almost invisible dab of *ersatz* jam or one of those silver paper bits of cheese which, like the tables in the cells at Loos prison, are designed for the use of Singer's

Midgets. Also a mug of imitation coffee. And sometimes instead of the cheese or jam we had those slivers of sausage which I have referred to as 'rubber heels', purple in colour like an angry sunset and snapping back like elastic when you bent them.

Occasionally – very occasionally – there were great days when the internee in charge of the dining-room would call for silence at lunch and intone these words:

'Gentlemen, bring your bowls tonight.'

This meant that in addition to the ordinary ration there would be soup for supper, a soft, clinging soup made from yellow peas, very grateful to the palate and, what was better, filling.

For breakfast next morning we had what we had been able to resist eating of our bread overnight and a mug of coffee.

The luncheon menu was more varied. There were always potatoes – three per man during the first two months and then suddenly a welcome increase to eight or nine – but different days brought different things to go with them. The great danger was always that the cook, a man of lethargic mentality, would lose his inspiration and fall back on swedes. If he did not, we would get a fish stew once a week, an odd sort of barley porridge once a week, and on other days cabbage, carrots, sauerkraut or black pudding.

From start to finish of my career as an internee I lost forty-two pounds in weight. I don't say it has not made me feel better and look better. It has. I feel terrific and I look like Fred Astaire. All I am saying is that that amount of me has perished from the earth. It is rather sad in a way – all those lovely dimpled curves vanished, probably for ever, but that's how it goes. If you have global wars, you can't have plump, well-fed authors.

The official diet in a camp being on the somewhat ascetic lines which I have indicated, it will be readily understood that the arrival of a parcel is a big event in an internee's life. If you have a parcel, you are in a position to laugh at barley porridge and sneer at swedes. The list goes up in the dormitory after lunch, and the lucky ones proceed in groups to the building where parcels are distributed and wait there till their numbers are called.

This may not be for a considerable time, and in cold weather the conditions of waiting are not too agreeable. In the parcels room itself there is a stove, but in the stone-flagged hall where you keep your vigil you get the Upper Silesian air untempered. For this reason kind donors should be careful what they put in an internee's parcel. I suppose there is no spiritual agony so keen as that caused by the discovery, after you have hung around for three-quarters of an hour and got frostbite in both feet, that your little bit of burlap contains not cake and chocolate but a jigsaw puzzle.

Close friends generally arranged to share their parcels. Which brings to my mind the story of the two Belgian buddies.

These two buddies agreed to share and share alike, and one day Buddy A. went to Buddy B. and told him regretfully that this time his wife had been able to send only a small piece of gingerbread, and here was his, Buddy B.'s, share with comps. At the same time exhibiting something that looked like a Huy biscuit.

Buddy B. thanked him and suggested that, as there was so little, Buddy A. should take it all. Buddy A. said he would not dream of it, and Buddy B., as he started to dig in, said that if there were more fellows in the world with big, generous hearts like Buddy A.'s, the world would be a better place.

So far so good. A pretty little incident, you would say, and one reflecting great credit on human nature.

Unfortunately a few days later Buddy A. got a letter from his wife, a Flemish girl, written in Flemish, which he could not read, and took it to Buddy B., who could read Flemish, for translation. The gist of the letter was that Mrs Buddy A. was in the pink and trusted that this found Buddy A. as it left her at present, and she hoped he had enjoyed the parcel she had sent him containing the two cakes, the two bags of biscuits, the three tins of sardines, the four pieces of gingerbread and the jar of home-made jam. No blood was spilled, for internees who spill blood get bunged into the cells for from two to five days, but I should be deceiving my public if I said that this beautiful friendship was ever quite the same again.

Sometimes unfortunate misunderstandings would occur. One afternoon Smyth found his name on the parcels list, and having only recently recovered from pneumonia, asked me to go down for his parcel. (You give the substitute your disc, and this enables him to collect.)

When I got back, Smyth gratefully presented me with a packet of sliced ham by way of agent's fee. I gave a bit to Arthur Grant and a bit to Czerny and a bit to Joe McCandless and another bit to Sandy Youl and then took a bit myself, and we were all munching happily when there was a stifled cry and we saw Smyth standing there aghast. Apparently he had meant me to take a slice for myself, and give the rest back.

Madness, of course, to go handing packets of sliced ham about in an Ilag if you ever expect to see the contents again. I told him so. It didn't go very well.

All this luxurious living, I should mention, took place in the later stages of my internment. Long months passed during which we were entirely dependent on the camp meals, such as I have described, and after a year of camp meals I am still only slowly re-learning the technique of dining.

Even now it sometimes seems to me that the only way of dining is to wait till somebody blows a whistle and then grab a bowl and cigar-box and queue up till one's turn comes, and I still cannot accustom myself to the peace-time method of securing potatoes. In Camp, when you want potatoes, you hold out the cigar-box and old George Marsh plunges both hands into the crate and comes up with the spuds and dumps them in. And if it is old George, he will catch my pleading eye and add a brace of small ones.

If it is old George, I repeat. There were servers, I regret to say, who lacked his splendid humanity, servers with hearts of flint. Yes, I am looking right at you, young Hoddinott.

Though, of course, even hard-hearted servers were better than no servers at all. I had a great respect for the servers, who did a lot of hard work and got not much in return except an occasional 'Hoy! Where's my ninth potato?'

We took our food in three sittings. As soon as the carriers had delivered the stuff, staggering over from the cookhouse with enormous baskets, we formed up in a queue, each man with a porcelain bowl for the *plat du jour* and a plate or a tin or a cigar-box for the potatoes. The servers then started serving, and it was extremely interesting to watch and compare their various styles.

Too many nervous young servers, I noticed, trying for distance, were apt to overswing and to forget that what puts ginger into the shot is that last-second crisp snap of the wrists. The moment a really first-class server started his swing, you could recognize his mastery of the ladle. He had learned the fundamental lesson – slow back, don't press, and keep your eye on the bowl.

With the low handicap man what you got was a nice easy half-swing, the ladle never rising much above the shoulder; and then, as you braced yourself to take the shock, down came the fish stew, bursting right in the centre of the bowl. A server anywhere near amateur championship class, like George Marsh, could always hit the bowl three times out of four and only splash you in odd spots.

* * *

Early in April, 1953, I sent Plum the script of this book, and received the following reply:

* * *

April 18th, 1953.   *1000 Park Avenue, New York.*

Dear Bill,

The book arrived safely a couple of days ago, and I have just finished a first quick perusal.

It gives one an odd feeling reading letters one has written over a period of thirty years. Rather like drowning and having one's whole life pass before one. How few of the people I mention are still alive. Flo Ziegfeld, Al Woods, Marilyn Miller, George Gershwin, Jerry Kern, George Grossmith, Bill McGuire, Lorimer, Kipling, Molnár ... dozens of them, all gone.

The impression these letters have left me with is the rather humbling one that I am a bad case of arrested mental development. Mentally, I seem not to have progressed a step since I was eighteen. With world convulsions happening every hour on the hour, I appear to be still the rather backward lad I was when we brewed our first cup of tea in our study together, my only concern the outcome of a Rugby football match.

Though I believe there are quite a number of people like me in that respect. I remember lunching with Lord Birkenhead once, and my opening remark: 'Well, Birkenhead, and how are politics these days?' left him listless. He merely muttered something about politics being all right, and crumbled bread. But when I said 'Tell me, my dear fellow – I have often wanted to ask you – what came unstuck at Oxford in 1893, or whenever it was? Why was it that you didn't get your Rugger blue?' – his eyes lit up and he talked for twenty minutes without stopping, giving me no chance to tell him what I did to Haileybury in 1899.

You ask: Do I approve of your publishing this book, with all the stuff about my German troubles? Certainly. But mark this, laddie, I don't suppose that anything you say or anything I say will make the slightest damn bit of difference. You need dynamite to dislodge an idea that has got itself firmly rooted in the public mind.

When I was interned, a man on *Time*, sitting down to write something picturesque and amusing about me, produced the following:

> When the German army was sweeping toward Paris last Spring, 'Plum' (to his friends) was throwing a cocktail-party in the jolly old pine woods at Le Touquet. Suddenly a motor-cycle Gendarme tore up, shouted 'the Germans will be here in an hour', tore off. The guests, thoroughly familiar with this sort of drollery from Wodehouse novels, continued to

toss down cocktails. The Germans arrived punctually, first having taken care to block all the roads. They arrested the Wodehouses and guests, later permitted Mrs Wodehouse and celebrants to depart southward.

You wouldn't think anyone would have believed such an idiotic story, but apparently everyone did. In 1941 someone wrote in the *Daily Express*:

He lived in Le Touquet. He was drinking a cocktail when the Germans arrived, and he was led away quite happily into captivity.

And in 1945 someone else thus in the *Daily Mail*:

He was, in fact, just sinking a cocktail when, in 1940, someone dashed in and cried that the Germans would be there in an hour or less. The party stayed put with a phlegm worthy of Drake's game of bowls.

So after four years the thing was still going as strong as ever, and presumably still is. It is embedded in the world's folk-lore, and nothing will ever get it out. I wonder where I am supposed to have collected these light-hearted guests whom I am described as entertaining. By the time the Germans were threatening Paris, the resident population of Le Touquet had shrunk so considerably that the most determined host would have found it impossible to assemble even the nucleus of a cocktail-party, and the few of us who had been unable to get away were not at all in the mood for revelry. We were pensive and preoccupied, starting at sudden noises and trying to overcome the illusion of having swallowed a heaping teaspoonful of butterflies.

Odd, too, that a motor-cycle Gendarme should have torn up and shouted: 'The Germans will be here in an hour,' when they had been there two months. They entered Le Touquet on May 22nd. I was interned on July 21st. At the time when the incident is supposed to have taken place we were all confined to our houses except when we went to Paris Plage to report at the Kommandatur to a German Kommandant who had a glass eye.

This matter of glass-eyed German Kommandants, by the way, is one that should be carefully gone into by the United Nations. One recognizes, of course, that in modern total warfare the innocent bystander can no longer consider himself immune from unpleasantness, but there are surely limits to what should be inflicted upon him.

I used to amble down to Paris Plage of a morning like Pippa passing, and I would go in at the door of the Kommandatur and meet that eye and wilt. It was like the Boss's eye you read about in the advertisements, and everyone knows how hopeless it is to try to meet that without wilting unless you have subscribed to the correspondence course in character-building and self-confidence.

But writers on daily and weekly papers always will go all out for the picturesque. When they interview you, they invariably alter and embroider.

As a rule, this does not matter much. If on your arrival in New York you are asked 'What do you think of our high buildings?' and you reply, 'I think your high buildings are wonderful', and it comes out as 'I think your high buildings are wonderful. I should like to see some of these income-tax guys jump off the top of them', no harm is done. The sentiment pleases the general public, and even the officials of the Internal Revenue Department probably smile indulgently, as men who know that they are going to have the last laugh. But when a war is in progress, it is kinder to the interviewee not to indulge the imagination.

When I arrived in Berlin, I told an interviewer that I had found it difficult to be belligerent in camp, a mild pleasantry by which I intended to convey the feeling of helplessness – of having to be just a number and a well-behaved number at that, which comes over you when you find yourself on the wrong side of the barbed wire. But it did not get over. It was too subtle. The interviewer sniffed at it, patted it with his paws, wrinkled his forehead over it. Then he thought he saw what I was driving at, and penned the following:

'I have never been able to work up a belligerent feeling,' said Mr Wodehouse. 'Just as I am about to feel belligerent about some country, I meet some nice fellow from it and lose my belligerency.' (Have you ever heard me talk like that?)

With the result that I was accused of expressing unpatriotic sentiments and being indifferent to the outcome of the war.

Even George Orwell, who was writing in my defence, said:

He was placed under house-arrest, and from his subsequent statement it appears that he was treated in a fairly friendly way, German officers in the neighbourhood frequently 'dropping in for a bath or a party'.

From Orwell's article you would think I had *invited* the blighters to come and scour their damned bodies in my bathroom. What actually happened was that at the end of the second week of occupation the house next door became full of

German Labour Corps workers, and they seemed to have got me muddled up with Tennyson's Sir Walter Vivian, the gentleman who 'all a summer's day gave his broad lawns until the set of sun up to the people'. I suppose to a man fond of German Labour Corps workers and liking to hear them singing in his bath, the conditions would have been almost ideal, but they didn't suit me. I chafed, and a fat lot of good chafing did me. They came again next day and brought their friends.

Some of the charges made against me at the time of the broadcasts were, of course, quite true. W. D. Connor, for instance, in his article in the *Daily Mirror* and subsequent speech on the B.B.C., accused me, not mincing his words, of having the Christian names of Pelharn Grenville, and he was perfectly right.

In the year 1881 I *was* christened Pelham Grenville – after a godfather, and not a thing to show for it except a small silver mug. I remember protesting at the time, vigorously, but it did no good. The clergyman stuck to his point. 'Be that as it may,' he said firmly, having waited for a lull, 'I name thee Pelharn Grenville.' All I can do is to express my regrets to Mr Connor, coupled with the hope that his Christian names are Walpurgis Diarmid or something of that sort, and that some day he will have to admit this in public.

The complaint of E. C. Bentley is that I was given a D.Litt. by Oxford University under false pretences, being nothing but a wretched humorist – one who 'has never written a serious line in his life'. He doesn't like it and I don't blame him. Nobody would. And again I have no satisfactory answer to make. If it is any comfort to Bentley and the thousands of others who have grudged me the honour, I may say that never in a career greatly devoted to feeling like thirty cents have I felt more like $.30

than when in a borrowed cap and gown (with scarlet facings) I stood in the Senate House, taking the treatment.

With Sean O'Casey's statement that I am 'English literature's performing flea', I scarcely know how to deal. Thinking it over, I believe he meant to be complimentary, for all the performing fleas I have met have impressed me with their sterling artistry and that indefinable something which makes the good trouper.

But Mr Colin Vincent of Cheltenham, who wrote in the *Daily Telegraph*, 'Pick up any book by Wodehouse and you will find it peopled by men who have never worked and are moneyed and bored', I can answer.

Moneyed, forsooth! It is true that Mr Donaldson, president of Donaldson's Dog Biscuits, Inc. of Long Island City and father-in-law of the Hon. Freddie Threepwood, had a pittance, but as he explained to Lord Emsworth, it did not amount to more than nine or ten million dollars at the outside. And as for the rest of my characters, I look back over the long line of them, and it seems to me that, whether their name is Bingo or Pongo or Ronnie or Archie or Stanley Featherstonehaugh Ukridge, they are all down to their last bean and peering about with gleaming eyes for someone into whose ribs they can get for a fiver. And those who in an iron age like this have succeeded in prising fivers out of a hard-hearted world cannot be said never to have worked. It is a task that calls for all that a man has of energy, courage and the will to win.

And as for being bored, if the experiences through which they have passed in my books induced ennui in Bertie Wooster or the Efficient Baxter or Lord Emsworth's pig, they must have been extraordinarily *blasé*.

Yours for fewer and better Vincents, Plum.

INDEX

TITLES IN THE EVERYMAN WODEHOUSE